D0553587

On Silver Wings

THE WOMEN AIRFORCE

BALLANTINE BOOKS • New York

Wings

1942-1944

SERVICE PILOTS OF WORLD WAR II

Marianne Verges

Foreword by Senator Barry Goldwater

Library of Congress Cataloging-in-Publication Data

Verges, Marianne.
On silver wings: the Women Airforce Service Pilots
of World War II, 1942–1944 / Mariane Verges. — 1st ed.
p.   cm.
Includes index.
ISBN 0-345-36534-8
1. Women's Air Service Pilots (U.S.)
2. World War, 1939–1945—Aerial operations, American.
3. World War, 1939–1945—Participation, Female.
4. Women air pilots—United States.
I. Title.
D790.V47 1991
940.54′4973′082—dc20   91-91907
CIP

Text design by Debby Jay

Manufactured in the United States of America

First Edition: November 1991

10   9   8   7   6   5   4   3   2   1

For Rita Murphy Wischmeyer, WASP Class 44-3, who introduced me to the venturesome spirit and enthusiasm possessed by these extraordinary women, and to my daughter, Stasi, who reminds me so much of them.

CONTENTS

$\mathcal{A}$CKNOWLEDGMENTS

THIS BOOK is the product of two and a half years of research and interviews—and it has only reached completion because of the support of many wonderful women from the Women Airforce Service Pilots. Special thanks also go to Duane Reed of the Air Force Academy, Colorado Springs, Colorado; Vivian White and Hugh Morgan of the USAF Museum, Wright-Patterson AFB, Ohio; Bob Kopitzke of the Frontiers of Flight Museum, Dallas, Texas; Virginia Qualline of the Ninety-Nines, Oklahoma City, Oklahoma; Carol Brown and Lynn Gamma of the Air University, Maxwell AFB, Alabama; Melissa Keiser of the National Air and Space Museum, Washington, D.C.; Laura Parker Castoro of the Greater Dallas Writers' Association—and to Mr. Rufus Fort and Miss Margaret Love.

Finally, *On Silver Wings* owes its greatest debt to Joe Blades, executive editor of Ballantine Books, for his never-failing enthusiasm for the Women Airforce Service Pilots and for his patience and encouragement.

You'll go forth from here with your silver wings,
You'll go forth from here with your silver wings,
Santiago blue and a heart that sings—
'Cause you ain't gonna be here no longer.

Graduation Song
Class 44-W-1
February 1944

$\mathcal{F}$OREWORD

DURING THE SECOND YEAR of my involvement in World War II, I received orders transferring me from the confortable warm desert of Arizona, which I knew so well, to a town on the East Coast that I had heard of, but never visited—Wilmington, Delaware—for the purpose of serving with the 2nd Ferrying Group, which was stationed at New Castle Army Air Force Base. Transferring in the military is always rather exciting, but then, with my orders sending me clear across the United States, I began to wonder.

I was to become Operations Officer for the 27th Ferrying Squadron and I'll never forget the first morning I reported for work; as I began scanning the roster for my troops, I discovered a number of girls' names listed as pilots. This must be a mistake, I thought to myself, but being a well-trained officer, I called on my first sergeant and asked him what was going on. He told me that our squadron, plus two others in the group, had admitted women pilots, to help fly airplanes around this country and, yes, around the world. These were the first ladies who had joined the WASP and the requirement was that they have about four hundred hours of time in heavy horsepower. I would say that in the entire wing, we had about twenty to twenty-five of these girls. It wasn't until later that Jacqueline Cochran talked to General Hap Arnold, and out of that conversation came the flying school for girls in Texas.

These girls did a wonderful job. They could handle any aircraft we had. They were very amenable to discipline. They came to their ground school classes, they checked their aircraft carefully, and they really knew as much about the airplanes they were flying as many, if not most, of the men pilots.

I had occasion one day to deliver a P-47 from Farmingdale to Oakland, California. There was a young lady who was going to deliver one too, so she asked me if she could fly under the hood, and I would fly observer, which I gladly did, talking her down on each approach. She did a fine job getting that single engine fighter plane across the United States, under the hood—with the exception of the landing, which wasn't done in a single engine aircraft under the hood!

The only difference between the girls who first volunteered for the ferry service and those who followed them after being trained at the WASP school in Sweetwater, Texas, was that the former relied on previous flying experience and training in their squadron to get the job done. They were available on call, just looking for a plane to ferry to a user.

The great thing about all of these young women, both those who first came on a volunteer basis, and those who became members of the Women's Airforce Service Pilots as graduates of the school, is the fact that they were ladies, and I think that is just as important to the business of flying airplanes as being gentlemen is a business of male pilots who ferry airplanes. They took instructions rapidly and avidly, they became thorougly engrossed in their aircraft, and they were completely familiar with the operating procedures of each of them.

Reading *On Silver Wings* and remembering these women of nearly fifty years ago has been a very, very enjoyable experience for me. This book reveals the story of these young ladies and their dedication to everything that Americans should dedicate themselves to. Not just in times of war or stress, but in the daily, hourly, living of being an American, of being free, and being proud of it. I was honored to know many of these aviation pioneers and I respected their qualifications, their patriotism, and their devotion to duty at a time in our history when that became an absolute necessity.

I wish I could take each of you readers by the hand and escort you personally on a guided tour of what these ladies did for the cause of victory fifty years ago. And that is precisely what Marianne Verges has accomplished in the pages that follow.

SENATOR BARRY GOLDWATER

On Silver Wings

1.

War Begins: Isn't There Anything a Girl Can Do?

THE FIGHTER WAS ON THEM before Cornelia saw it. She jerked the controls of the yellow Piper Cub away from her student and jammed the throttle wide open, just as the glistening plane screamed past them. It came so close that the windows on their tiny trainer rattled violently. The red orbs on the wings of the fighter blazed into their eyes. The Rising Sun! Cornelia gasped. Incredibly, there it was—the bold symbol of Japan's might branded on the intruder that was slicing through the soft morning sky—down, down toward the sea, the island below. Then beneath them Cornelia saw crooked fingers of billowing black smoke reaching across Pearl Harbor. God! This is either some kind of military maneuver or a crazy miscalculation. Stunned, she watched as flames seared the navy ships resting in their berths. The harbor's blue waters seemed to boil. Explosions whipped on shore, shattering rows of trim aircraft, smashing neat barracks. It might be a mistake, it *must* be, Cornelia thought. For surely, dear God . . .

IN 1941 CORNELIA FORT, a twenty-three-year-old belle from one of Nashville's finest families and a recent graduate of Sarah Lawrence College in Bronxsville, New York, was working as a flight instructor in Hawaii. She was a happy expatriate who loved the beauty of the islands and the freedom there, away from the Nashville Junior League and her beloved mama's fretting.

At dawn on December 7, Cornelia drove from Waikiki to the John Rodgers Civilian Airport next to Pearl Harbor. Her Sunday-morning student was waiting for her. Shortly after six thirty, the two of them were practicing takeoffs and landings, just as wave after wave of ferocious, glittering planes, marked by the Rising Sun, began to bury Hickam Field and Pearl Harbor in bombs—thereby hurling America into World War II.

Cornelia pointed the Piper Cub's nose down and got on the ground fast. She taxied the trainer through a spray of machine gun bullets toward the nearest hangar. Her student still hadn't caught on. Why were they landing? What about the rest of his lesson? "Not today, brother," Cornelia shouted as she jumped out of the plane and sprinted for cover.

By that afternoon everyone at the airport knew that two instructors and their students were missing. The bodies were found washed up on the shores of Pearl Harbor the next day.

Cornelia remained in Honolulu for three months after the Japanese surprise attack. Thousands of people were waiting for evacuation to the States. Her eldest brother, Rufus, who had gone on active duty with the army, was tapping all of his resources to expedite Cornelia's return to Nashville. Their mother was fussing and their baby sister was anxious. Nobody back home considered Hawaii a safe place for Cornelia.

When she finally got to Nashville in March, Cornelia discovered she was a celebrity. First the local papers requested interviews, and then every civic group in town asked her to provide a firsthand account of the attack on Pearl Harbor. Next she narrated a short promotional film to sell government War Bonds. This film was such a success she was soon speaking at War Bond rallies in several states. A famous New York society reporter devoted an entire column to her. Cornelia was even offered a contract for a lecture series, but she turned it down.

Cornelia Fort was one of a handful of experienced women pilots in America, and she was determined to use her skills in the service of her country. In the meantime she gave private flying lessons at the Nashville airport on the weekends and in the evenings. Because of wartime restrictions and shortages, instructing was about the only way Cornelia could fly at all.

She knew civilians were delivering aircraft from the production lines to the military, and she believed this was work American women pilots could do. She had read newspaper stories about women who were ferrying planes in England for the British Air Transport Auxiliary (ATA). Cornelia thought about joining them, but she was ready to stay in the States for a while.

Then out of the blue, on September 6, 1942, she got a telegram from the War Department announcing the organization of the Women's Auxiliary Ferrying Squadron (WAFS) and ordering her to report—at her own expense—within twenty-four hours, if interested. She left at once.

Cornelia and twenty-four other elite women pilots became the nucleus of an unparalleled experiment that would put over a thousand young American women into the cockpits of military aircraft on a variety of noncombat missions for the Army Air Force (AAF) during World War II. During the course of this experiment Cornelia Fort became the first woman pilot in our nation's history to die while on wartime military orders.

America's love affair with flying and flyers began in earnest on May 21, 1927, with Charles Lindbergh's triumphant arrival in Paris after the first solo transatlantic flight. He landed in the dead of night after flying alone thirty-three hours and thirty-nine minutes across the wild North Atlantic. Six men had already lost their lives attempting this same feat. Tall, young, and handsome, Lucky Lindy became an everlasting hero.

Lindbergh and his comrades in the air were bright lights during

[5]

the gloomy Depressions of the thirties. The spirit of these early flyers helped Americans forget their troubles. All around the globe long-distance and over-ocean records were set, one after another. The great Amelia Earhart, who resembled Lindbergh enough to be his sister, became the first woman pilot to cross the North Atlantic alone, on May 21, 1932, exactly five years to the day after Lucky Lindy's landing. Fifteen hours and nineteen minutes after leaving New Jersey she set down her plane, *Friendship*, in a farmer's meadow near London. In July 1933 Wiley Post, a tough, one-eyed Oklahoman, was the first to fly solo around the world. He did it in an amazing time of seven days, eighteen hours, and forty-nine minutes.

Flying circuses and barnstormers toured the country, drawing crowds from all around. After the show the pilots charged twenty-five cents for a ride. Air races, as documented in movie newsreels, were audience favorites. Howard Hughes, eccentric millionaire oilman and movie producer, built and raced some of the most advanced aircraft of the decade.

Air passenger service, an indulgence of the rich and famous, demanded headlines. In May 1934 American Airlines began transcontinental Sleeper Service, which took eighteen hours. The press rode along and photographed everything, including the pajamaed passengers slipping into their curtained bunks. Pan Am's exotic Clipper Ships, those high-winged flying boats, carried passengers from New York to Southampton, England, via the Azores, Lisbon, and Marseilles. The fare was $345.

Americans' infatuation with aeronautics grew apace. Ironically, the crash-related deaths of the thirties only added to the drama and the romance. Wiley Post and his passenger, cherished humorist Will Rogers, were killed in 1935 during a foggy takeoff at Point Barrow, Alaska. Rogers, a great believer in the future of aviation, was out to prove air travel was safe. In 1937, at the age of thirty-nine, Amelia Earhart disappeared over the Pacific. She and her navigator were attempting to fly around the world when, at the end of a grueling eighteen-hour leg off the Howland Islands, all radio transmission ceased.

Women flyers, sporting jodhpurs, leather flying helmets, and goggles, were the heroines of the era, front-page glamour girls. In 1935 a brassy newcomer named Jacqueline Cochran elbowed her way into the Bendix Trophy Race, the most competitive national air race, ignoring a ban on women. At the finish she stood side by side with the men while flashbulbs popped and movie cameras rolled. Young people of both sexes longed to fly.

However, learning to fly remained nothing more than a dream for most. In 1938 a private pilot's license cost between $500 and $750 while the average person's income was less than $2,000 per year. Flying was for the privileged few.

AFTER HER GRADUATION from Sarah Lawrence in May 1939, Cornelia returned home to Fortland Farms near Nashville. Her debut ball at Christmas had been a beautiful party. Now, because it made her mama happy, she was trying to be an active, interested member of the Girls' Cotillion Club and the Junior League.

Cornelia was very tall and lanky. She was a good athlete, a fine horsewoman who loved to fox hunt. She had a broad, clear forehead, a patrician nose, and wide, intelligent eyes. Her expression was gentle, and even at the age of twenty-one she carried herself with dignity.

She loved books and music and the company of her dogs. For years Cornelia kept a journal, and she had been on the staff of her college newspaper, where she composed emotional editorials about Hitler's rise to power and his swastika, the symbol of victory for the Aryan man. And the Jews. She felt strongly about the obligations of free people to the Jews. In one editorial she wrote: "But surely this campaign of horror will turn on its creator and smash him also. . . . We shall aid the persecuted Jews with one hand and try to hasten retribution with the other."

Sarah Lawrence and New York City had awakened Cornelia politically. Most of her family and friends in Nashville couldn't envision the threat of the Nazi party and the Third Reich, the new German state Hitler proclaimed would last a thousand years. Most Americans didn't feel the threat either and had no interest in fighting anyone else's battles. The powerful isolationists in the Congress and the press echoed the sentiments of the people. The United States of America was safe and happy behind her protective shores.

Cornelia knew she was idealistic. Integrity and loyalty were important to her, but she also realized her privileged circumstances allowed her to pursue these values above all else. She took this fluke of birth as a responsibility. Besides, the comfortable life at Fortland made her restless.

Of course Cornelia loved being home with her parents and her sweet thirteen-year-old sister, Louise. Her big brothers were all wonderful, too—all three of them had graduated from the Virginia Military Institute, the West Point of the South. But she sensed that something was missing from her life.

In the spring of 1940 Cornelia decided to try flying to see if being disconnected from the earth could help her find where she was. Flying spoke to her soul as nothing else did, except for her books and music. Then in March her dynamic father—Dr. Rufus E. Fort, the firm center of the family—died. After losing her father and then, a month later, making her first solo flight, Cornelia knew her life had changed, perhaps forever.

By June she qualified for a private pilot's license, and in jubilation she flew over two thousand miles in the first week, celebrating with friends from St. Louis to Louisville.

That same month, on June 22, 1940, France surrendered to the Germans. The Nazi forces spread relentlessly as Hitler's Panzers rumbled to the edge of the English Channel.

Within a year after her first flying lesson Cornelia had both a commercial pilot's license and an instructor's rating. She was the only woman flight instructor in the state of Tennessee. Flying was a real challenge!

By now she knew aviation had an important future, and she was convinced that women would be part of that future. Cornelia went on to get ratings for twin-engine aircraft and seaplanes.

Cornelia's family often found her new passion bewildering. They had long suspected that a rebellious spirit lived within her gentle being. Even so, her brothers were proud of the big, beautiful planes their little sister flew.

In 1940 NANCY HARKNESS LOVE was a sales and demonstration pilot at Inter City Aviation at the East Boston Airport. She was a smart, witty beauty with sultry blue eyes in her mid-twenties. Even then, she had steely gray hair. Nancy was from a prominent Midwestern family and had married into a prominent East Coast family. Nancy and her husband, Bob, owned Inter City Aviation. They were one of the most attractive young couples around.

[8]

Ten years earlier, when she was sixteen, Nancy Harkness became the youngest woman in the United States to get a private pilot's license. She had her first plane ride, with a barnstormer, only a few months before. That same night she told her parents she wanted to quit school for airplanes. Her father said she could take flying lessons—*and* go to school.

Nancy was a boarding student at the Milton Academy in Massachusetts when she soloed. She wrote a poem for English class about the exhilaration of it and how flying set her apart from ordinary things. "Shows considerable ability for original thought," the teacher remarked on Nancy's report card.

Two years later, as an undergraduate at Vassar, she also became the youngest woman to qualify for a commercial license. Nicknamed the Flying Freshman, Nancy padded her allowance by giving rides at the Poughkeepsie Airport until her family and the college grounded her. One sunny weekend afternoon Nancy got caught buzzing the Vassar campus with her date and another joy-riding couple on board. Somebody got the tail number off the plane as they breezed by at treetop level, and the airport manager was waiting when Nancy landed. She was sent home for two weeks and furthermore had to promise to stay out of airplanes for the rest of the semester.

Following her sophomore year Nancy Harkness left Vassar. She was majoring in history, but suddenly she realized a lot of people were *making* history, not studying it—because of the airplane. She had no interest in college anymore. Nancy vowed to embark on a career in aviation. However in 1934 those jobs were few, even for old-timers. Jobs for girls with only three hundred hours and no practical experience didn't exist.

Nancy started selling airplanes on a commission basis out of the East Boston Airport, but it was hard going, even for a stunning young woman whose circle of acquaintances included almost anyone who had money left in the midst of the Depression. She tried for five months to sell a plane to millionaire Joe Kennedy at his offices in Manhattan. All the while, and unknown to Nancy, Kennedy was having private detectives check her out. Papa Joe thought Nancy Harkness looked like a highly suitable marriage candidate for young Joe, the oldest Kennedy son and heir to the family hopes and dreams.

Despite Kennedy interest, Nancy had romantic plans of her own. Bob Love had earned his pilot's license in 1929 when he was a student at Princeton. Aviation took a firm hold of him. By 1933 he left graduate studies at MIT, joined the Army Air Force as a reserve flying officer, and bought the Curtis-Wright Air Terminal at East Boston Airport to start his own company. Nancy met him around the hangars when she first got into town.

In 1935 Nancy and four other women pilots were hired by the federal government to airmark the United States. Their job was to comb the entire nation, sixteen thousand towns and cities, for rooftops where a mark would be visible from the air as a navigational aid. At last Nancy had a regular paycheck from flying.

In May 1936 Bob and Nancy were married. This time she was dubbed the Flying Bride as the couple took off for a flying honeymoon. The local press adored Nancy. Women flyers were rare, and Nancy's serene beauty and sensual eyes drew reporters like magnets. After the honeymoon Nancy returned to the airmarking program for a while and then, in August 1937, she went to work as a test pilot for the Gwinn Aircar Company in Buffalo, New York. Spending several hours daily perfecting unconventional planes and equipment gave Nancy a unique and thorough graduate course in aviation.

She also entered occasional air races and practiced tight turns by flying around the lighthouses in the Boston Harbor. However, the Loves' resources were earmarked for Inter City Aviation, not hot planes for air races, so the competitions were few and far between.

By 1938 Nancy was working full-time with her husband at Inter City Aviation. In four years their company had grown from two planes to eight and a staff of fifty. At Inter City Nancy and Bob ran flying classes and charters, and they demonstrated and sold several types of airplanes.

When American factories began turning out war planes for Great Britain, Nancy tried her hand at ferrying. She flew the aircraft as far as Halifax, Nova Scotia, where, under a treaty agreement, they had to be pushed, not flown, across the Canadian border before being picked up by British pilots for transport to England.

By this time Nancy had logged over a thousand hours. She held a CAA instrument card and a seaplane rating; she was qualified to fly planes of six hundred horsepower. She was convinced that ferrying—that is, delivering planes from the factories—was a meaningful job that experienced women pilots like herself could do. Through Bob's reserve contacts, Nancy started promoting a woman's ferrying group to the Army Air Force.

On May 21, 1940, she wrote to Colonel Robert Olds, who was in charge of AAF planning at GHQ. Her letter suggested that qualified women could serve in some manner: "I've been able to find forty-nine I can rate as excellent material . . . there are probably at least fifteen more. I really think this list is up to handling pretty complicated stuff." Colonel Olds agreed that Nancy was on to something, but the idea of women in the cockpit of military planes was too radical for AAF headquarters. Olds filed Nancy's suggestion for future reference.

Inter City Aviation continued to thrive, and Bob and Nancy bought a small weekend retreat near Boston to get away from the grind. They also joined the Aviation Country Club on Long Island where they could spend time with real pilots and people like themselves.

Nancy Love was urbane. She liked rum and Coca-Cola. She smoked. She was a wonderful dancer. She knew how and when to swear—very, very effectively. She looked smashing—womanly soft and curvy—in the slacks she always wore at the airfield. Nancy had the respect of the men she worked with because she knew her stuff, from top to bottom. As her flying experience increased, so did a bearing of cool detachment, the mark of many great pilots. Cool, crisp, and always a lady. Because of her background, Nancy Love was always a lady.

IN 1937 JACQUELINE COCHRAN took first place in the women's division of the Bendix Air Race, broke Howard Hughes's New York-to-Miami speed record, and was awarded the first of several Harmon International trophies as the outstanding woman aviator in the world. The First Lady of the United States, Eleanor Roosevelt, presented the trophy. The following year Jackie won the Bendix Air Race in a modified Army Air Force P-35, set a new woman's coast-to-coast transcontinental speed record, and received the annual Billy Mitchell Memorial Award, presented to the person making the greatest contribution to aviation. Jackie had only had a pilot's license for five years.

She went at flying the way she went at life—with gusto. She loved flying, but more than this she had seen from the first what it could do for her. Jackie was a rascal, out to make her mark and make a difference.

By 1939 Jackie Cochran was a national sensation. Not only did she have a successful cosmetics business, a rich and powerful husband, an illustrious social circle, and several flying records to her credit, but her childhood was a rags-to-riches story to rival Little Orphan Annie's. She was a foundling adopted into a poor family of factory workers, itinerants who scraped by in the sawmill camp towns of northern Florida and southern Georgia. From this heartbreaking beginning Jackie created herself, constantly reinventing herself as she went along. She even chose her own birthday, May 11, but the year always varied—from 1906 to 1910, depending.

Jackie got a kick out of telling about going to work in the mills at age eight for six cents an hour on a twelve-hour shift, and about the good Catholic priest who saw such promise in a skinny, little, blonde girl. With his help she determined not to be like her shiftless foster family, and the Catholic church became Jackie's good-luck talisman for the rest of her life.

As a teenager she got a job in a beauty shop in Montgomery, Alabama, and quickly learned all there was to know about hairdressing in that sleepy southern city. A kindly customer, a lady judge in the juvenile court, was another person who saw Jackie's promise. She encouraged her to try nurse's training. Jackie's sketchy education made nursing school rough work, but she finished with high ideals and went to work in the impoverished mill towns where she had grown up. One night after the long and bloody ordeal of delivering a malnourished young mother of a sick, scrawny baby, she abandoned nursing. What could she do about the grinding poverty all around her? Walking back to her rooms, Jackie decided she had to leave, to make something of herself.

She went back to work in a beauty shop, this time in Pensacola, Florida. And this is where Jackie got her first exposure to the glamour and excitement of flying—and of flyers—at the cadet dances at the Naval Aviation Station. She met a new kind of man: tanned and handsome, in navy summer whites, living on the edge of danger, facing a new challenge every day.

[12]

In 1929 Jackie struck out for New York, where she talked herself into a hairdresser's job at Antoine's Salon, Saks Fifth Avenue. Sassy and talented, she caught on with the sophisticated clientele. During the winter social season she worked at Antoine's shop in Miami Beach. In 1932 in Miami Beach, twenty-six-year-old Jacqueline Cochran met Floyd Bostwick Odlum, aged forty, who became her Daddy Warbucks. Floyd was a tycoon. The son of a poor Presbyterian minister, he had made his first million by the time he was thirty-six. Now he was a tremendously influential financier, famous for a Midas touch in investments, and a major contributor to the political campaigns of Franklin Delano Roosevelt. He was also a married man with a family back home in Forest Hills, Queens.

Floyd was the first to suggest that Jackie learn to fly. He bet her the price of lessons she couldn't secure her private license in six weeks' time. He lost. The summer after they met, Jackie got her license on Long Island during her three-week vacation from the beauty salon. This was not the last time she would charm Floyd by accepting a challenge.

Suddenly Jackie, the pilot, became a major presence in the aviation world. She had access to all the latest, fastest planes and the best instructors. Men at the top liked Jackie. She was young, blonde, and gutsy with a thoroughgoing intelligence behind her big brown eyes.

In the meantime, assisted by Floyd, she started her own company, Jacqueline Cochran Cosmetics, Inc., with offices at 630 Fifth Avenue near Rockefeller Center, a laboratory in New Jersey, and a salon on North Michigan Avenue in Chicago. At Floyd's suggestion Jackie also bought several hundred acres of land in the California desert for an investment and eventually a home.

During the winter of 1935 Jackie made a crash landing, with Floyd as her only passenger. This was a soul-searching experience for her. It also provoked an embarrassing news story, with awkward details about the so-called famous couple. Jackie detested this kind of notoriety. Soon afterward, on May 11, 1936, her birthday of sorts, Jackie and Floyd were quietly married, four years after their Miami Beach meeting. Jackie Cochran and Floyd Odlum began a marriage and a partnership that lasted for forty years. In his divorce settlement Floyd gave his first wife Bonwit Teller in New York, one of the several department stores he owned.

Floyd doted on Jackie's roughneck spirit. Her courage and her accomplishments delighted him. He collaborated, he encouraged, and he financed, while Jackie's ambitions got bigger and bigger. She had met Amelia Earhart at air races, and Floyd's Atlas Corporation put together the financing for Amelia's 1937 attempt to fly around the world. When Earhart disappeared over the Pacific, Jackie claimed to have had a revelation, a psychic message from Amelia when she went down.

Five months afterward Jackie was the speaker at a memorial tribute to Earhart. "Amelia did not lose, for her last flight was endless. Like in a relay race of progress, she had merely placed the torch in the hands of others to carry on to the next goal and from there on and on forever."

Jackie saw herself as Amelia Earhart's natural successor. She continued to set speed and altitude records, one after another, followed by newspaper stories and congratulatory calls from the White House. Floyd stood by, beaming. After she won the Bendix Trophy in 1938, he gave her a gold cigarette case with a map of the race traced in diamonds and rubies. When she received her first Harmon Trophy, he had a pin made for her, a silver propeller with a large, perfect diamond in the center.

In September 1939, the day after the Nazi tanks rumbled into Warsaw, Jacqueline Cochran sent a letter to the First Lady, outlining the valuable contributions she felt women pilots could make in case the United States was pulled into the war. She envisioned a women's air corps that would handle almost any noncombat flying job, thereby releasing men for duty overseas. Mrs. Roosevelt, a most progressive woman, liked Jackie's ideas and told the nation about them in "My Day," her regular newspaper column.

All during 1940 and the first half of 1941, Jackie Cochran kept pushing for a separate women's air corps, with a woman commander. In addition to her influential connections, Jackie was president of the Ninety-Nines International Organization of Women Pilots for the 1941–43 term, so she was in a good position to make herself heard. However, no one in the military establishment was ready to listen to such revolutionary concepts.

AMERICA WAS JITTERBUGGING to the big bands, going to see Gary Cooper in *Sergeant York*, and trying to ignore the headlines. Bugs Bunny made his debut in *The Wild Hare*, and Bob Hope, Bing

Fortress, was obsolete, and the pilot training program was totally inadequate.

The $300 million approved by Congress finally gave AAF Commanding General H. H. "Hap" Arnold the means to start building a modern air force. At fifty-four General Arnold was a robust, handsome man with an energy level that trampled that of his aides. His nickname had followed him from his cadet days at West Point, where his mischievous charm had made him popular with his classmates—if not always with faculty. A maverick who forsook the traditional army for aviation, Hap Arnold learned to fly soon after his graduation in 1907. He was the second officer in the army to be certified for flight, and his teachers were Wilbur and Orville Wright. "More than anyone I have ever known or read about, the Wright brothers gave me the sense that nothing is impossible," he said.

By 1939 Arnold felt a strong need to do the impossible immediately. He rushed to develop new aircraft, fast pursuits, and bombers—the P-38 Lightning, the P-47 Thunderbolt, the B-24 Liberator, the B-25 Mitchell. Factories sprang up across the country. Arnold knew it took years to design, test, and produce a new plane, so in 1940, without specific authority, he persuaded Boeing to begin designing the successor to the B-17, a Superfortress that would become the B-29 bomber.

The AAF had less than 1,000 officers, and the current training system was only turning out 300 pilots annually. General Arnold knew that control of the air would be critical to America's survival, and he felt that soon, very soon, the country would need at least 100,000 trained pilots. So in 1939 he also started the Civilian Pilot Training Program (CPT) to put a large number of potential military pilots through primary flying instruction. As usual the rambunctious Arnold plunged into the CPT program without authorization for funds by the Congress—because he believed he had to.

Most often CPT was offered through colleges because they had both young men and the classroom space necessary for the ground school. The flying was done nearby at small airstrips. For a forty-dollar lab fee, students academically in the top of their class could get their private pilot's license.

Arnold's Civilian Pilot Training was a pioneering equal opportunity program, open to all regardless of race or sex. Usually one woman was accepted into a CPT course for every ten men. By 1941 over three thousand adventuresome young women would have their private pilot's licenses.

CORNELIA FORT accepted a job in Fort Collins, Colorado, as an instructor in the CPT program offered through Colorado State University. She had been hired to give primary flying lessons to young men who were applying for Army Air Force and Naval Aviation. She looked forward to being involved in a more strenuous flying program than the private lessons she was giving on the weekends in Nashville. Cornelia was also eager to gain experience with the tricky air currents around the Rocky Mountains and to learn about the performance of light planes at high mountain altitudes. However, her mother absolutely forbade the twenty-two-year-old single girl to travel alone by car halfway across the United States. When Cornelia left Nashville to train future AAF pilots in Colorado, her mother sent the family chauffeur along as her chaperone.

THE EPIC CLASH between the Luftwaffe and the Royal Air Force during the Battle of Britain sent a message to America: a new type of warfare and warrior had been born in the skies over Britain. All at once Congress and the people discovered Hap Arnold, the dynamic general who had been fighting throughout his army career just to keep an air force alive. They wanted a leader who understood air power, and the exuberant, if often stubborn, senior officer with the boyish smile and dimpled chin became a celebrity.

During the late spring of 1941 General Arnold and Jackie Cochran were both invited to a ceremony in Washington. Jackie cornered the military's rising star and drummed up the idea of women pilots. Arnold's environment was and always had been male. Women made him nervous. He had a hunch that a women's air corps, with Cochran in command, could really stir up the Army Air Force. Instead, suggested the smiling general, why didn't Cochran consider ferrying American-made bombers to the British? The Brits were already using women in their Air Transport Auxiliary. After sustaining huge losses during the Battle of Britain, England had a critical need for planes and the pilots to move them. The efforts of a prominent flyer like Jackie Cochran might generate some helpful publicity for their cause in the States.

She jumped at the idea. The first woman to fly a bomber to Great Britain! Floyd rented a Lockheed Lodestar to help Jackie get the heavy, twin-motored aircraft experience she needed and he hired Northeast Airlines pilots to coach her for the flight check. Floyd's friend Lord Beaverbrook, head of the Ministry of Procurement for Great Britain, facilitated matters with the British ferry command headquarters in Canada. But none of this was enough to get Jackie through all the flight tests on the Lockheed Hudson bomber once she got to Montreal. The British check pilot there rated her lacking in the physical strength to operate the bomber's hand brake "under all conditions."

On June 17, 1941, Jacqueline Cochran became the first woman to fly a bomber across the Atlantic. However, she had to turn the Lockheed Hudson over to her male copilot for takeoff and landing.

Jackie was back in her Manhattan penthouse on the first day of July. She called a press conference in the apartment's huge foyer, lined with display cases of her trophies, to talk about her ferrying mission.

The very next day she was invited to lunch with President and Mrs. Roosevelt at their Hyde Park estate. The president asked her to research a plan to train and organize women pilots for the Army Air Force and he gave her a handwritten note to that effect for his military staff in Washington. Eleanor Roosevelt commented on their lunch in her syndicated newspaper column.

Jacqueline Cochran headed for Washington, with seven of her New York office staff in tow and the president's note in her hand. Somehow during the next months the note disappeared, but not before it had opened all the right doors. She held meetings with General Arnold and several bewildered AAF colonels and put her staff to work combing the records of every licensed pilot in America. Since the government files were not separated by sex, finding the names and qualifications of women flyers ended up taking four weeks. Meanwhile reporters got wind of what was up and began making a nuisance of themselves at AAF headquarters. All the top brass knew Jackie Cochran was in town.

Colonel Robert Olds, who had been contacted the previous year by Nancy Love, decided that it would be beneficial to have a list of qualified women pilots on hand. He called Nancy down to Washington to do some research of her own.

The Air Transport Command (ATC) also had an interest in the outcome of Jackie's investigation. They calculated that perhaps a hundred American women might have over five hundred hours of flying time. These women could be used to ease the crucial shortage of ferry pilots with practically no additional training.

Of course Jackie had much bigger plans. She wanted to train a large auxiliary corps of women pilots to serve in a variety of non-combat roles. The government records showed that over three thousand women had at least some flying experience. These were the ones that interested Jackie.

On August 1 the ATC and Jackie submitted a joint report to General Arnold. It was a compromise for her. The report proposed to hire women with over five hundred hours as civilian ferry pilots on a ninety-day test. If the trial was satisfactory, the women would be commissioned into the Air Force Reserve and Jackie would serve as chief of the Women Pilots' Section. For Jackie at least it was a beginning.

Two days later Mrs. Roosevelt wrote in "My Day" about the British Air Transport Auxiliary, which had been employing women pilots for more than a year: "I have been hearing lately about how much women pilots are doing in England. I wonder if we have begun to train women so they may perform such duties. It would seem wise. . . ."

Nevertheless General Arnold rejected the joint plan. He still wasn't ready to consider women in the air force, so he fast-stepped around Jackie again. Why not recruit these experienced women pilots to ferry for the ATA in Great Britain? Their organization was already set up for women. The ATA had solved numerous major problems—specifically the billeting, training, and messing of women at normally all-male military facilities. As leader of a group of American women volunteers, Cochran would gain valuable first-hand information about how to integrate women into the Army Air Force—when the country seemed ready for it.

Jackie decided to do exactly that. Maybe it would prove her point to the army. Once again with the intervention of Lord Beaverbrook, Floyd's friend, she made the necessary contacts in England

and began scouring her lists to select the right women. These volunteers would have to be bold women, no weak sisters. England was being bombarded daily by the Germans. The ATA worked under combat conditions. Also Jackie had to be careful not to draw off too many of the top American women, so she would still have a corps of experienced pilots for a women's auxiliary air force later on.

HALFWAY AROUND THE WORLD the warm sea breezes in the Pacific bore the sharp scent of Japanese aggression. After conquering eastern China and brutally decimating the population of Nanking in 1937, Japan was meeting tough resistance in the rest of China. The Empire of the Rising Sun looked to Southeast Asia and the Pacific for possible expansion: Burma, British-held Singapore, and the United States possessions of Wake Island, Guam, and the Philippines. Lured by the Nazi triumphs in Europe, the Japanese signed a military alliance, the Axis Pact, with Germany on September 27, 1940.

KAY MCBRIDE lived in the Philippines with her family. She was an army brat. Her dad was a colonel, a career officer and a West Pointer, stationed on Corregidor—the Rock—America's island fortress at the mouth of Manila Bay. Colonel McBride had brought Kay along and enrolled her in the University of the Philippines in Manila, the capital city. She had been happy at college back in the States, but her father wanted her with the family. So there she was.

Kay was a handsome girl with black curly hair, and she was tall, very tall, like her dad. She really liked to have fun and was always the first to accept a dare.

Even though the University of the Philippines had about seven thousand students, almost all of them were Filipinos. At least, Kay wrote to her friends back in the States, the classes were in English. Kay spent a lot of time at the Army-Navy Officers' Club, swimming and dancing, and for the *Manila Sunday Tribune* she wrote a column of army social news called "From the Rock."

Whenever a military transport arrived from the States there was a welcome party at the club for the newcomers. In May 1939 Lieutenant Al D'Arezzo walked into the Army-Navy Club on Corregidor. His ship had docked in the Philippines just two hours before. Al was handsome and tall, very tall, like Kay. She saw at once he was also very special.

Al was from an Italian immigrant family in California. They were farm workers and poor. Al got an appointment to the United States Military Academy in 1934, the worst year of the Depression. He couldn't believe his good luck. He graduated and received his commission in 1938, when he was twenty-four years old.

Kay and Al married, under an arch of gleaming sabers, in June 1940, the same month France fell to the Nazis. Soon after, Colonel McBride and the rest of the family returned to the States. The young couple, however, stayed in the Philippines. They were having a fine time. There were rumors around about Japanese spies, but no real worries. Europe's war was far away.

Even so, in February 1941 evacuation orders came for the army families. Kay had a week to pack and crate their furniture for transport by ship. She and Al had been married eight months. Since she had been in the Philippines for quite a while, Kay was in the first group the army sent out.

She joined her family in Austin, Texas, where her mother had set up household while one of Kay's younger sisters attended the University of Texas. Colonel McBride was stationed on the Gulf Coast. He told his daughter when she arrived in Austin, "Kay, you're not going to see Al for about five years."

"Oh, Daddy, that's crazy. You're just being pessimistic."

Within the month America embargoed gasoline and other key commodities going to Japan. In July 1941 the Japanese occupied Indochina, claiming to be desperate for raw materials. The United States immediately froze Japan's bank credits in America. In October Al D'Arezzo got his orders stateside, but within days General Douglas MacArthur canceled all transfers out of the area.

About this same time Cornelia Fort left Colorado to become a CPT instructor with the Andrews Flying Service in Hawaii. Pearl Harbor was the home port of the United States Navy, and Waikiki was a boom town, full of military and defense workers, many of whom wanted to learn to fly and had the money for lessons. Cornelia was busy and happy. She wrote to her eldest brother Rufus back home in Nashville: "And if I leave here, I will leave the best job that I can have (unless the national emergency creates a still better one), a very pleasant atmosphere, a good salary, but far the best of all are the planes I fly. Big and fast and better suited for advanced flying."

In late 1941 a letter from a young wife in Queens appeared in the *New York Herald Tribune:* "Isn't there anything a girl of 23 years can do in the event our country goes to war, except to sit home and sew and become gray with worrying? I learned to fly an airplane from a former World War ace and I've forgotten how many parachute jumps I've made. If only I were a man there would be a place for me."

Marjorie Stevenson arrived at Linwood College to begin her freshman year with several black metal trunks full of clothes and new riding tack.

On Sunday afternoon, December 7, 1941, she was in a bridge game in a friend's dorm room. Suddenly a girl Marge disliked as much for her glamorous blonde looks as for her histrionics burst into the room. She threw her back against the door and flung an arm across her forehead. From this melodramatic pose she announced, "The Japs have just bombed Pearl Harbor!"

The room was dead quiet. Marge's friend stopped with the last bridge trick still in her hand. She looked puzzled and asked. "Pearl Harbor? Who's she?"

The surprise attack had been brilliantly conceived and executed. A Japanese fleet of six aircraft carriers, two battleships, and several cruisers had silently slipped within two hundred miles of Pearl Harbor, where most of the U.S. fleet was in port. On a sleepy Sunday morning, just after eight o'clock, the Japanese carriers launched a total of 360 planes, in several waves. Two hours later most of the American navy ships in the harbor, including six of the eight battleships, were in flames, and half of the aircraft on the island were wrecked. Some 2,400 American servicemen were dead. Hundreds of military and civilians were wounded. There was only one saving factor amid the disaster: The group commander of the navy's three aircraft carriers had taken his ships out to sea the day before.

Within hours of the attack on Pearl Harbor, Japanese planes struck Clark Field in the Philippines. Even though the United States

command had had word of the enemy strike in Hawaii, the AAF
pursuits and bombers stationed at Clark were caught on the ground.
In less than twelve hours the Japanese had not only crippled the
navy but had wiped out American air power in the Pacific. Nothing
stood between the Japanese Empire and the West Coast of the
United States.

2.

Uncle Sam Wants You!

ON DECEMBER 8, 1941, both the United States and England declared war on Japan. Three days later Germany and Italy declared war on America. By the end of the week half of the population of the world was at war.

After Pearl Harbor America was in shock, besieged by a frenzy of rumors and panic. A Japanese attack was expected at any second on the Pacific Coast. But the Japanese troops were busy elsewhere, devouring British Hong Kong and the American-held islands of Wake, Guam, and the Philippines. By the middle of December they had established an airfield in the Philippines, and the day after Christmas General Douglas MacArthur withdrew his forces from

Manila across the bay to the mountainous peninsula of Bataan and the rocky island fortress of Corregidor. Lieutenant Al D'Arezzo, Coastal Artillery Corps, moved with his men onto Bataan.

Two weeks earlier Kay D'Arezzo had joined the State Women's Defense Corps in Austin, Texas, as a private. She was learning about fire fighting, first aid, map reading, and marksmanship.

In the Atlantic Hitler unleashed his U-boats, launching a submarine offensive against the East Coast of the United States. Coast watchers, on the shore and from the air, patrolled constantly, looking for any sign of the enemy. Boston Harbor, New York, and Norfolk were protected by antisubmarine nets and floating mines. Every community near the shore blacked out at night, and all civilian airfields within fifty miles of either coast were closed.

Bob and Nancy Love's Inter City Aviation at the East Boston Airport shut down. Within a week Bob was on active duty with the Air Transport Command as deputy chief of staff at headquarters in Washington, D.C. Nancy went with her husband to Washington, but she was out of a job.

ONCE THE FIRST SCARE wore off, Americans got mad. For five years the United States had simply ignored the misfortune and disorder. But the Japanese attack aroused the Yankee giant and endowed it with a single purpose: to win the war. No sacrifice was too great.

Great sacrifices would be needed. America was simply not prepared for war. After the havoc created by the Japanese Zeros in Hawaii and the Philippines, the Army Air Force had only 1,100 planes fit for combat. Many of these were slow and outdated. The best available fighter planes couldn't even reach the cruising altitude of enemy bombers.

Even though General Hap Arnold and his staff had been going full tilt for two years in trying to build air power, there were still almost no combat pilots or the instructors and facilities to train them. And even with Arnold's Civilian Pilot Training program, months of training separated a civilian pilot from a combat pilot.

Now at the start of 1942 America was fighting two separate air wars half a world apart, in Europe and in Asia. Hap Arnold and the struggling air force hung on grimly, waiting for America to deliver new planes and the trained men to fly them.

Factories and shipyards roared twenty-four hours a day, seven days a week. The government rationed nearly everything in order to supply the army and navy. Gasoline and tires. Shoes. Sugar. Meat, butter, and coffee, the staples of the American diet. Civilians swapped ration coupons to get by. Everybody who was capable planted a Victory Garden and raised a few chickens. People saved tin cans and bought War Bonds.

The nation learned to live with shortages and with loneliness. Over the next three and a half years, sixteen million American men would leave home to serve in the armed forces. Families, sweethearts, and friends split apart. Babies were born who would walk and talk before they saw their fathers' faces—if ever.

Women were vital to the war effort, and newspapers, magazines, radio, and movies never let them forget it. During the Depression women had been encouraged to stay home. In fact married women were often denied jobs. No family deserved two jobs. Now the media cranked out wartime propaganda. Women must go to work "for the duration." They were urged to join the struggle for freedom and democracy "to make the world secure for your children."

All sorts of barriers dropped overnight. Women went into the factories, shipyards, offices, ordnance plants, and they were making salaries they had never dreamed of before. Rosie the Riveter on the assembly line, decked out in cute overalls and fetching turbans, received the publicity, but all women had new career opportunities—as musicians, pilots, college professors, scientists, athletes. Several states even dropped bans against women jurors, and women's baseball teams started to play the minor leagues.

Women in the nation's work force doubled. Nearly forty percent of women worked, and three-quarters of those were married. Even for those who stayed home, there were significant volunteer jobs— the Red Cross, the Office of Civilian Defense. War work, they were told, even included canning foodstuffs and making supplies last longer. Every American woman had a contribution to make until the men came home again.

Without their husbands and fathers, women discovered they had to take care of themselves. They were replacing men in nearly every area and assuming the full responsibilities of citizenship for the first time.

Tens of thousands of women would serve in the various branches of the military during World War II. For two years prior to the war there had been discussion about using women in routine jobs behind the lines, but the generals and admirals weren't sure how to deal with females in what had always been an exclusively male domain. By the spring of 1942, a growing manpower shortage, particularly in jobs women were already doing in civilian life (clerks, typists, and switchboard operators) forced a change in thinking. Male enlistments were starting to drop off. Every community in the nation had turned to draft boards to secure its quota of young men for the armed services. The army decided it needed women, and it wanted them in the military, under control.

Because of the crisis the army's proposal for the Women's Army Corps (WAC) faced slight opposition in Congress. When similar legislation had been proposed in 1941, the Congressional Record was riddled with outraged objections: "Take the women into the Armed Service, who then will do the cooking, the washing, the mending, the humble homey tasks to which every woman has devoted herself? . . . Think of the humiliation! What has become of the manhood of America!" Now three months after Pearl Harbor there was only muttering in the back of the congressional chambers about the "sanctity of the home," the traditional order when the army assistant chief of staff testified, "We have found difficulty in getting enlisted men to perform tedious duties anywhere nearly as well as women will do it."

In March 1942 the Women's Army Corps Bill passed the House, and in May the Senate. The women's corps was composed entirely of volunteers, who were entitled to almost the same benefits as the men: insurance, health care, and the new G.I. Bill, which included educational opportunities and help to buy homes after the war. Married women could enlist, but mothers with children under fourteen were ineligible for the WAC. The earliest discharges were reserved for women whose husbands were being mustered out of service, so that couples could return home together.

In June 1942 Oveta Culp Hobby, the publisher of the Houston *Post* and an ardent Democrat, became the director of the WAC, with the rank of colonel. She was married to a former governor of Texas and was the mother of two children. Mrs. Hobby was the first woman officer in the army, and she had a strong sense of mission. She told an early group of WAC recruits, "You have a debt and a date. A debt to democracy, a date with destiny."

During World War II more than 100,000 army women would serve in noncombat roles, not only in the United States but in every major overseas theater. Posters and newsreels proclaimed that WACs were "doing a man-sized job," for it was a "woman's war too." Still, more often than not, the commentators called them *gals*, not soldiers—women working to bring their men home safely.

LIKE MRS. HOBBY, Jackie Cochran also had a mission: to establish a corps of women pilots in the Army Air Force under their own woman commander. So far she hadn't made any progress. Neither Mrs. Roosevelt's support in her newspaper column nor Floyd's connections had helped. Even now with the country at war the Army Air Force, particularly General Hap Arnold, it seemed, wasn't ready for women—yet.

So Jackie went ahead with plans to take a group of female volunteers to Britain to fly with the Air Transport Auxiliary. The ATA would keep interest up and give her a chance to keep talking about a Women's Army Air Force. If her recruits did a good job in England, it would also help prove her point to the folks—*and* the generals—back home.

The Air Transport Auxiliary worked under rugged conditions. They had to deal not only with German attacks but with some of the worst weather in the world. The pilots navigated by maps, memorized landmarks. No radio contact was allowed. The Royal Air Force was using 120 different types of aircraft. An ATA pilot might fly several different kinds of planes in a single day, quickly referring to *Ferry Pilots' Notes* for technical information on each one while taxiing down the runway. Flying for the British would take extraordinary women.

Jackie knew from the research she had done in Washington that there were only a small number of women pilots of the right age with the qualifications to do this job. Jackie sent selected prospects a sensational two-foot-long telegram, with all the details about the ATA and interview instructions. After personally talking with each candidate, she selected forty women to send, in groups of five or six, to Canada for the British flight tests.

Several of the candidates had been trying to find a way to fly for the United States and had heard scuttlebutt about an AAF program for women. Helen Richey, a former airline pilot with over a thousand hours of flying time, asked Cochran about this. Jackie told her, "There isn't going to be any military flying for women in the States."

In January Cochran put the whole British scheme on hold. The first group's passports were being delayed by red tape. Fears were rife in England that the Germans would invade at any time, so Jackie refused to take her girls overseas unless they were protected by American passports.

During the postponement Jackie got wind of trouble: the commander of the AAF Air Transport Command was planning to hire women almost immediately as ferry pilots. Jackie dashed off a strong letter to Hap Arnold telling him that this idea was in direct conflict with the project for women pilots the two of them had discussed:

> In addition, it would wash me out of the supervision of the women flyers here . . . as we contemplated.
>
> I cannot approach the women to go to England except on the basis that for some months to come, at least, there will be no opportunity to serve here in the air.
>
> His plan should be put on ice for a least the next six months or my program for England should be stopped. . . . I will check your office for word Monday afternoon.

General Arnold forwarded Cochran's note to the ATC on January 19, 1942, and advised them, "You will make no plans or open negotiations for hiring women pilots until Miss Jacqueline Cochran has completed her present agreement with the British authorities and has returned to the United States."

By February enough pressure had been brought to bear that Jackie's ATA recruits were issued passports. Cochran and the first group of five "ATA-girls" left for England.

The minute she was gone, there was more trouble. The recruits being sent to Canada began failing their check rides and washing out. Jackie remembered her own humiliating experience in Montreal when the check pilot for the Hudson bomber had labeled her test "lacks sufficient upper-body strength." Those guys just didn't like women! Lord Beaverbrook asked a few well-placed questions about prejudice, and twenty-five of Jackie's original list finally made the cut for the Air Transport Auxiliary.

GRACE STEVENSON didn't get a recruiting telegram from Jackie Cochran, but another instructor at Spartan Aviation did. Grace had never seen a telegram that long! It described the ATA and requested an immediate reply if interested. Grace figured she met all the qualifications. "And I sure am interested in meeting Jackie Cochran," she told her fellow instructors. So Grace replied.

Jackie answered by return mail, saying she was going to be in Kansas City. Would Grace come there for an interview—expenses paid? Grace would have gone anywhere for a chance to meet Jackie Cochran. She was a famous pilot, a woman with real clout.

When they met, Grace thought Jackie was smaller than she seemed in her pictures. She was about five foot five and slender. Her eyes were large and brown, and she had the most beautiful skin Grace had ever seen. Her hands, though, were chunky, almost masculine. They looked as if they could pilot a plane to new records.

Cochran was gracious and full of enthusiasm. The more she talked about the ATA, what it meant, what women could do, the more Grace got sold on the idea.

Cochran stopped and looked at her. "Would you like to go?"

"Yes," Grace replied without another thought.

Afterward she went home to Holdenville, Oklahoma. When she told her mother what she had done, her mother cried. Grace cried too. Seeing her parents, seeing her mother's tears, suddenly made Grace realize she was going to England!

Grace landed at Bristol on May 6, 1942. She was with a group of five American ATA recruits who had come across the North Atlantic in a ship convoy, dodging German U-boats all the way. The enemy subs roaming in groups, Wolf Packs, were hunting down and sinking nearly a hundred Allied ships a month, and the convoy's crossing had taken two weeks.

Stacked on the dock at Bristol were a wardrobe trunk, a steamer trunk, and three suitcases, all belonging to Grace. Her mother had outfitted her well. The British officers sent to meet the women were extremely polite and took Grace's luggage with them into London for storage—until she might need it.

Cochran invited the new arrivals to her suite at the Savoy Hotel for tea. Several dignitaries and reporters were guests as well, and Jackie was dressed to the hilt. She helped each woman send a cable home to say that she was safe. Later Jackie treated everyone to an elegant dinner and a performance of Noel Coward's *Blithe Spirit*. Grace had never seen a stage play before, and she would never forget this one. "Nothing is too good for my girls," Jackie told the group. What an introduction to the job, Grace thought.

The next day Jackie drove the five women to Maidenhead, where they signed an eighteen-month ATA contract. Then she took them on to Luton to start training. Grace thought this was wonderful. How else could they have managed in a strange country where all the road signs had been destroyed to confuse the Germans—and everyone else! Jackie was really looking after them.

Regardless of past experience, all pilots joining the Air Transport Auxiliary went through a three-month basic training program at Luton Airfield, thirty miles north of London. Cochran had never completed this training. She said she didn't need to prove herself as a pilot because she was there to prove something more important— that women pilots could make a real contribution in wartime. Instead Jackie Cochran was commissioned as an ATA flight captain and withdrew to London to study the details of administration.

Before Jackie left Grace's group at Luton, she reminded them, "Keep your noses clean, be on your best behavior—you are representing the United States."

In February, when the British doctors ordered the American women to strip for their physicals, Jackie raised Cain. Under no circumstances, she declared. Some of the women pilots began to suspect Jackie might be a prude, at least the ones old enough to remember when she married Mr. Odlum after he divorced his *first* wife.

Grace made dozens of practice fights at Luton to learn the countryside. England was a small country, but there were so many cities! They all looked alike from the air, and all the checkpoints seemed to be buried in camouflage. Thank God for the Iron Compass, the system of railroad tracks winding over the landscape, or she would have landed in the drink more than once!

Within a short time Grace got her Air Transport Auxiliary uniform, made of good English wool, with a USA patch on each shoulder. Cochran had the standard blue uniforms especially tailored for the American women by Austin Reed, Ltd., Regent Street, London, with a skirt, a tunic, a greatcoat, and two pairs of slacks. Slacks were daring attire for women, particularly in England. However, Grace was from the Wild West, and she thought trousers were a great idea. She won the nickname Oklahoma Kid.

Meanwhile Jackie Cochran was cutting a wide swath through London. Her apartment at the Savoy was always stuffed with celebrities, politicians, and visiting U.S. generals. She served wonderful meals with food and whiskey nobody else ever seemed able to purchase. She had a Rolls-Royce at her disposal and more than one fur coat. This didn't necessarily make Jackie the most popular American in London, but she was undeniably one of the most recognizable.

She refused to go to the underground shelters during the air raids. She'd done it once and that was enough for her. Jackie liked to be out in the open, watching the planes and the fires. She stayed in almost daily contact with Floyd. He was in Washington volunteering for the duration as head of the government's Department of Defense Contract Distribution. He kept Jackie apprised of developments in the nation's capital, and she shared her London adventures with him.

IN MID-FEBRUARY the Japanese took Singapore and started a land assault on Indochina. They spread through the East Indies and in March landed on the Solomon Islands. At some points the Japanese were only a few hundred miles from Australia. In the Philippines U.S. Army supplies were running out, and thousands of soldiers were trapped. America had no way of helping them.

President Roosevelt ordered General MacArthur to leave his Philippine command. The situation there was hopeless, and America needed MacArthur's considerable talents for the future. On March 12 the general went to Australia. He sent back an order to his troops on Bataan and Corregidor: "If food fails, you will prepare and execute an attack on the enemy."

The United States forces attacked on April 4, but the soldiers were so weak by this time that the Japanese easily broke through their lines. Bataan surrendered and thousands of Americans were taken prisoner. The island fortress of Corregidor managed to hold out until May 5.

In Austin, Texas, Kay D'Arezzo was enrolled in courses at the University of Texas and continued training with the State Women's Defense Corps. She had been promoted to an officer in the corps. The physical activity made her feel much better. During fire-fighting drills, Kay had to jump off a fire tower into a net, and the sensation was terrific.

What the country was getting from the Philippines was more rumor than news. If the military bigwigs in Washington knew what was happening, they weren't telling. The American troops had almost starved before they surrendered. How many were killed? Some had escaped into the hills to join guerrillas, and there were prisoners, thousands of them. Kay had no word of her husband.

Her father had been sent out to California. Her mother did what she always did when the colonel was away. She took care of all five kids and the details of everyday life—and played bridge as often as possible. Kay was glad to be with her mother.

She decided what she needed was a job, so now she enrolled in secretarial school. For a while she thought about joining the WAC. Her application was approved, but just before the interview Kay came down with the mumps. Somehow she never got around to doing anything more. Then in the fall Kay went to work as a secretary in the adjutant general's office at the state capitol.

She hadn't seen Al in eighteen months. The American Navy had won a major sea and air battle in the Pacific during June, but they were still thousands of miles from the Philippines. She had no idea if Al was dead or alive. The United States Army had declared him missing in action.

IN THE FACE of world conflict the U.S. Army was reorganized, with all activities grouped under air forces, ground troops, and supply, each with its own commanding general. H. H. "Hap" Arnold, after thirty-five years in the service, was promoted to lieutenant general in charge of the expanded Army Air Force. Air power had finally and formally been recognized.

On the morning of May 26 General Hap Arnold arrived in London. He had flown via Montreal and Goose Bay, Newfoundland, across the North Atlantic with several other general officers. The storms over the ocean were so severe, it had taken them two tries to make the treacherous crossing.

Arnold had come to England with bad news for the British Air Ministry: the Brits would not be getting the large number of B-17s they had been expecting. The United States needed the planes themselves. Most of these bombers would still be operating out of England, but Americans rather than RAF pilots would be flying them.

General Arnold only had a few days in England, but he did his best to rub elbows with all the necessary British swells. He also visited American pilots based near London, took notes on changes in squadron command, and, while he was at it, endeavored to have the army chief of staff sack the head of army operations in England, an old rival who was too conservative for Arnold's tastes.

He saw Jackie Cochran too. She asked him again about women pilots in the air force. Arnold admitted that there were still no plans. "But I foresee a need in the near future," he added. He asked when Jackie was returning to the States.

She told the general that the last of her recruits wouldn't complete flight checks in Canada and be sworn into the ATA in England until August. After that she'd be back, perhaps during the fall. Arnold told her to come see him as soon as she returned.

Arnold and his party left London on June 2 and landed in Goose Bay at three in the morning, after a long flight against strong headwinds. They ate a cold, greasy breakfast in the air force mess hall. The food was awful, and Arnold said so—vehemently! He telegraphed his staff in Washington for a planeload of the best provisions to be on the way to Newfoundland by the next morning. His boys were entitled to good food, and Goose Bay AAF Base, a major link in the North Atlantic air route, was going to be a top-notch mess hall. "And if it's not, you're in trouble," his message warned.

The chaos in the early days of the war suited Arnold just fine. It gave him every excuse to operate outside channels, which had always been his preferred modus operandi. He could accomplish a lot more.

When he got back to the States, Arnold pounded the aircraft manufacturers hard. The American pursuit aircraft in the Pacific were hopelessly outclassed by the Japanese Zero. Development of new fighters had to be speeded up. Bomber production was falling behind schedule. Worse yet, the huge B-29 Superfortress still had not made its maiden flight. On Arnold's authority, the government

[35]

had been spending huge amounts of money on this plane for over two years, and he had bet his reputation that the B-29 would deliver.

Because the air force had to have thousands of thoroughly trained combat pilots in an incredibly short time, no matter what it took, Arnold gave the Training Command encouragement and anything they asked for. The general's expanded Army Air Force also was assigned the task of hauling military supplies and equipment all over the world and delivering planes across both the Atlantic and the Pacific. The AAF Air Transport Command (ATC) would become the largest airline the world had ever seen. In the summer of 1942 Arnold put two men he trusted in charge of this effort: General Harold George, an experienced pilot and military planner, and Colonel C. R. Smith, who was the president of American Airlines and a legend in the business. Bob Love was promoted to lieutenant colonel and assistant deputy chief of staff.

The Ferry Division of the Air Transport Command had a vital role in the colossal transportation operation: to deliver airplanes. Before long, American factories would be turning out an incredible four thousand planes a month. Finding pilots, particularly ones who could handle many different types of planes, was tough. One day a ferry pilot might pick up a 200-horsepower, single-engine primary trainer and the next a 1,200-horsepower bomber. They had to be able to fly anything, anywhere.

The Army Air Force needed these flyers for combat overseas, not in transport work, and the Ferry Division (FERD) wasn't set up to train inexperienced pilots. Eventually a system was worked out to allocate a few recent AAF flight-school graduates to FERD, and "transition" them to more complicated aircraft, step by step. But in the early months of the war ferry pilots were, for the most part, men who were not qualified to fly combat, usually because of their age. They were a mixture of civil service and military, and the supply was exceedingly limited.

THE NOTION of using women pilots in the Ferry Division had been dropped in January following General Arnold's orders not to poach on Cochran's turf. However, by June 1942 the severe shortage of trained pilots brought the idea to life again.

Nancy Love was working in the northeast office of the Ferry Division in Baltimore, Maryland, and she was as positive as she had been in 1940 that experienced women flyers could handle ferry assignments. Nevertheless she was plotting delivery routes and schedules in operation. "Flying a desk" was her term. At least, Nancy thought, she was doing something useful and staying visible, just in case.

Bob worked at ATC headquarters in Washington, so the Loves lived in the capital, and Nancy flew the sixty miles back and forth to her job every day. It was much easier for a FERD employee to get fuel for a plane than tightly rationed gas for a car. Before long this unusual means of commuting caught the attention of the new commanding officer of the Ferry Division, Colonel William Tunner.

Tunner had his office near Bob Love's at ATC headquarters, and when he heard that Love's wife *flew* to work, he was very interested indeed. William Tunner, thirty-six years old, West Point, class of '28, had a brilliant career in store that would include three stars and directing the heroic Berlin Airlift. But in the summer of 1942 the harried young colonel was scouring every backwoods airport in the nation for experienced pilots.

Nancy Love had 1,200 hours logged flying time and ratings for 600-horsepower engines, instrument flying, and seaplanes. She also had a unique solution to some of Tunner's problems: a squadron of experienced women pilots, like herself, in the Ferry Division.

A squadron of women pilots! Tunner wasn't sure. How could they make long flights? Women could never make use of cockpit relief tubes. What would they do if they had to stay overnight, away from their base? How would females be billeted? He wondered if the Army Air Force was prepared for women. Tunner wasn't even certain *he* was.

Still, Nancy Love insisted, there were probably a hundred women who could handle ferry work. Colonel Tunner needed pilots desperately, so he sketched out her plan in a memo and sent it upstairs to ATC headquarters. He also discussed it with his Ferry Division staff. His staff thought Nancy's idea was lousy, but General George, the ATC commander, and his deputy, Colonel C. R. Smith, felt differently. On June 11, 1942, just a week after Hap Arnold and Jackie Cochran had their meeting in London, General George wrote orders for Tunner: "It is desired to use commissioned officers of the Women's Auxiliary Army Corps for the ferrying of airplanes under this command, to replace and supplement male pilots insofar as qualified women may be available."

With help from Nancy, Colonel Tunner returned guidelines to General George within a few days for finding, training, and utilizing women pilots. Each woman had to have five hundred hours' flying time, be between the ages of twenty-one and thirty-five, and have a high school education. Tunner wanted only the most qualified women, and they had to be of legal age, twenty-one. FERD, he said, had no intention of baby-sitting.

The women would ferry only primary and liaison types of aircraft within the continental United States. Candidates would apply directly to the commanding officer of the 2nd Ferrying Group at Wilmington, Delaware, for a flight test and physical. After a ninety-day trial period their names would be reported to Colonel Oveta C. Hobby, who would take the necessary steps to have them commissioned as second lieutenants in the Women's Auxiliary Corps. During the trial they would have to pass thirty to forty-five days of ground school, with instruction in military procedures, ferry routes, and how to fill out the paperwork that went with delivering a plane. Tunner proposed that the first, experimental squadron be held to twenty-five women and that it should be the only one for the remainder of the year.

Next Tunner went to Wilmington, Delaware, to see the commanding officer of the 2nd Ferrying Group, Colonel Robert H. Baker. This ferrying group was based at New Castle AAFB near several firms manufacturing primary aircraft.

Baker was willing to give the women a try. He said he had enough separate barracks space for more than twenty-five women, so why not increase the proposed number? Fifty perhaps? The new officers' mess would be open almost immediately, and the women could eat there. Colonel Baker said he could be ready for the women's squadron by July.

He requested Nancy Love as operations officer for the squadron and thought she should be commissioned as a first lieutenant. Baker wanted Nancy to report to New Castle at least two weeks before the others in order to establish operations.

After checking with Colonel Hobby to see if a fifty-woman unit was standard for the WAC, Tunner updated ATC headquarters on his progress. His Army Air Force heart was struggling with the concept of women flying military aircraft. His *main* concern was finding fifty truthfully qualified women pilots. Their credentials and capabilities would have to be thoroughly checked.

AT NEW CASTLE Colonel Baker's *only* concern was getting the supplies to revamp the plumbing in a barracks built for soldiers so that it would be suitable for ladies. He decided he needed Nancy there right away.

Two weeks later Nancy discovered a major problem: Women pilots could not be legally commissioned into the WAC. On July 13 General Arnold summed up the predicament when he wrote a bread-and-butter letter to a member of Congress. He explained that he wasn't using any of the nation's trained women pilots, who had been clamoring for months to join the army, because there was no authority to commission or pay female flying officers. However, the ATC was working on a plan. He added, "I understand an amendment is now being drafted for submission to Congress. When and if the amendment is adopted, it seems probable that a place will be found for women fliers to the extent that they are available and qualified."

Nancy realized that getting an amendment through Congress could take forever. The Ferry Division needed pilots now. By the middle of July she and Tunner had another proposal ready. The two of them suggested hiring the women as civil service employees until a bill could be introduced and passed in Congress. This new proposal also cut back the size of the first group because of the mounting problems renovating the barracks and latrines.

Love also increased the requirements for the women pilots. Candidates had to be U.S. citizens, present two letters of recommendation, and have 200-horsepower ratings. After the public announcement of the program, there would be a two-week period for the women to come to Wilmington to have their credentials checked, take a test flight, and undergo an AAF physical. The same board who reviewed males would check the women pilots, and Nancy would sit in attendance, as a nonvoting member. The women pilots' pay would be $250 a month plus per diem, which was about $600 a year less than civilian men in the Ferry Division were paid.

At New Castle AAFB the barracks plumbing was *still* coming

slowly, but Venetian blinds had been installed over all the windows. Each room was also furnished with a small dressing table and a wall mirror.

ON JULY 18 General Harold George wrote Hap Arnold about the Ferry Division's latest proposal to employ women:

> "I feel sure we can go to bat on this plan and come out with an answer that will be satisfactory to all concerned. If you approve this we will go ahead at once with the organization although you intimated, when we discussed this about three weeks ago, that you wanted to mention the matter to the President thinking that he would like to announce the formation of a Women's Pilot Corps for use in the domestic ferrying of aircraft."

He added that although the women would be hired through the civil service, they would live as a unit and wear some type of uniform. They were to have the normal privileges of officers. He also recommended Nancy as the director of women pilots. Not only was she an experienced pilot, she was "one who has been indoctrinated in the system of operations of the Air Transport Command by employment therein in various administrative capacities."

Arnold wanted to wait a little longer. Over the next few weeks General George brought up the subject to Arnold whenever he had a chance. Then, on September 1, 1942, Eleanor Roosevelt went to bat for the women again in her *Washington Daily News* column.

> "We know that in England, where the need is great, women are ferrying planes and freeing innumerable men for combat service. It seems to me that in the Civil Air Patrol and in our own Ferry Command, women, if they can pass the tests imposed upon our men, should have an equal opportunity for non-combat service. This is NOT A TIME WHEN WOMEN SHOULD BE PATIENT. We are in a war and we need to fight it with all our ability and every weapon possible. Women pilots, in this particular case, are a weapon waiting to be used."

After such strong support, in print, from the president's wife, General George decided the time might be ripe to approach Arnold again—in writing. He sent a memo, dated September 3, repeating most of what Arnold already knew about the ATC plan. He added that the Ferry Division could have the women's pilot program under way within twenty-four hours. All they needed was his approval.

At last, on September 5, Arnold said okay, get started. Arnold was famous with his staff for verbal orders and they had learned to proceed carefully, but General George decided it was worth a gamble to get thirty or forty experienced pilots into service at once. That night, on George's say-so, Nancy sent telegrams to the women listed in the government files as having the required qualifications. They were requested to report as soon as possible, at their own expense, for flight checks and a physical.

ON THE MORNING of September 10, 1942, General George and Nancy were invited to Arnold's office for a public announcement of the Air Transport Command's new program—the Women's Auxiliary Ferrying Squadron (WAFS), with Mrs. Nancy Love as the director of women pilots. When they arrived, they discovered that Arnold had been suddenly called out of the city and that Secretary of War Henry L. Stimson would make the announcement during his regular press conference. If General George had any suspicions, he kept them to himself.

Mr. Stimson made the announcement with flourishes of whimsy and old-school gallantry. After telling the press that forty or fifty skilled women pilots were to be appointed to the Ferry Division, he read a list of Nancy's qualifications. Then he said, "Come, Mrs. Love, will you let the ladies and gentlemen have a look at you?"

Nancy stood, a twenty-eight-year-old beauty in a softly tailored suit and pillbox hat. The audience gave her a burst of applause. She smiled, returned a little bow, and sat down.

"Of the two most important ladies who have so far come in contact with the army," the secretary of war said with a smile, "one is named Love and the other is named Hobby. That will show you how respectable the army is."

After the conference General George and Nancy handed out a press release, answered questions, and posed for photographers. By that afternoon they were shaking hands on the front page of every major newspaper in America.

Almost the minute Arnold gave General George the word to establish the WAFS, Jackie Cochran heard about it in London through her husband, Floyd Odlum. She had to get home at once and put a stop to this plan or be left out in the cold. The last of her ATA recruits had just been sworn into service, so Jackie was on a plane headed for New York within twenty-four hours. The first thing that hit her eye coming off the airliner on September 10 was *The New York Times* with a front-page story about the WAFS. Too late! She was furious.

Jackie was in Arnold's office in Washington the next morning. And she was steaming. *Mrs. Love?* Hadn't he promised Jackie for nearly two years that *she* would be in charge of the women pilots' program? He had told her to come see him as soon as she returned from England. Well, here she was. What was she supposed to do now?

In her final report three years later, Cochran hinted that the WAFS were slipped over on Arnold and that they were announced "without his knowledge and not in accordance with his intentions." But on the morning of September 11 she was ready to wring Hap Arnold's neck.

He had to think fast. Jackie was different from any of the women Arnold knew. Seeing her so angry set him back on his haunches. She was right. He had invited her to discuss her pet project, a women's air corps, as soon as she got home. Why had she waited so long?

The Air Transport Command had been after Arnold for months to authorize the use of women pilots in the Ferry Division. They had presented a workable plan too. When Mrs. Roosevelt got back into the fray the week before with her column about women being "a weapon waiting to be used," Arnold decided to okay the ATC experiment. He didn't remember exactly what he had said to whom, but now Jackie Cochran was fuming. Arnold had to fix the situation.

The general called both General George and his assistant, Colonel C. R. Smith, into his office and told them he couldn't have two women's pilot organizations—that they had to find a way to get together with Miss Cochran. The potential for women pilots was a bigger proposition than just flying for the Ferry Division.

The next four days were rousing at the Air Transport Command headquarters. Hap Arnold had ordered General George and Colonel Smith to solve the difficulty between Mrs. Love's ferry squadron and Jackie Cochran, and they tried. For a short time George thought he had even found a solution. He brought Arnold a plan for a two-pronged women's program. The WAFS, a squadron of experienced women pilots, would be part of the ATC. Nancy Love would be their commander. The Women's Flying Training Detachment (WFTD), under the direction of Jacqueline Cochran, would be a separate program with the mission to train additional women pilots.

It seemed fair, Arnold thought. He left on a fact-finding trip to the Pacific theater of war thinking his woman troubles were over. While he was away, Arnold had some other hopeful news. On September 21, the B-29 Superfortress made its first successful test flight.

No matter what the generals and colonels thought, Jackie was determined that the women pilots' program in the Army Air Force belonged to her. This was just the opening skirmish, she told Floyd. Wait and see.

Nevertheless, for the time being she agreed to compromise. On September 15, five days after the secretary of war announced Nancy Love's WAFS at his weekly press conference, Miss Jacqueline Cochran was publicly named director of women pilots' training, AAF. She was assigned to the Office of the Director of Individual Training, and asked to train five hundred women pilots for eventual service in the Women's Auxiliary Ferrying Squadron of the ATC.

3.

The Originals

THIS TELEGRAM was sent on the evening of September 5, 1942, to
eighty-three of the women on Nancy Love's list. Each of those who
responded had to pass the tough AAF flight physical and a thorough
check ride in a 175-horsepower primary trainer, just like the male

[44]

applicants. Love knew these women would have to prove themselves many times over, so she was very selective.

The first Women's Auxiliary Ferrying Squadron would be made up of twenty-five elite pilots. These originals, as they soon came to be known, averaged 1,100 hours and were among the most experienced young pilots, male or female, in the country. Less than a hundred American women could match their qualifications, and a quarter of those were in England with the ATA. In 1942 women of the right age with this much flying behind them were a privileged and determined few.

Thirty-two-year-old Betty Huyler Gillies was the first to report to the 2nd Ferrying Group. On September 7 she flew from her home on the north shore of Long Island to New Castle AAFB in her own slick, twin-engine amphibian. A five-foot-one dynamo, she had logged over 1,400 hours since getting her license in 1928, and she worked as a utility pilot, an airborne gofer, for Grumman Aircraft.

She started flying when she was eighteen because a handsome young navy aviator, Bud Gillies, had caught her eye. Betty, who was from a wealthy Long Island family, was a student nurse. She continued nurse's training and earned her pilot's license on her days off.

The next fall Betty was invited to the charter meeting of the Ninety-Nines, International Organization of Women Pilots. Amelia Earhart suggested the group's name during the meeting, since there were ninety-nine charter members—ninety-nine out of 117 licensed women pilots in 1929! Tiny Betty was overwhelmed to be in the same room with Amelia Earhart.

When Curtis Aviation offered her a job demonstrating for their flying school, Betty had to make some choices about her life goals. She chose flying—and the navy aviator—over nursing.

By 1942 Bud was a Grumman vice president, and Betty had just finished a two-year term as president of the Ninety-Nines. She had become one of the best-known and respected women in aviation.

When Nancy Love called for Betty to help launch the WAFS, her family was all for the idea. Nine months earlier, right before Christmas 1941, the Gillieses' four-year-old daughter had died of leukemia. Friends and family agreed that being involved in a significant venture like the first women's ferrying squadron would be therapeutic for Betty, and her mother offered to supervise the Gillieses' two older children, who were both in school. "You don't have to stay for long," Nancy had promised, "just the first ninety days, until we get started."

Betty Gillies and Nancy Love roomed together at New Castle AAFB. They knew each other from the tight group of pilots who were members of the Aviation Country Club on Long Island. Both came from similar backgrounds—distinguished schools, good families—and held similar ideas about what was and was not proper behavior. Both were top-notch pilots. They became close friends. Betty served as the WAFS executive officer and later commanded the squadron at New Castle.

Cornelia Fort was the second woman to report. She was in upstate New York taking a Link-trainer-operator class when the AAF telegram arrived. She dashed off a quick note to her mother: "The army has decided to let women ferry ships and I'm going to be one of them." Cornelia was in Wilmington by the next day.

Within three weeks ten WAFS had been hired. The majority of this first group was true to a type—debs, Junior League, money, and as much alike as such an amazing group of women could be. Most arrived wearing neat, tailored suits with simple blouses. Nearly all were in their late twenties and married. Three had children. Cornelia was one of the youngest and also one of the richest. These women came prepared to work hard and make a go of the opportunity Nancy was offering them, if they could. Cornelia wrote later, "All of us realized what a spot we were in. We had to deliver the goods or else there wouldn't ever be another chance for women pilots in any part of the service."

Meanwhile women who had heard the news about the women's ferry squadron began arriving at New Castle AAFB clutching their log books. Colonel Baker, the commanding officer of 2nd Ferrying Group, was anxious because many of the qualified women on Nancy's list had not applied. Nancy assured him that the best of these young pilots were working as CPT instructors and would arrive as soon as their current round of classes was over. Besides, Nancy was looking for more than just flying know-how. She wanted women who could be trusted to act as a team.

Some of the ones who did show up were either too young or too old or just plain too nuts. They made Colonel Baker even more anxious. And so did the reporters that had been swarming all over the 2nd Ferrying Group ever since the secretary of war's news conference.

When the first eleven women were sworn in as civilian pilots of the Air Transport Command on September 21, 1942, Colonel Baker insisted there would be absolutely no distinction between men and women in the 2nd Ferrying Group. The WAFS would have all the privileges of officers. They would also be expected to stand in formation for roll call at 8:00 A.M. and to adhere to all other regulations—including no smoking in the headquarters building.

As Nancy had suggested, the WAFS were designated civil service to get them in the air while the details of their status were worked out with the army. They were hired temporarily at $250 a month. Although this was less than civilian men were paid, the Ferry Division thought the salary seemed equitable—since the women would be restricted to lightweight, simple aircraft.

In spite of Baker's apprehensions, New Castle had its full complement of twenty-five women pilots by the middle of December. During the ninety-day test period two of the original squadron washed out, one for flying deficiencies and another for attitude. Nancy was able to fill their spots immediately from a lengthy waiting list.

SINCE THE WOMEN'S BARRACKS were still not completed, the ten women hired in September stayed at a nearby mansion that was a victim of hard times and had become a guest house. They started training at once, learning to "fly the army way." Each was issued khaki flight overalls, a parachute, goggles, and a white silk AAF flying scarf. Their classes lasted four weeks. In the mornings they studied navigation, ferry routes, military jargon—and paperwork! Each aircraft delivery would require forms and more forms, all with proper signatures. They learned to fill out transportation requests, the chits they needed to get back to New Castle by the quickest means. The women also discovered the army kept time on the international clock, 0100 to 2400 hours, and ferry pilots had to keep track of when the sun went down every day. The FERD wanted all airplanes safely on the ground by dark. Before doing anything else a pilot had to telegraph operations each night with the exact location of the plane in his or her custody.

In the afternoon when the fog from the Delaware River had burned off, the WAFS flew. They became familiar with military procedures and the trainers—the Cubs and PT-19s—they had been hired to ferry. Most of the women had always piloted heavier planes with bigger engines, so the tiny 65-horsepower Piper Cub was a challenge. Top speed, under perfect conditions, was one hundred miles per hour. Against a stiff breeze cars on the highways below could beat a Cub out almost all the time. During descent the plane drifted and wafted, and it was nearly impossible to land predictably on all three landing gears.

The first women were able to move into their barracks before the second group arrived in October. Compared with what most of them were accustomed to an army barracks was a jolt. They lived two to a room with a shower and a laundry room down the hall. The furniture, except for the window blinds, was military issue. Some roommates tried to spruce up their surroundings with throw pillows and family photos, and one room set up a bar on top of a dresser for cocktail hour.

The second group hired was, on the whole, younger and more savvy about the military. Like Cornelia Fort, they had been through CPT advance courses, and several had Link trainer time. Most were single, and the phones in the barracks hallway started jingling. Colonel Baker decided the women needed a housemother, as in a college sorority, for the sake of decorum.

To the dismay of the originals, part of learning to fly the army way included learning to march the army way. As squadron leader Nancy led the formation and gave the commands during close-order drill. Bawling orders at the top of her lungs wasn't her style. Nancy hated this so much that she sometimes drew a blank. One morning the WAFS were drilling on an inactive runway, marching smartly down the paved runway toward the end, where there was a dropoff of about ten feet. As they reached the edge, Nancy lost track and absolutely couldn't remember, "To the rear—march!" Off the edge went all twenty-four WAFS, still in close formation and roaring with laughter, straight down the embankment and into the open field, leaving Love standing at the end of the runway, still speechless. Three of these happy young women would die in the service of their country during the next eighteen months.

A majority of the originals, at least twenty-one out of the twenty-five, were not only first-rate pilots, they had also been instructors. And they had been making considerably more money teaching than they ever would in the Women's Auxiliary Ferrying Squadron.

Esther Nelson operated a flying school in California, and Dorothy Fulton had run her own airport in New Jersey before the war. Nancy Batson taught flying at Embry-Riddle in Miami. Batson had not received one of the AAF telegrams but had read about the WAFS in the local paper. She immediately packed her bags for Wilmington.

Delphine Bohn, of Amarillo, Texas, was the first woman in the Panhandle to get a commercial license. Katherine Rawls Thompson had won two gold medals in swimming for the United States at the 1936 Olympics in Berlin. She married her coach, and now he was off flying with the RAF in England.

Helen Richards, the youngest of the originals, completed CPT at the University of California and had been instructing in Idaho. She had just turned twenty-one when she came to Wilmington. Aline Rhonie, the oldest member of the squadron, was an heiress and bona fide woman of the world. She had lived everywhere and knew everyone. Not only had Aline spent most of the past year in France driving an ambulance, she was *divorced*!

Teresa James worked in air shows as a stunt pilot besides giving flying lessons. She had caught the flying bug from an older brother and earned her license in 1934. She loved acrobatics. Teresa could fly inverted and do spins that made an audience's hair stand on end. A month before she joined the WAFS she married one of her former students, George Martin, who had joined the Army Air Force.

Nancy Love held the allegiance of all the originals. As far as they were concerned, she'd pulled off a miracle. Women pilots all over America had been trying to get the army or the navy to let them fly, but Nancy had actually persuaded the ferry service to give women a chance. The WAFS weren't going to let her down.

Getting the confidence of the men in the Ferry Division was another matter. Most of the senior officers had known Nancy and her husband, Bob, for years through the Air Force Reserve. She was a woman who did business without fuss or femininity, and they respected her flying ability. But a squadron of women flying for the army was something else!

Nancy had made an important friend in 1940 when she had approached Colonel Robert Olds in AAF Planning with the idea of employing women pilots. Olds was now a major general, and on October 2, 1942, he wrote Nancy cheering her on and telling her he was sure she could build the WAFS far beyond the scope authorized. He foresaw WAFS towing targets and carrying messages, parts, and passengers. He urged Nancy to keep her chin up and added, "The smartest thing we ever did was to lay low after Jackie Cochran flared up." General Olds closed with, "As ever, Bob."

Bob Love kept his wife up on the scuttlebutt at Air Transport Command headquarters in Washington. He wrote her a quick note about the latest complaint: "Listen, Bud, your girls are in everything from khakis to cerise jodhpurs. How about checking it out?"

Almost immediately, on October 8, 1942, headquarters announced that the WAFS would wear "standardized attire for recognition purpose." Nancy picked a jacket, skirt, slacks, and overseas cap in a soft shade of gray that almost matched her hair. The originals also wore the wings of the Civilian Pilot, Air Transport Command, and leather flying jackets, with a Ferry Division patch. In spite of the subdued choice the prospect of women wearing a uniform with slacks was risqué enough to put the WAFS back in national headlines.

Colonel Baker ordered the men and women at New Castle AAFB to stay away from each other, at least during the WAFS ninety-day trial period, but it was a big base, with over ten thousand men, and the WAFS were young and pretty. A few looked like movie stars. Besides, they ate all their meals in the officers' mess, even if the women did have to sit at their own table and they had the privileges of the Officers' Club. Any evening of the week young men and women could be found in groups at the bar, and whenever Nancy showed up at the club, she drew a flock of admiring young AAF officers.

The bomber pilots at New Castle began offering the younger WAFS joyrides in the heavier, faster aircraft available to them. In the middle of October another set of orders came down from Colonel Baker. Under *no* circumstances were WAFS to ride in bomber-type airplanes. Not only were the girls forbidden to go up for a spin, they weren't to hitchhike back from ferrying missions either.

1. *Above*: Fifinella, the girl gremlin created for the WASP by Walt Disney, checks out rookies arriving at the front gate of Avenger Field, Sweetwater, Texas.

2. *Right*: Fifinella, the Women Airforce Service Pilots' emblem.

3. Nancy Harkness Love, who founded the Women's Auxiliary Ferrying Squadron in September 1942, wearing an A-2 flight jacket with a Ferry Division patch and a helmet and goggles.

4. *Right*: Nancy Harkness Love, Executive Officer of the Women's Auxiliary Ferrying Squadron, in the WAFS gray uniform.

5. *Below*: Betty Gillies and Nancy Love at Goose Bay trying to put up a good front after just being ordered out of the B-17, Queen Bee, in favor of a male flight crew.

6. Jacqueline Cochran, head of the Women Airforce Service Pilots, wearing the organization's silver wings and Santiago blue uniform.

7. Jacqueline Cochran demonstrates flying technique for a crowd of admiring trainees in the ready room at Avenger Field.

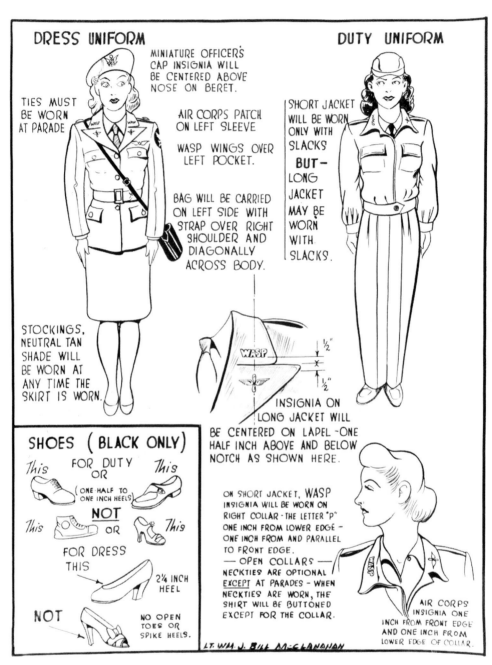

8. Instructions for the new Santiago blue WASP uniform and insignia.

9. Zoot suit! You gotta be kidding! Micky Axton, 43-W-7, gets a fitting from a classmate, Leonora Horton.

10. *Above*: Ground school class: trainees learn to take down an engine.

11. *Below*: Cornelia Fort (second from left) seated on the wing of a BT-13 at Long Beach in March 1943 just a week before she was killed. On the wing with her are Evelyn Sharp, who also died in the line of duty, and B.J. Erickson. Standing are two more of the originals, Barbara Towne and Bernice Batten.

12. *Above*: The six WAFS who were part of a flight of twenty-three PT-17 Stearmans ferried from Montana to Tennessee. The women piloted the first planes to arrive after the long cross-country trip and they beat most of the men in the group by several days. Teresa James (far right) was flight leader. To her left are Florene Miller, Delphine Bohn, Nancy Batson, Katherine Thompson, and Phyllis Burchfield.

13. *Right*: Florene Miller, the squadron commander of the women stationed at Dallas Love Field, in the cockpit of an AT-6 Texan trainer.

14. Jane Straughan, one of the first women pilots recruited by Jackie Cochran for the WASP, strides away from a delivery with her parachute and B-4 bag.

15. *Above*: WASP Louisa Thompson with a parachute standing in front of a P-38 Lightning.

16. *Right:* Margaret Harper in the WASP duty uniform, a short jacket and slacks, climbs on board a B-26 with her parachute.

17. *Left*: Shirley Slade in a wistful pose on the cover of *Life* magazine, July 19, 1943.

18. *Right*: Ruth Craig Jones in her silver wings and Santiago blue WASP uniform.

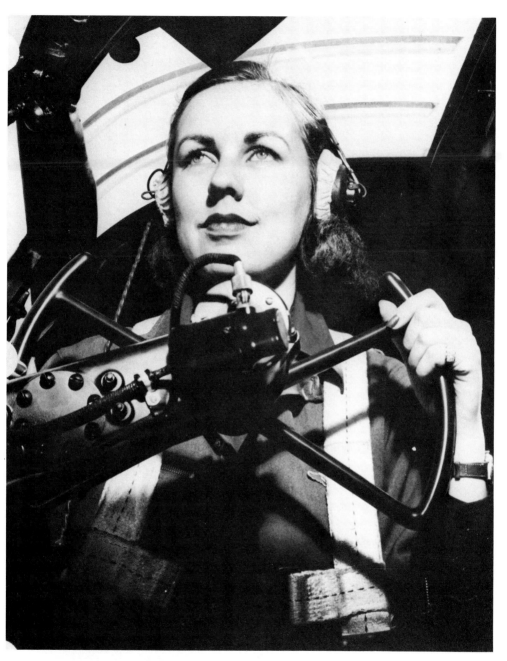

19. Shirley Slade, the winsome trainee who posed for the cover of *Life*, dolled up and on operational duty at the controls of a B-26 bomber.

20. Trainees Millie Davidson and Kay D'Arezzo wearing the required Urban's turbans.

21. All together now: Army exercises in matching gym shorts.

22. Madge Rutherford 43-W-4, climbs into at AT-6 wearing her parachute and clutching a pair of booster cushions.

All members of the women's squadron were supposed to return to Wilmington via commercial carriers, unless the ferrying group sent a special plane for them. This regulation caused problems later on, but the Army Air Force felt it was protecting the WAFS' reputation, something the top brass was eager to do.

The regulations on men and women traveling and working together were enlarged upon several times. The WAC was already a victim of gossip, and the women ferry pilots were getting so much attention, even a small slip could cause a scandal.

The Ferry Division had been unhappy since the first week about the WAFS' notoriety. They were on the front page of *The New York Times*. They were in *Cosmopolitan* and in all their hometown newspapers. Nancy Love had a full-page glamour shot in *Life* and was picked, along with Dorothy Lamour and Gracie Allen, as one of the six American women in public life with the Most Beautiful Legs.

Colonel Tunner asked the War Department to put a lid on publicity. All the fuss made his staff uncomfortable. Nor did it give the women a fair chance. Tunner wrote the War Department, "Stories of this type are not considered to be for the best interests of the Ferrying Division and will tend to over-glamorize the members of the WAFS in our opinion."

As his request moved upward through channels, it was stopped by Air Transport Command headquarters in Washington. General Harold George and Colonel C. R. Smith had their own troubles with the War Department and didn't want any more. Headquarters advised Tunner the WAFS experiment was a natural news story and "as such needs to be treated with diplomacy and delicacy."

Meanwhile Jackie Cochran, a celebrity with an inspired gift for publicity, decided she needed to protect the WAFS from the press in order to protect her own plans. At her request the War Department hired Hazel Taylor to clear all public relations material on the women pilots. Requests for stories, interviews, and appearances were supposed to come through her office.

In November Hazel Taylor paid a visit to the squadron at New Castle AAFB. Nancy stonewalled her. In her report to Cochran, Taylor specified that Nancy should not meet with the press. She was showing signs of fatigue. Perhaps the Ferry Division should relieve her of administrative work for a few weeks and let her fly. Nancy Love, she wrote, was a "spoiled brat."

THE ORIGINALS got their first assignment on October 22, 1942. They ferried five bouncy Cubs from the Piper factory at Lock Haven, Pennsylvania, to Mitchell Field, New York. Betty Gillies led this short mission, and Cornelia Fort was a member of the flight. Four days later Cornelia delivered another Cub to Nashville, where she was met by her mother, her baby sister Louise, and of course a photographer from the local paper.

Most of the AAF primary training bases were in the southern states or out on Texas plains. These were regular destinations for WAFS ferrying Cubs and, more often now, the slightly larger, faster PT-19. Before leaving the ground the women flew every mission on paper, plotting each leg of the trip with maps and a compass. There were no radios in the trainers, so they used towns, rivers, railways, and roads for checkpoints. As their confidence grew, the WAFS began to copy the men and fly in loose formation.

During the winter months the temperature might dip to ten degrees in the open cockpits of the PT-19s at cruising altitude, and the wind was so severe the WAFS had to lash their maps to their legs to keep them from blowing away. They froze even in their regulation leather, fleece-lined winter flying suits. Nevertheless the women regularly got where they were going and almost always on time.

FLORENE MILLER, a tall Texas beauty who had learned to fly on her family's isolated ranch, was leading a flight of six PT-19s west when suddenly she looked down and saw the the others circling below her for no apparent reason. Since the trainers had no radios, Florene flew down, straightened the planes out and headed the flight west again. Within minutes the five other PT-19s were circling again!

Once more Florene descended and got the flight back on course. This routine went on until a distraught Florene spotted an alternate airfield on their flight plan and signaled for everyone to land. The runway was thick with ice and snowbanks piled high on either side. Florene brought her plane in and prayed fervently as the others followed her down safely, one by one.

The WAFS jumped out of their planes and rushed at one another, chattering and gesturing. Florene stalked up to the giddy group and demanded to know what was going on.

"Look," said the girl who had been designated navigator of the flight, "I lost my maps, all of them blew right out of the cockpit! I kept circling to let you know something was wrong and to signal for someone else to take the lead. Of course every time I circled, you all followed me. I was the navigator! But couldn't *someone* figure out I must be lost?"

As COLONEL BAKER'S confidence in the WAFS grew, they made longer ferrying trips, which kept them away from New Castle several nights in a row. Very few of the bases where they had to remain overnight (RON) had suitable places for a woman to sleep. In fact most officers on duty at these air bases were flabbergasted when a woman climbed out of an AAF plane. After ten to twelve hours of flying, the WAFS secured their planes, notified FERD of their location, and headed for the nearest town to find somewhere to spend the night and grab a bite to eat. In a strange location this usually took quite awhile. By the time they got to bed, there weren't many hours left until takeoff at dawn.

A flight of WAFS in Cubs was forced down at the Marine base at Quantico, Virginia, because of weather. The Marines were anxious to be hospitable. They partitioned off part of a barracks with a sturdy wall and posted a sign: KEEP OUT! LADIES PRESENT. Regardless, the officer on duty posted an armed guard, who also personally escorted each of the WAFS to the latrine.

THE LAST BATCH of originals was through training and on the job by the middle of December. By now the 2nd Ferrying Group used a regular shuttle to take the women to Hagerstown, Maryland, to pick up PT-19s, and the WAFS' own Lockheed Lodestar flew them to the Piper Cub factory in Pennsylvania.

In spite of his earlier doubts, Colonel Baker still had his sanity. In fact both he and Tunner were beginning to think the WAFS might work out. Their performance in just the few weeks they had been on duty was encouraging. Baker reported the women were enthusiastic and dependable, and their delivery record was excellent— equal to or better than that of the men.

However, the very idea of Jackie Cochran's flying school put Tunner and the FERD staff on the defensive. They weren't interested in employing a large number of women pilots, but only in finding as many pilots as they could, of either sex, who met Ferry Division standards. In Colonel Tunner's opinion, there were probably only fifty qualified women available in the country, and he resolved not to hire Cochran's graduates unless they could prove their ability.

TERESA JAMES was assigned to lead a flight of twenty-three PT-17 Stearman trainers from Great Falls, Montana, to an air base in Tennessee. Six of the planes would be flown by WAFS and the rest by men. The pilots traveled together by train from Wilmington to Montana.

The Stearman was a tandem-seat, open-cockpit biplane with the most powerful engine of any the WAFS had been allowed to fly so far. Once they had taken off from Great Falls, the pilots scattered out so that each could set his own pace for the long cross-country flight. By the second day the flight began to arrive in Tennessee. The first six to land were piloted by the WAFS. Two days later only six of the seventeen men had appeared.

The ATC headquarters was horrified. As the reports came in, it seemed the missing members of the flight had gotten lost or were paying social calls along the way. Headquarters couldn't miss taking note of who had completed the mission successfully. But just in case, Nancy reminded them.

LIKE IT OR NOT, the Ferry Division was told to expect the first graduates of Cochran's Women's Flying Training Detachment sometime in January. Colonel Tunner dispatched Nancy to find suitable locations for new WAFS squadrons. She selected ATC bases near plants assembling light planes and where housing for women was immediately available. She planned to split the originals up into groups of five or six and use them as the core of these new squadrons.

Before the end of the year Love was ready with three additional bases: Dallas Love Field; Long Beach, California; and Romulus, Michigan. All were near factories turning out primary trainers, but at Love Field and in Long Beach there would be plenty of opportunities to fly other types of aircraft as well.

[54]

Nancy decided to request a transfer. She was bored with Piper Cubs and her desk. "There haven't even been that many Cubs!" she wrote Bob.

For the most part she had spent the past six months in meetings and shuffling government forms. Nancy wanted to fly. By now she was convinced Colonel Baker wasn't going to give women a shot at anything except primary trainers, and she told him so. Betty could handle the 2nd Ferrying Group's squadron, and she had to stay near her children on Long Island. Nancy asked for Dallas Love Field.

CORNELIA DELIVERED three to four PT-19s a week during the first part of December. Once in a while she was able to stop in Atlanta to see Rufus. Her brother was stationed there as a WAC recruiting officer! Rufus would pick her up at the airfield and they would have dinner.

Cornelia went home to Fortland for Christmas with her mother and sister. A year earlier she had been in Hawaii with the whole family wondering and worrying if they'd ever see her again.

The day after she got back to New Castle, a telegram came from friends in Nashville:

FIRE FROM DEFECTIVE WIRING BURNED FORTLAND COMPLETELY THIS MORN-
ING ABOUT TEN STOP NO ONE HURT STOP YOUR MOTHER IS WELL CONSID-
ERING THE SHOCK STOP . . . MOST THINGS DOWNSTAIRS WERE SAVED BUT
NOTHING UPSTAIRS END

Cornelia was stunned. Fortland was the family. She felt as if she had lost her father all over again. Her mother's jewelry. Letters and photographs. Her own diaries and books. Everything she'd always kept in her room.

At the end of a very long letter to her mother Cornelia wrote, "I am about to lead a flight to Texas which will, weather permitting, bring me thru Nashville. My transfer to Long Beach is official but won't take place for three or four weeks. When it does, I think I can manage a few days in Nashville with you."

THE 5TH FERRYING GROUP at Dallas Love Field had eight rooms in the nurses' quarters capable of accommodating sixteen WAFS, and the ATC issued orders to build a separate WAFS barracks within sixty to ninety days. The five women going to Dallas to kick off the new squadron would be ferrying much more powerful airplanes than before, including the AT-6 Texan, with a big, loud 600-horsepower engine and capable of speeds over two hundred miles per hour. The Texan was flown by every AAF cadet during advanced training and was the most familiar and numerous Army Air Force plane built during World War II.

The FERD headquarters watched over the transfer of the WAFS, shepherding their movements from Wilmington to Dallas, mile by mile. Nancy Love flew to Dallas on New Year's Day, via American Airlines, after spending the holidays with her husband in Washington. The same day, two of the women left by car, and the two remaining members of the group arrived in Dallas by airline on January 5, 1943. Colonel Baker wired FERD every detail of the women's travel plans, and the commander of the 5th Ferrying Group was instructed to notify headquarters as soon as the WAFS arrived at Love Field. Sometimes the women pilots laughed about being the Ferry Division's little *girls* and sometimes it made them mad as hell.

As Nancy Love moved into the nurses' quarters at Dallas Love Field, Jackie Cochran was just fifty miles away at Flying Training Command Headquarters in Fort Worth. This was big news in Texas, and Pearl Beer ran a large ad in the Dallas newspapers welcoming the WAFS to town.

Nancy Love was happy now out on the flight line and away from her office. She was the first woman assigned to ferry a Texan trainer. In the meantime Jackie Cochran was at her desk every day, going full-throttle on arrangements for her school. Nancy loved to fly. Jackie loved to plot and plan. Army Air Force headquarters in Washington, a military kingdom where females had never dwelled before, usually didn't know what to say or do with either of them.

WITHIN DAYS after the first groups of WAFS left New Castle for Dallas, five more were ordered to report—by January 15, 1943— to the 3rd Ferrying Group at Romulus, Michigan. Romulus had a temporary barracks that could house about twenty-five women and plans for a new facility in three months.

Even though Tunner had set up new squadrons for the WAFS,

the Ferry Division had yet to receive any pilots from Cochran's school. With no firm commitment when to expect the WFTD graduates, Tunner and Nancy thought they should continue to hire women pilots on their own. They decided to put qualified applicants through the same four-week training as the WAFS already on duty. Almost at once Tunner received a directive from AAF headquarters that in the future all women pilots *must* enter the Ferry Division from the WFTD school.

Betty Gillies knew Jackie—and she didn't like her. They had been acquainted with the same flying crowd on Long Island, and Betty had just turned the presidency of the Ninety-Nines over to Cochran the year before. Jackie was always maneuvering. Betty was sure the directive on WAFS hiring was just more of her meddling.

Cornelia wasn't so certain. Jackie had spent nearly six months in England with the British Air Transport Auxiliary. The ATA required all pilots, male or female, to have at least three months of basic training. Aline Rhonie had more flying time than anyone in the WAFS, and she had just been washed out for her attitude. Aline thought she knew everything, and absolutely refused to obey any orders she didn't like. Maybe more training in flying the army way wouldn't be such a bad idea.

The rest of the originals were suspicious of Cochran. Several of them also knew her. Jackie Cochran liked things her way. She was probably trying to take over. Besides, Aline always contended that Jackie was older than she was, no matter how she might lie about it. If that was the case, Jackie was too old to qualify to be a WAFS herself.

THE FINAL GROUP of WAFS did not leave New Castle for the 6th Ferrying Group, Long Beach, California, until the middle of February. There was no base housing available until then. Baby-faced B. J. Erickson, a former government CPT instructor, was in charge of the squadron. Long Beach assigned the five WAFS to ferrying BT-13s, a low-wing, closed-canopy, basic trainer. However, with all the aircraft manufacturers in southern California, the women felt they were going to have plenty of exciting flying opportunities.

Cornelia arrived at Long Beach on February 18. She had wrangled a day in Nashville on the way and had gone fox hunting in a blinding snowstorm. Long Beach was a busy station, and the next morning Cornelia was checked out in a 450-horsepower BT-13, with the minimum allowable time. Within two weeks she knew the route to Dallas so well she felt as if she was following a groove cut in the sky by a BT-13, over the Guadalupe Pass and across west Texas. She barely even needed to use her radio during the ten-hour flight from Long Beach.

BETTY GILLIES was in charge of the WAFS in New Castle, the largest of the four squadrons, with eleven of the originals on duty. More and more often these women discovered they were delivering trainers to bases where boys they had taught to fly during Civilian Pilot Training were preparing for combat. Before too much longer the women were getting news of deaths—former students and fellow instructors killed in action overseas.

The February issue of *Look* magazine ran a photo story on WAFS with pictures of the best-looking girls zipping up leather, fleece-lined flying suits and putting on a last touch of lipstick before heading for the flight line. A glamorous story, the piece depicted the WAFS as the elite of America's auxiliary services, a squadron of twenty-five girls leading the way for women fliers because "tomorrow there will be hundreds."

The pilots in the Ferry Division were embarrassed by this magazine spread. Ferry pilots felt compelled to justify their work at every turn. They were sick and tired of arguing with bums and drunks who called them yellow because they weren't overseas flying in combat. This daffy response to the WAFS, all the publicity, only made matters worse.

The WAFS had posed for the *Look* photographers right after starting at New Castle, nearly three months before the issue came out. It had seemed like a good idea at the time. Now Universal Pictures was making a movie about the WAFS, *Ladies Courageous*. General George was right in the first place: pretty young women performing extraordinary tasks created news—particularly when America was still losing the war on all fronts. However, many of the older men in the Ferry Division were furious about the glamour girls.

DURING THE FIRST MONTHS of 1943 the WAFS worked seven days a week. From their point of view there was no glamour at all ferrying airplanes. They had to be ready to leave at a moment's notice, lugging winter flight gear, a thirty-pound parachute, and their B-4 bags—packed with a clean shirt, a uniform skirt, a toothbrush, and maps. A pair of high heels and a can of leg makeup went into the bag, too, since they had orders to wear a skirt when returning from a mission. Every one of them learned how to iron shirts and collars on hotel radiators, how to catch a quick nap on benches in airport waiting rooms. They knew they could be away from base three days or three weeks.

In Ohio a flight of four WAFS was grounded for three days during a winter storm. Once the weather cleared, the planes were packed with ice and snow. The women worked all morning clearing out the cockpits and scraping off the wings before they could get the planes into the air. After takeoff all four women sighed with relief. They felt lucky. Just a month before, in the same vicinity, another WAFS had been weathered in for twenty-one days.

DURING THE LAST TWO WEEKS in February Nancy Love checked out in advanced, challenging aircraft, not at her home base in Dallas but at the 6th Ferrying Group in Long Beach. This was the oldest and most important ferrying group, and it was surrounded by large established aircraft manufacturers. The commanding officer had a critical shortage of pilots, and he welcomed the WAFS.

Nancy worked her way up through these bigger and faster planes as quietly as possible. While Air Transport Command headquarters spurred her on to find out what types of equipment qualified women were capable of flying, the Ferry Division's policy still restricted all WAFS to light aircraft.

On February 27, 1943, Nancy Love became one of the first pilots of either sex to fly the P-51 Mustang, "the Cadillac of the air." The 440-miles-per-hour Mustang, the most celebrated fighter plane of World War II, would not even be ready for combat until the fall of 1943.

Less than a week later Betty Gillies became the first woman to fly the P-47 Thunderbolt. ATC headquarters quietly but firmly recommended to Colonel Baker that he ought to give his qualified WAFS a chance to fly bigger planes. Since Gillies was the squadron leader, he put her at the head of the line.

Before she started transition training in the P-47, Betty called a test pilot at Grumman who was almost as short as she was and still managed any type of plane. She discovered that he had made special wooden blocks to go over the pedals in the cockpit so that he could reach them easily with his feet. He made Betty a set of wooden extenders like the ones he used. She found them handy more than once.

Nancy Love requested a transfer to California from Dallas Love Field the first week in March. The attitude at Long Beach made transition simpler for the WAFS stationed there. On March 7 Nancy and B. J. Erickson, the squadron leader who also was taking every mission she could get, delivered a twin-engine C-47 cargo plane, the Gooney Bird, to Memphis.

The Ferry Division used transition into larger aircraft for pilot training. New personnel came into the division as Class I, rated to fly single-engine planes, and were gradually upgraded to Class V, which meant they had checked out in four-engine transports. Eventually an incoming pilot was prepared to leave the domestic operation and ferry bombers overseas or fly the supply lines in China and across the North Atlantic.

Since women were hired to deliver light planes, the Ferry Division only had use for a limited number of WAFS. On the other hand, now that the AAF commanding general, Hap Arnold, had thrown his support behind Jacqueline Cochran's WFDT school, the division apparently was going to have to employ three to four hundred women pilots, no matter what. If this large group of women got frozen in a particular class, for example, Class I, the men could not pass through and continue their vital training.

General George and his Washington headquarters staff saw that the Ferry Division policy limiting the women pilots to trainers would have to be changed as the WFTD graduates came on line. They hoped Nancy Love's rapid transition to multi-engine and pursuit aircraft would convince Colonel Tunner to amend this policy on his own. Nonetheless on March 17 Tunner's staff drew up orders to all ferry bases limiting the activities of women pilots and emphasizing that they were not to fly bombers, even as copilots.

TERESA JAMES was the WAFS chosen to go to Hollywood. Universal Pictures needed a PT-19 for *Ladies Courageous*, the saga about the WAFS, and Teresa was assigned to deliver the plane from Maryland to California. Teresa was a tall, healthy-looking girl with a hearty laugh. She knew how to enjoy herself, and Hollywood was going to be right up her alley.

Delivering the PT-19 was better than Teresa ever dreamed. Paul Mantz, the producer of *Ladies Courageous*, arranged private tours of several movie studios. She had lunch at the Brown Derby with Bob Hope, and when she went to the famous Stage Door Canteen, the stars working there asked for *her* autograph!

Universal was shooting all the action sequences for *Ladies Courageous* at Long Beach with a WAFS acting as stand-in. When the fellows on the flight line saw the perfect hair and makeup on the actresses, they thought the new crop of women pilots was going to be quite an improvement. Nancy Love had a hunch the movie was going to be less than factual—in spite of the producer's assurances.

ON MARCH 10 Cornelia wrote to her mother from Long Beach with exciting news:

> Yesterday was a very eventful day—I bought a car, a dream car this time instead of a junk heap. I felt so helpless without one and distances are so tremendous out here. This is a gray Chevrolet convertible with radio and heater. It will be wonderful fun this summer to put the top down. All cars are ridiculously high out here, especially convertibles. Everyone says this was an excellent bargain, but at any rate, I love it altho [sic] it doesn't leave much balance in my savings acc't.
>
> If anything should happen to me—which I don't think it will—I want Louise to have the car.

4.

WFTD:
Up and Flying,
Off the Ground

NOBODY WAS MORE SURPRISED than Colonel William Tunner of the Ferry Division to read in the papers on September 15, 1943, that Miss Jacqueline Cochran was going to train five hundred new women pilots for him within the next year. He had no intention of hiring more than a few highly qualified women. In fact when Cochran returned from England raving about Mrs. Love's WAFS and General Arnold ordered a solution to the complication of *two* women pilots' programs, Tunner was so sure of his stance that he sent a junior staff member, a captain, to represent him during the meetings. All of the other officers present were at least colonels, so immediately Miss Jacqueline Cochran and the Ferry Division were off to a shaky start.

Nonetheless Miss Cochran agreed to accept the limitations that Tunner set on candidates for her flight training. She would only consider women with at least two hundred hours and put them through a curriculum that would graduate pilots with 200-horsepower ratings and commercial licenses—qualifications almost identical to the current WAFS standards. All of the graduates would also be American citizens with high school educations, between the ages of twenty-one and thirty-five and at least five feet four inches tall.

Even with her pledge Tunner had a hunch about Jackie's motives—a bad hunch. A day or two after the meetings a reporter for the *Washington Daily News* quoted her: " 'Yes, I've been called back by General Arnold to be head of a women's air corps in this country. Our goal is 1,500.' " Only very well-qualified women would be considered for the corps at first, she said, then women with less and less flying time. " 'I've had such success with my girls in England that I know this will work.' "

This interview riveted Colonel Tunner's attention. As far as he knew, Cochran had recruited the best pilots for the British Air Transport Auxiliary and then the Brits had schooled them in ATA procedures. Truly wary now, Tunner contacted a friend at the American embassy in London to ask about the performance of these women pilots—and about Miss Jacqueline Cochran. The Americans, his source reported, were in grand shape, doing an excellent job. On the other hand, what he said about Jackie was disturbing. She had held a volunteer, administrative position with the ATA, along with an honorary commission, and had no hand in training procedures. And Miss Cochran's flamboyant behavior while she was in London had stirred resentment, particularly in military circles.

After this troubling report from London and the surprising September 15 newspaper announcement, Colonel Tunner made up his mind he would not be herded into hiring Cochran's graduates. He wrote a memo to Air Transport Command headquarters: "[Graduates] will be employed at Headquarters, 2nd Ferrying Group, Ferrying Division, ATC, only if they meet the basic requirements for the position of women civilian pilots (including physical examination and flight test) and not because they have graduated from the course."

His boss in the Air Transport Command, General Harold George, knew this would never work. When Hap Arnold approved the arrangement—and the expense—to train women to fly the army way, the Ferry Division *had* to give them a chance. All the same, after the snafu over the Women's Auxiliary Ferrying Squadron, General George decided to lay low for a while.

Of course Tunner was absolutely right to be suspicious of Jackie. She felt from the start that two hundred hours of flying time was a ridiculous requirement for applicants to the women's training program. Men were being accepted into the Army Air Force with no previous flying experience at all. AAF Commanding General H. H. Arnold had told her to pick out five hundred of the best women flyers in the United States and prepare them for ferrying assignments—so Jackie wasn't concerned about her agreement with the Ferry Division. With the reluctant approval of the AAF Office of Individual Training, she dropped the requirement to seventy-five hours almost at once.

Jackie also tried to sidetrack the Women's Auxiliary Ferrying Squadron by suggesting an additional women's auxiliary, based in Texas, with herself as commander. This squadron would deliver trainers from factories in Dallas and Fort Worth. The ATC struck this idea down as a duplication of the WAFS' functions.

Next she proposed that her graduates be assigned to several new women's ferrying squadrons within FERD, each with its own WAFS executive. Nancy Love could remain in charge at New Castle, but her authority and influence would be greatly diluted. Colonel Tunner said no, just plain no. Jackie had too much clout as it was.

By the time Hap Arnold returned to Washington from his inspection tour in the Pacific on October 2, Jackie had made a number of influential enemies. The chief of the Office of Individual Training and she were at each other's throats. Colonel Tunner was hostile about the amount of time he had to give to the mounting WAFS problems. And up at New Castle AAFB, Colonel Baker was incensed to hear that the 2nd Ferrying Group was expected to employ all five hundred of Jackie's girls. Worse yet, Cochran had everybody so riled up that she hadn't made any progress on a facility, equipment, or staff for her school. Before Arnold left, she had promised that the women's flight school would be operational in thirty days.

General Arnold had always been a maverick himself, and he was learning to like Jackie. However, he had no idea how to corral her. Certainly it wasn't by telling her no. One solution was to get her out of Washington. He called his West Point classmate, Major General Barton Yount, at the Training Command in Fort Worth, and passed Jackie on to him—with verbal instructions to give her anything she wanted.

Before Jacqueline Cochran could even get to Fort Worth, the Training Command received a tip that a "bundle of trouble" was on the way. But it was a false alarm. Jackie and General Yount got along magnificently. "He's one of the loveliest men I ever met," she reported back to Arnold.

Jackie rented an office downtown and got to work. Her flight school needed everything: aircraft, instructors, a field, and sleeping and eating facilities for hundreds of young women. Nearly every airfield in the region was already taken, but General Yount found a temporary location at Howard Hughes Airport, next to Ellington AAFB, in Houston. He also discovered a company, Aviation Enterprises, Ltd., whose government contract was about to expire, and hired them to train Cochran's girls to fly—under army supervision. The only planes Yount had available were a collection of odds and ends—"claptrap equipment," Jackie said—but they were enough to get started. Cochran's school, built on a wing and a prayer, was christened the Women's Flying Training Detachment (WFTD), and the first class was scheduled to begin in mid-November.

ENGLAND WAS DAMP and cold. Nothing had heat. Everything was rationed. But London was splendid and only an hour away by train from Grace Stevenson's Air Transport Auxiliary base. Even during blackouts and the air raids London thumbed her nose at the Nazi bombers with parties, theater, nightclubs, and high spirits.

The wife of the United States ambassador set up a Red Cross club on Charles Street for the American nurses, and the ATA-girls were welcome anytime. The club served good coffee, Coca-Cola, and peanut butter in a country where every commodity was in short supply. The club had a reasonably priced dinner, perhaps the only one in London. Dormitory rooms rented for four shillings. There was even a jukebox, and in the evening an army band played dance music. It was London headquarters for Grace and the other American ATA-girls when they could get into London.

Grace had worked her way through various types of British aircraft and was assigned as a second officer to the 15th Ferry Pool in Hamble on the southern coast of England. The 15th was staffed exclusively by women, and ferrying new Spitfires from a nearby factory was their primary mission. The British Spitfire was a legend, a beautiful fighter plane that was one of the fastest aircraft in the world.

The women of the 15th Ferry Pool had come to England from far and wide—South Africa, Argentina, Poland—to fly for the British. England needed experienced pilots, male or female, and women had been flying for the ATA since 1940. If Grace were at home, she might be allowed to ferry military aircraft by now, but they would be primary trainers, not Spitfires.

In October 1942 Eleanor Roosevelt and Colonel Oveta Culp Hobby, commander of the WAC, traveled to England to learn about women in the British military. Of course they made a point of visiting the American women flying for the ATA. Grace was photographed, in uniform, shaking hands with Mrs. Roosevelt, and the picture appeared in *The New York Times* and *Look* magazine. Grace's mother made sure it was also on the front page of every newspaper in Oklahoma, Texas, and Arkansas.

WHILE THE PRESIDENT'S WIFE and Colonel Hobby were in England, Jacqueline Cochran, with Arnold's approval, made a fatal decision: for the time being the Women's Flying Training Detachment would be civil service employees, just like the WAFS, in order to avoid bureaucratic slowdowns. Cochran was eager to get her women "up and flying, off the ground." Military status and benefits would have to wait while more important matters were settled.

No one asked for congressional approval or funding for the WFTD, and there was still no legislation to commission or pay women flying officers. The money came from here and there in the civil service and Army Air Force budget.

On November 3 General Arnold wrote to Barton Yount, who had known Hap since they were both plebes at the academy, and preferred orders from the AAF commanding general *in writing*.

Arnold cited the strain the armed services were putting on the nation's manpower and instructed Yount's command—in almost exactly the words used by Cochran—to take immediate action on a program for women "to provide at the earliest possible date a sufficient number of women pilots to replace men in every noncombat flying duty in which it is feasible to employ women." A week later he wrote General Yount again saying that women in the air force was an idea whose time had come. "We must accept this principle without reservation and that literally, 'the sky is the limit' in our objectives for effecting it."

Simultaneously the Army Air Force distributed a public information directive on the WFTD/WAFS, who were defined as a "novel activity for the air force." This directive ordered AAF public information officers not to discuss militarization of the women pilots and included a statement for immediate release describing the positions of Miss Cochran and Mrs. Love and making it clear that Cochran was not a subordinate.

Even though she had dropped the required number of certified flying hours, Cochran nevertheless recruited the most experienced candidates she could find for the first few WFTD classes. The applicants also had to pass a regular AAF physical identical to the one given to prospective male combat pilots. She wanted to get her project off to a smooth start.

The revised admission standards stated, "Limitations of hours will not be published. Individuals will be selected based upon their own qualifications." These personal qualifications would be established by individual interviews with Cochran or Ethel Sheehy, the vice president of the Ninety-Nines, the new WFTD executive officer.

Jacqueline Cochran's ultimate goal was to prove that any healthy, stable young American woman could learn to fly the army way as well as her brothers, and she had her eye on the list of three thousand women with private licenses as a core of a Woman's Army Air Force Auxiliary. Interviews made it possible to screen out recruits with disturbing characteristics or undesirable backgrounds—no matter how much flying they had done. Jackie's girls had to be the best, above reproach.

With recruiting under way, Cochran urgently needed an administrator for the WFTD school, as well as a guardian for the girls, most of whom would be young women who in normal times would still be at home under their parents' care. A national field volunteer for the Red Cross, Leni Leoti "Dedie" Deaton was suggested for the position.

Mrs. Deaton, thirty-nine, married and the mother of an eighteen-year-old son, was from a pioneer Texas family in Wichita Falls. On the morning of November 8, 1943, she took a train to Fort Worth to talk about an exciting, top-secret project with celebrated Jacqueline Cochran. From the minute they met, Jackie knew Dedie was what the WFTD needed. Hardly before she realized it, Dedie Deaton had a civil service appointment, the title of establishment officer, and was on her way to Houston. That morning Deaton only expected to be away from home a short time, but she would be gone over two years.

Deaton was exhausted by the time her train got into Houston late that night. Her first and almost impossible assignment was to find housing and transportation in the sprawling city crowded with defense workers and military personnel.

Early the next morning she had a phone call from young army officer Lieutenant Alfred Fleishman. Somehow he had found out who she was and what she was up to. Fleishman was in charge of a supply depot next to Ellington AAFB, and he offered Dedie a ride out to the WFTD temporary facility at neighboring Howard Hughes Airport. He also helped her find a place to live, through his own landlady. Deaton was relieved and grateful. Lieutenant Fleishman said to let him know if he could do anything else.

JANE STRAUGHAN had learned to fly at a private airfield in Maryland, just for the fun of it. She worked for an aircraft-engine manufacturer as an assistant to the sales manager, and flying was a hobby she shared with her husband. In the fall of 1942 she had been married four years, and her husband was in the Army Air Force.

Jane was a member of the Ninety-Nines International Organization of Women Pilots. In October Jacqueline Cochran, the president of the group, invited Jane and several other members from the Washington area to a cocktail party in a suite at the Mayflower Hotel. Cochran had just gotten back from a well-publicized mission for the Air Transport Auxiliary in England, and the newspapers said she was now planning to train women for the AAF Air Transport Command.

The party was swell. Jackie told the Ninety-Nines about the work women pilots were doing in England, what an adventure they were having, and her vision of similar opportunities for women in America. "Which of you would like to do this?" Cochran asked them. After a drink or two Jane signed her name and address on a list.

The next thing Jane knew, she had orders to report to Houston, Texas. So did five others who had gone to the cocktail party. They were all curious, because neither Cochran's talk nor their orders gave them a definite idea what it was they were going to be doing.

Jane's husband told her, "Go ahead." He was flying mapping missions on the East Coast for the air force, but expected to be sent overseas at any time.

THE FIRST WOMEN'S FLYING TRAINING DETACHMENT class of twenty-eight women began November 16, 1942, just two short months after the program had been announced. The women were notified by a telegram from General Barton Yount that they had been selected for Army Air Force training and were ordered to report to the Rice Hotel in Houston at their own expense.

. . . BRING SUCH STREET CLOTHING AS YOU DEEM DESIRABLE TOGETHER WITH FUNDS FOR LIVING EXPENSES FOR THIRTY DAYS STOP PROVISIONS HAVE BEEN MADE FOR YOUR EMPLOYMENT ON CIVIL SERVICE STATUS AT THE RATE OF ONE HUNDRED AND FIFTY DOLLARS PER MONTH DURING YOUR SATISFAC- TORY PURSUANCE OF FLYING INSTRUCTIONS UNDER ARMY CONTROL STOP UPON SATISFACTORY COMPLETION OF ARMY INSTRUCTION COURSE AND IF PHYSICALLY QUALIFIED YOU WILL BE ELIGIBLE FOR EMPLOYMENT AS UTIL- ITY PILOT AT A RATE OF TWO HUNDRED FIFTY DOLLARS PER MONTH END

The women who gathered at the Rice Hotel that November morning looked each other over carefully. They were dressed in everything from tailored suits to cowboy boots. Some of them were career girls, others were college students, several were heiresses— and one was a movie stuntwoman. Over half the group was married. The average age was twenty-five, and they had all been flying for years. Each had logged more than two hundred hours of flying time, but for the majority flying was a personal interest, an enjoyment. For example, Jane Straughan had 250 hours, all of it in a Piper Cub on weekends and vacations.

A tall redhead dressed in a bright green jumpsuit with two equally redheaded Afghan hounds on leashes got everyone's attention. The dogs were even wearing bows to match their mistress's jumpsuit. She was Marion Florsheim, whose wealthy husband was related to the shoe magnate. Showing Afghan hounds was her hobby, and Marion had learned to fly so that she could transport her dogs to shows anywhere in the country.

The Rice had more uniforms per square inch in its busy lobby than any other hotel in Houston. Army Air Force cadets, naval officers, marines, coast guard, civilian-defense personnel, Red Cross volunteers—even Knights of Columbus. After sorting through this mayhem, the women discovered a civil service clerk waiting upstairs in a hotel room who gave them forms to fill out, in quadruplicate.

Before long Jacqueline Cochran swept into the room with an escort of Army Air Force officers and executives from Aviation Enterprises, the flight contractor. She was wearing an elegant suit with a striking lapel pin, a silver propeller with a large rosette diamond in the center.

She told them, "You have the honor and distinction of being the first women to be trained by the Army Air Force. You are very badly needed, and I hope that you will be out of here in two and a half to three months at the most." Cochran went on to say there was no hope of militarizing the women's unit. This sounded all right to Jane and the other married women. You could quit a job if you had to, but you couldn't quit the army.

The Women's Flying Training Detachment was top secret, they were warned. There would be no publicity, no glory. Just hard work. This was Class 43-W-1—not only because it was the first but also because the trainees were scheduled to graduate in 1943. The members of Class 43-W-1 were flying guinea pigs, and Jackie told them the future of women in military aviation depended on them.

Jackie introduced Dedie Deaton, using her puzzling title, establishment officer. Mrs. Deaton had been on the job a week. To this group of formidable, sophisticated women, she looked like a housewife and Red Cross volunteer. Dedie had never even been out of Texas, and right now she was unsure of herself.

Formidable women or not, the qualifications of Class 43-W-1 didn't cut any slack with the WFTD commanding officer, Captain Paul Garrett, who was introduced next. He had been shanghaied into the job by General Yount and he wasn't pleased. Garrett told the WFTD recruits, "If you think you're hot pilots, I'd advise you to forget it. You are here to learn to fly the way the army flies.

"The best way to get along here is to be where you're supposed to be and do what you're supposed to do.

"There are three things for which you can be washed out of this course. The first is that you can't fly. The second is that you can't do the ground-school work. The third is that your attitude isn't good."

Before the meeting Garrett had told Mrs. Deaton, "Keep the girls happy and out of my hair."

Class 43-W-1 took the oath of office, and Mrs. Deaton handed out a list of accommodations near Howard Hughes Airport. The hastily prepared list was meager, and since there were several cars in the group, the women decided to strike out on their own. By the next day one had an apartment over the gatehouse of an estate belonging to family friends, the du Ponts. Marion Florsheim, along with a French countess, and a blonde heiress (whose mailing address was c/o National City Bank, Park Avenue Branch, New York City), had each rented a suite of rooms in an uptown hotel. They were occupying an entire floor.

Jane Straughan teamed up with three other women from Washington and found rooms in a wealthy section of Houston where a few of the mansions had been turned into boardinghouses for working girls. Their rooms were in the former home of Oveta Culp Hobby, the head of the new Women's Army Corps, so the housemother accepted the story that they did classified work for the Army Air Force without question. But the other boarders were intrigued by their "secret" mission.

CAPTAIN GARRETT was absolutely right about learning to fly the army way. It was the most demanding flying most of the class had ever done, even though the new flight school was still essentially a catch-as-catch-can operation.

Before dawn they went to the field. Half of the day was spent flying in an odd collection of trainers, doing an endless variety of stalls, spins, and turns, as well as takeoffs and landings. Howard Hughes Airport was parallel to Ellington AAF Base, a huge facility where as many as five thousand male combat pilots were in training at a time. The air space swarmed with planes. Whenever a WFTD student came out of a spin and saw dark specks, she knew she didn't have spots before her eyes. Those were other planes.

The other half of the day was spent at ground school, where the trainees studied navigation, weather, communications, and mechanics. They learned ATC procedures and practiced instrument flying—staying on the beam—with high-pitched radio frequencies as their guide. Being back in a classroom with exacting instructors was the toughest part of the WFTD training for most of the women.

The trainees were at the field for twelve hours nearly every day. It was long after dark when they got back to their rooms, and they still had to do homework and laundry before going to bed.

The Women's Flying Training Detachment had an array of administrative difficulties. The only place to eat at Howard Hughes Airport was a small, crowded café in the terminal building. Since it was almost impossible for the women to find breakfast before they arrived at the field, many of them went all day without anything to eat but Cokes and candy bars. The trainees had no standard uniform. Captain Garrett got a kick out of encouraging them to buck discipline, assuring the class since they were civilians nobody could force them to obey military regulations. However, by far the most urgent problem was rest room facilities—only one john was available for twenty-eight women!

Dedie Deaton had her work cut out. She had been captured by Jackie Cochran's vision, but she knew she had to establish some order—and her authority—or the future of the women's flying program was in jeopardy. Deaton's inexperience limited her influence with the trainees in the first class. They seem to have agreed among themselves to give the chief establishment officer the cold shoulder and go about their business. Deaton was determined to be better prepared when the second class reported.

Lieutenant Fleishman, who chauffeured Dedie Deaton around her first day in Houston, had been watching the mob scene at Howard Hughes Airport since classes started. He decided to be the WFTD's Dutch uncle and straighten the situation out in his spare time. First he gave Deaton his copy of *The Officer's Guide and Army Regulations*, which she devoured looking for guidance. Her original instructions from Jackie—to "look after the girls"—had been thin.

Fleishman wrote a military indoctrination bulletin for the trainees. He appointed himself the WFTD athletic director and attempted to teach them how to march.

The women in 43-W-1 thought he was a pain in the neck. Just like the men in the AAF, they had decided that marching was for the infantry. The class wisecracked and talked in formation until they realized Fleishman was right about one thing: They were the first women to be trained to fly by the Army Air Force, and they ought to start looking and acting the part.

The members of the first class agreed during a private get-together that it was childish to continue in such an undisciplined manner. They decided on a dress code. They would obey the rules and do calisthenics and march, but Class 43-W-1 still resented the way Fleishman had butted in.

On the other hand, his help meant so much to Mrs. Deaton that General Yount transferred him from supply to the Flying Training Command as a special service officer. Despite his bumpy relationship with 43-W-1, Fleishman was immortalized by later classes in a marching cadence:

> Tramp, tramp, tramp, the girls are marching
> Marching everywhere we go
> First we march and then we drill
> If that won't kill you
> Fleishman will
> Listen boys, oh listen to our tale of woe.

MARIE MUCCIE was trembling all the way up in the elevator at Rockefeller Center. She was actually going to meet Jacqueline Cochran. Marie had a scrapbook full of news clippings and photographs of Cochran. She couldn't believe it when she had received a telegram at her parents' home in New Jersey asking her to meet Miss Cochran in her office for an interview. She knew Jackie was in charge of a program to train women pilots to fly for the air force. As the elevator door opened on the thirty-fifth floor, Marie prayed for a chance to join.

Before she was out of high school in Trenton, New Jersey, she had decided that somehow she was going to learn to fly. She also decided she'd better not tell her folks. Marie's parents had been born in Italy. They had twelve children, and their notions about their kids' futures, particularly their girls', were old-world. Daughters married and made homes for their husbands and children.

After graduation Marie got a job at a civilian airport near home. She put as much of her earnings as she could spare into flying lessons. Lessons were ten dollars an hour. Extra flying time was six dollars an hour. Marie cajoled and gassed planes to earn more time in the air. Every time she went up, Marie had to take along at least one pillow to sit on. Her five foot two inches needed help in reaching around the cockpit.

After the war started, Marie lost her job because the airport was too close to the coast. Civilian aviation in her part of New Jersey was finished for the time being, and it took her several weeks to find more work. Nothing else paid as well as the airport, so she ended up working two jobs.

Cochran sat at her desk in an office filled with antiques and samples of her cosmetic line, Wings to Beauty, looking over Marie's log book. When she saw over three hundred hours' flying time, she said, "We can use you."

She told Marie the first few classes would have to be outstanding because they were an experiment to see if a women's pilot program would succeed with the air force. Jackie wanted her to be part of the second class forming in Houston.

Marie couldn't believe it. "What about college? I don't have a college education."

"That's not required," Jackie assured her. Marie was nearly two inches too short, but that wasn't a problem either. Just one thing: Marie was still a minor; she wasn't twenty-one. "Can you get your parents' written permission?"

Marie would do it somehow. Then Jackie asked, "When can you leave? You need to take a physical when you get to Houston."

"As soon as I can get some money," Marie told her. "I'm flat broke. I lost a good job at an airport, and right now I don't have a dime."

Cochran told Marie she would lend her the seventy-five dollars' train fare to Houston. A beautiful fairy godmother had just tapped Marie with her magic wand. Now all she had to do was tell her father she knew how to fly—and get him to sign the WFDT release.

He said no.

[74]

"Then I'll join the ATA," she threatened, telling him what women pilots were doing in England.

"And fly where they are bombing and shooting?" He cried, wringing his hands. "You'll be killed for sure."

Marie had already tried the Air Transport Auxiliary and had been turned down due to her size. Since there was no way her father could know this, she watched silently while he signed the Women's Flying Training Detachment form.

When Marie Muccie got to Houston in the middle of December, she was told to check into the Alamo Inn about fifteen miles from Howard Hughes Airport. The rooms were two dollars a night.

Mrs. Deaton had decided the next class must live together, rather than be scattered all over the city like the unruly members of Class 43-W-1. She knew unity and discipline were required from here on out if Cochran's plan for a women's air corps was to succeed. She persuaded several tourist courts adjacent to one another to rent blocks of rooms to house the incoming WFTD students.

Cochran was shocked when she found out. Tourist courts had a horrible reputation! Her girls were having enough trouble maintaining their good name because of the odd hours they kept and the secrecy of their work.

Deaton talked fast—before she got fired. She convinced Jackie that under the circumstances the tourist courts were the only solution to locating the girls in groups so that they could have proper supervision and be transported to the airfield by buses.

The day Marie and the sixty members of class 43-W-2 arrived, Aviation Enterprises finally opened a mess hall. It was three-quarters of a mile from the hangars and classrooms, and Fleishman marched the recruits in formation to every meal. They lined up for roll call each day before sunrise. The class was organized into squadrons with student officers, just like the male cadets, and introduced to a set of regulations adopted from the AAF Training Command, complete with demerits for infractions.

Marie Muccie and her classmates were younger and living together from the start; they tended to group together. They smuggled radios into the mess hall and jitterbugged together. To the first class they seemed noisy and too self-assured. Even worse, they were apparently going to settle right in without any complaints and accept all of Deaton and Fleishman's rules.

There were many outstanding pilots in the second and third classes. While the majority of 43-W-1 came from the East Coast, the women in the next two classes were from all over the United States. Many had learned to fly because it had been practical. They lived where it was a long way to anywhere else—Oklahoma, California, and rural areas in the Midwest.

By the time these classes reported, Mrs. Deaton had set up an infirmary with a nurse on duty and a doctor and dentist on call. The medical problems of the young women in her charge ranged from an outbreak of the crabs to an epidemic of measles. The cold, damp climate put five of the girls in bed at the same time with pneumonia.

Because there were no recreational facilities at the airfield, Deaton made arrangements for the girls to have use of the YMCA swimming pool one night a week. She got them seats at the Houston Symphony and tried to hold dances with the AAF cadets at Ellington, but the strenuous training schedules for both groups ruined this idea.

None of the WFTD trainees had uniforms except for AAF coveralls and leather flying jackets. The regulation khaki coveralls were so huge on most of the women that the crotch hung down between their knees. They rolled up the arms and legs, belted the middle, and composed songs about the baggy coveralls, which they nicknamed zoot suits.

> Once we wore scanties, now we're in zoots
> They are our issue GI flying suits
> They come in all sizes, large, Large, and LARGE
> We look like a great big barrage.

At first the only bus available to transport the new classes from the tourist courts was one that had been used by a Tyrolean orchestra. Eventually the army provided trucks that pulled covered trailers outfitted with wooden benches, but for several weeks the trainees rode in a fancy white bus decorated with red-and-white striped awnings and edelweiss. Mrs. Deaton quipped to Jackie that this bus certainly helped maintain the secrecy of the WFTD mission.

In any case keeping the women's flight training hush-hush was a joke by the time the third class began in January. When the women were out in a group and people asked what they were doing in Houston, a favorite answer was, "We're a women's basketball team." Since about a third of the trainees were five feet two inches or less, this reply guaranteed hilarious reactions.

After the first of the year a Houston radio program asked for permission to interview some of the trainees. Indignant, Jackie rushed to Houston from her office in Fort Worth to stop the leak. Since the request had come from a Houston station, she decided to blame Sidney Miller, because she was the only Texan in the first class.

Despite her anger, Cochran had to admit there was no practical way of keeping what was now over 150 young women on an important, classified mission for the Army Air Force entirely invisible. She made a deal with the radio station. She would allow interviews—they could even use Sidney, the good-looking daughter of the mayor of Mineral Wells—if they promised not to put them on the air until the first class graduated. By then Cochran would be ready to tell the world that her flight school, her girls, were a success.

Something occurred when the third class reported that contributed immeasurably to this success. The Women's Flying Training Detachment got a new commanding officer, Major Walter Farmer, a young West Point graduate. He took them seriously. He worked seven days a week planning schedules, checking on instructors, and talking to the WFTD students. He also assembled a staff of air force officers who respected the trainees and supported Mrs. Deaton. Major Farmer was a boost to self-confidence and morale because he believed the women pilots could realize their goals, and he was tremendously popular with the girls.

Major Farmer's presence plus the military routine and discipline were having a positive effect on the Women's Flying Training Detachment, and the atmosphere at Howard Hughes Airport in Houston changed. For Jane Straughan and her classmates the work became more serious and concentrated as they moved into advanced trainers and started making cross-country flights in twin-engine aircraft. The members of 43-W-1 began to accept the role of upperclassmen and a real sense of esprit de corps was obvious among the trainees and the staff.

Songs took on more significance, even though Cochran sometimes objected to the earthy lyrics. The weather, the food, patriotic sentiments, men, washing out of flight school—even the early difficulties in the detachment—all provided musical inspiration. One ditty in particular, sung to the tune "There'll Be Some Changes Made," reflected the trainees' new attitude.

> There'll be a change on the flight line
> A change on the bus.
> From now on there'll be a change in us
> Our walk will be different
> Our style and our dress
> No more shirttails hanging out in the mess.
>
> We're gonna change our way of living,
> And if that ain't enough,
> We'll change the way we use our powder and puff.
> Our slacks will be pressed
> And our shoes will all shine.
> We'll wear our hairnets when we're out on the line.
>
> And when the lieutenant calls attention
> We will give him no sass
> 'Cause from now on we'll be cooking with gas!
> We'll get demerits if we don't obey
> There were some changes made today.

By now the Women's Flying Training Detachment even had its own insignia. During World War II these distinguishing emblems were an important way for military units to express spirit and unity. Walt Disney, who designed the insignia for the Flying Tigers, gave the women pilots Fifinella, a spunky little female gremlin with long eyelashes, hip boots, and gossamer wings, who came zipping merrily out of a bank of clouds. Fifinella's job was to scare off male gremlins—who were widely known to be the cause of most aircraft malfunctions.

One day a WFTD flight instructor and a young captain from Ellington AAF Base were exchanging cigarettes on the flight line and watching the planes circling overhead. A trainer banked, put its wheels down, and made a final approach. The captain said, "If it's a gal, I'll bet she bounces the landing.

"A dollar says she doesn't," replied the WFTD instructor.

"I'll match my boys against your girls."

"It's a deal. I'll give you a dollar for every bad landing the girls make, and take a dollar for every one the boys mess up."

"It's a deal."

It was a bad day for the young captain, and the WFTD instructor was all smiles. The girls couldn't seem to miss. Every landing was smoother than silk. Before the afternoon was over, the captain was borrowing dollars to pay off his bet from the boys who bounced in.

GENERAL HAP ARNOLD had been to North Africa and then to China to check on AAF operations for himself. He even flew over the Hump, the deadly five-hundred-mile supply route over the mighty Himalayas into China.

The day after Arnold returned to Washington, the second B-29 test plane took off from the Seattle municipal airport. Half an hour later, with a wing on fire, the bomber smashed into a packing plant, killing the crew and several people on the ground.

When General Arnold heard about the tragedy in Seattle, he knew he was in trouble. Ever since its maiden flight in September, the sophisticated Superfortress had developed one problem after another. Now it would be months before the bomber could be ready for combat. Arnold had to deliver the B-29, make it do the job for the air force, or in spite of his popularity in Congress, he would have a lot of explaining to do.

The next day, on Sunday, February 28, Hap Arnold was spending the afternoon at home after meeting all morning with the president. He complained to his wife, Bee, about pains in his chest. Much against his will, the general was taken to Walter Reed Army Hospital, where he was diagnosed as having had a severe heart attack.

The attack was kept quiet, and he was flown to an army convalescent hospital in Florida to recuperate. His wife chose not to go with him.

The Arnolds had been married over thirty years and had four children, a married daughter and three sons. They had always been an army family, but something was different now—the war. One of their boys was with the army in Italy, another was about to graduate from the United States Military Academy, and their son-in-law was a naval officer. Arnold was never home. He was either out of the country or in his office working eighteen-hour days. The general was popular and important, very important. Bee and Hap had seen little of each other for two years.

CLASS 43-W-1 was night flying. The lighting at Howard Hughes Airport was primitive, and the new, inexperienced controllers in the tower had problems issuing clear instructions. Many nights the traffic pattern over the field was a confusion of circling planes attempting to obey conflicting orders from the tower—and stay out of each other's way. It made everyone nervous—the girls, their instructors, and Major Farmer.

The wet winter weather in Houston was also causing problems. Flight training was often delayed due to fog and rain. Class 43-W-1 was under pressure to finish the required number of hours so that they could graduate.

On February 15, 1943, sixty-three members of class 43-W-4 reported to Howard Hughes Airport. The rookies looked around at their small numbers. Something was cockeyed. Cochran would never train five hundred pilots, as she promised, at this rate. The fourth WFTD class worried about the future of the women's program—and their own.

The first week in March Jackie Cochran flew to Houston in her souped-up Beechcraft Staggerwing, named *Wings to Beauty* for her cosmetics firm. As the fast and flashy biplane approached Howard Hughes Airport, her voice crackled over the radio, "This is Jacqueline Cochran. Clear the air. I'm coming in for a landing."

The little trainers in the busy traffic pattern scrambled to get out of the way as Cochran roared straight in for a landing. She taxied up to the WFTD hangars, cut her engine, and climbed out of the cockpit with a full-length mink coat draped over her arm. "What an entrance!" whispered Sidney Miller, who was on the flight line.

Jackie had come to tell her four WFTD classes that the air force was expanding the women's program. Instead of 500 pilots, they now wanted 750 by the end of 1943, and another 1,000 in 1944. In order to accomplish this task, the Women's Flying Training Detachment would move to its own training facility, Avenger Field, Sweetwater, Texas, where they would have much better equipment, including all the PT-19s and AT-6 Texan trainers they needed.

Cochran had hired more administrative staff. Aviation Enterprises, Ltd., would continue to be the civilian contractor at the new location, and extensive construction was already under way on additional runways, a mess hall, classrooms, offices, and a chapel.

Since there were still AAF cadets at Avenger finishing primary training, the women's detachment wouldn't leave Houston before May. However, she added, there were already more than eighty trainees at Sweetwater, the additional members of 43-W-4 who had reported a week later than those in Houston.

Jackie's announcement was heartening news! It made everyone in Houston feel as if they were right on the beam, that they were a success. The brass in Washington thought they were okay.

Shadowing Cochran's triumphant visit, death visited the Women's Flying Training Detachment for the first time. Margaret Oldenburg, a novice from the fourth class, and her instructor died in the crash of a PT-19 on March 7. Margaret had been in Houston for only three weeks. Since an instructor was in the plane, he got the blame. Major Farmer immediately flight-checked all of the instructors and replaced a few of them. Mrs. Deaton mothered the grieving trainees and arranged to have Margaret's body shipped to her family. On orders from the Training Command, the accident was kept quiet—an unfortunate incident during a secret project.

Afterward Deaton flew to Sweetwater to see the new facility and meet the women who were already there. Because of the AAF cadets at Avenger, the chief establishment officer was the one who had to give the okay for these women to begin training. Tourist courts aside, Cochran had learned to trust Deaton completely and to rely on her good judgment. Cochran told Deaton the decision to mix girls and boys on the same base was hers, and any trouble would be hers too.

By this time Deaton had several helpers, assistant establishment officers, not only at Avenger but in Houston as well. However, because Deaton felt obligated to be both places at once, she commuted back and forth between the two bases for a month or more. After five months she had become the final authority on everything to do with the trainees, except flying. When the girls talked about her now, she was Dedie.

Her office at Avenger Field was finished just before 125 rookies of the fifth class reported to Sweetwater in mid-March. On April 5, 1943, only seven weeks after beginning training, the 43-W-4 trainees in Houston flew the detachment's primary trainers up to Avenger to join their classmates. Major Walter Farmer, their commanding officer, led them north, with two girls in each light plane. They took turns flying, and at a hundred miles per hour the trip took several hours. They stopped for a picnic lunch on the way. With all of the fourth and fifth classes, over 250 young women, at the field in Sweetwater, Deaton moved to Avenger on a permanent basis.

In Houston the twenty-three women remaining in the first class, the guinea pigs, were ready to graduate, five months after starting in the training program, not two and a half or three as Cochran had originally hoped. She decided to introduce her girls to America at the graduation and delayed the ceremony even further, until late April, when all the details were to her satisfaction. In the meantime the class got in extra Link trainer time at Ellington Army Air Force Base and practiced marching. With over a hundred trainees from the other two classes marching in formation with them, the 43-W-1 graduation parade was going to be impressive.

The women decided on a uniform, of sorts, for the occasion. They bought long-sleeved, open-neck white shirts, khaki overseas caps, and trousers from the Ellington Post Exchange. The loose, high-waisted khakis were dubbed general's pants because the fit resembled the baggy seat on an elderly commander's trousers. This outfit became the WFTD standard dress, even on duty, while the final decision on the *right* uniform for the women pilots bounced between AAF commands for many months.

Just before the appointed day Deaton realized that the graduates had no wings, the official symbol of all pilots. She went to Major Farmer, and he agreed. There had to be wings, even if he had to make them himself. "Now, you get them some," he ordered.

Deaton couldn't find Cochran anywhere, so she called Floyd Odlum, Jackie's husband. He quickly approved and said, "Send me the bill."

Deaton and Lieutenant Fleishman bought regular AAF wings at the Ellington P-X and had a local jeweler buff off the center shield. Then he engraved the women's class and training detachment number in its place.

April 28, 1943, was a hot, muggy day in Houston. The Women's

Flying Training Detachment rode to Ellington Field in steamy buses for Class 43-W-1's graduation ceremony. Flags were flying, bunting billowed in the breeze, and army brass filled the reviewing stand. Much to the women's surprise they weren't top secret anymore. Reporters were everywhere. The local papers were nearly smothered by the United Press, Associated Press, and Movietone newsreels. The Army Air Force general delivering the commencement address said, "I guess you've done it again. You've shown us that one of the things we thought was a male prerogative can be done just as well by women. You girls who have just completed training have shown that you can take the training men can take and can achieve the same degree of efficiency. We are proud of you." Jacqueline Cochran added God's blessing.

The commanding officer of Ellington Field was chosen to pin the graduates' wings on their chests. He wasn't too sure how to go about it, so he whispered to the girls, "I've done this for hundreds of cadets, but I've never pinned wings on a woman before. If I stick you, for heaven's sake, don't jump. My wife is in the first row, and I'd never live it down."

Flashbulbs popped when Admiral L. C. Colbert pinned the wings on his daughter, Mary Lou. Father-daughter, navy-army: the picture was in every major paper the next morning.

After two weeks' leave the graduates of the first WFTD class reported to the women's squadrons at Dallas, Long Beach, Wilmington, and Romulus. Jane Straughan was assigned to the original squadron at New Castle AAFB and immediately went to work delivering planes.

May 16, 1943, after four months at Houston, the forty-four trainees surviving out of the third class flew to Sweetwater to complete their training. The girls felt like real ferry pilots as they transferred the 450-horsepower BT-13s halfway across the state of Texas to the new WFTD flight school. The formation stopped at an AAF base for lunch, where the elated girls sat together in the cafeteria and whistled at every good-looking soldier who walked in the door.

Less than two weeks later, on May 28, 1943, the day before their graduation ceremony, forty-three women of 43-W-2, Marie Muccie's class, brought the fast, powerful AT-6s and the twin-engine AT-17 advanced trainers up from Howard Hughes Airport. After the ceremony Marie handed Jackie Cochran seventy-five dollars in cash. She was repaying the money her fairy godmother had lent her for a train ticket to Houston.

The exodus of 43-W-2 marked the close of the WFTD training program in Houston. Five classes of the Women's Flying Training Detachment, with over four hundred young women, were under way in Sweetwater, and sixty-six newly trained women pilots were on duty with the Women's Auxiliary Ferrying Squadron. Jacqueline Cochran's program was indeed up and flying, off the ground.

5.

The Women Airforce Service Pilots

AFTER NANCY LOVE CHECKED OUT in a P-51 Mustang at Long Beach in late February 1943, she transferred to the 6th Ferrying Group permanently. This group moved a large number and variety of aircraft from the multitude of factories in southern California, and only the most experienced and self-confident WAFS were assigned here. Due to the scarcity of seasoned pilots, these women ferried basic and advanced trainers from the first, even though this was against the Ferry Division policy, which restricted the WAFS to primary-type aircraft.

Nancy continued taking transition in heavier, faster planes at Long Beach. Because of General Arnold's enthusiastic reaction to the concept of women pilots in the air force, ATC headquarters urged Love to prove what a woman could do. She reveled in the task and got a kick out of teasing her husband, Bob, who was stuck behind a desk in Washington, about the extraordinary planes she was flying—most of which he would never have an opportunity to handle.

However, after Nancy Love and B. J. Erickson, the WAFS squadron leader at the 6th, delivered a twin-engine C-47 Gooney Bird to Memphis in early March, the Ferry Division flexed its muscles and issued orders *again* that no WAFS were to pilot or copilot multiengine aircraft.

Colonel William Tunner was on edge over the women ferry pilots. All in all he didn't like the way the situation was shaping up. Scuttlebutt had the expanded Women's Flying Training Detachment near Sweetwater, Texas, turning out hundreds of women pilots. Tunner had no intention of letting his command be a dumping ground for all of Jacqueline Cochran's graduates, but the attitude of ATC headquarters toward Nancy Love's illicit flying indicated that a large number of women might soon be ferrying. Worse yet, several Army Air Force generals—besides H. H. Arnold—seemed to have jumped on the women's air corps bandwagon.

DESPITE HIS DREAD, by March Colonel Tunner had yet to lay eyes on any of Cochran's graduates, although he had the nucleus of four WAFS squadrons ready and waiting for over six weeks. Meanwhile the originals stationed at these squadrons continued to pile up excellent delivery records. The women at the 5th Ferrying Group, Dallas Love Field, made hops all over the Southwest delivering trainers to AAF flight schools. The five originals on duty at the 6th Ferrying Group in California proved to be so valuable that the group's commanding officer was clamoring for more women pilots.

At New Castle AAFB, Delaware, Betty Gillies and Colonel Baker, the ferrying group commander, got along well, and she was able to turn the routine paperwork over to a WAFS who had been grounded because she and her husband were expecting a baby. Betty was out of her office and in the air nearly as often as the women under her command.

While most of the 2nd Ferrying Group WAFS continued to ferry trainers and utility planes, after Betty transitioned into the P-47, two other veteran women pilots also learned to fly the Thunderbolt. Morale was high.

The situation at Romulus AAFB was another matter. Not long after the orignals arrived in January they agreed the only thing frostier than the winter weather in Michigan was the behavior of the officers and men of the 3rd Ferrying Group.

Romulus was a huge AAF modification center, and the women's barracks were half a mile from the ferrying group with no reliable means of transportation. Operations took the regulations restricting women pilots to light aircraft seriously. They were invariably assigned to open-cockpit PT-19s, and during the freezing weather at least one or two of the WAFS were usually grounded with runny noses and coughs. Because they were not allowed in the officers' mess in slacks, the women had to change out of their flying clothes before every meal. They never seemed to be able to get Link trainer time or transition training. From the first the WAFS faced a cold, courteous conspiracy at Romulus.

BY SPRING all of the originals were flying longer missions, and they were often away from base several days at a time. For the women of the 2nd Ferrying Group, delivering Piper Cubs from the factory in Lockhaven, Pennsylvania, to flight schools in the Southwest was a week's work. Just before sunrise they flew to the factory in the WAFS transport plane, hauling all their flying gear. In mild weather a flight of Cubs could usually get as far as Atlanta the first day.

Even though this airport was the largest military base in the area, there was no place for the women to sleep. They had to take a taxi into town and find a bed, safely away from the men. By dawn of the next day the WAFS were hopping across the South between fuel stops to Shreveport, Louisiana, the second night's stop.

The third day they landed in Dallas and then flew on to an AAF training field in some desolate place farther west. Once the paperwork on the Cubs was finished, the women put on their uniform skirts, spruced up, and caught the late bus from the nearest small town. After riding several hours back to Dallas, the WAFS took the first American Airlines flight to Washington.

In spite of their notoriety, the WAFS' official gray uniform wasn't

familiar to most people. They were mistaken for nurses, WACs,
Red Cross workers—or airline stewardesses. Someone in the airport
waiting room was sure to ask if lunch was served on the flight or
what time the plane got to Kansas City.

It was eleven hours' flying time to Washington, where they
boarded a train to Wilmington and then grabbed a taxi out to New
Castle AAFB. They still had to file reports before they could wash
their hair and get some sleep.

THE LATE AFTERNOON AIR was springtime soft. Flimsy clouds
brushed against the brilliant blue sky. Across the rolling rangelands
a few bluebonnets and bright Indian paints mixed with snatches of
new green grass, and the sagebrush was in full bloom. March 21,
1943, was a beautiful day in west Texas.

A loose formation of seven Army Air Force BT-13s was heading
east, away from the late afternoon sun. The pilots from the 6th
Ferrying Group had left Long Beach, California, at dawn, and
when they sighted the rugged, blood-red mesas near Big Spring,
they knew Love Field, their final destination, was only a little over
an hour away. The planes had just passed Sweetwater, Texas, a
few minutes before, and Abilene was coming up next.

The sun was very warm, and the trainers' canopies were pushed
back to catch the wind. Cornelia Fort looked down at the flat ranch
land below. She heard that Jacqueline Cochran had moved her
women's flying school to an airfield around here. Well, this was
sure the wide open spaces, nothing to get in their way. Maybe she'd
land and check out Cochran's new setup on the next delivery. But
not today. Cornelia had been having trouble all day with the guys
flying in formation with her. She just wanted to get to Dallas.

One guy in particular thought he was hot stuff, flirting and showing off. When Cornelia landed at Love Field, she planned to go out
to dinner with whoever was around the WAFS' quarters. She didn't
want to take a chance on running into this dumb lug at the Officers'
Club.

The plane on Cornelia's wing suddenly peeled away from the
formation. Holy smoke, there he goes again. The stray BT-13 pulled
up above the formation and then nosed into a rolling dive. Cornelia
looked up through the open canopy as the plane closed in on her.
Hey, brother . . .

It appears that the landing gear leg on F/O Stamme's aircraft No. 42450 broke off the left wing tip of Pilot Fort's aircraft No. 42432, and peeled approximately 6 feet of the leading edge of the wing toward the center of the aircraft. . . . F/O Stamme's aircraft did not go out of control. Pilot Fort's aircraft apparently went out of control, and after executing a series of rolls, went into an inverted dive, slowly rotating to the left. There was apparently no attempt to recover or to use the parachute. The emergency latch on the hatch release was found to be locked. . . . the aircraft apparently hit vertically and did not move from the point of contact. The marks outlining the wings were very distinct on the ground, and the engine was buried approximately two feet in the ground, and showed no movement after impact. [AAF description of accident, April 2, 1943]

Amazingly, Cornelia's plane did not catch fire when it spun into the ground. Four of the other trainers, including F/O Frank Stamme's, dropped down and circled over her shattered BT-13 for about fifteen minutes. There was no sign of life. How could this have happened? It had only been a game. She hadn't even tried to pull out. Had she hit her head, been knocked out, on the first roll? She was out when she hit the ground, don't you think? It had only been a game.

After a while the circling planes left. Frank Stamme made an emergency landing at Abilene, the nearest AAF base, to report the accident and to find out how badly his own aircraft had been damaged. The others proceeded on their flight plan to Dallas.

The next morning Cornelia's mother received a telegram from her daughter's commanding officer at the 6th Ferrying Group, Long Beach, California.

IT IS MY SAD DUTY TO INFORM YOU OF THE DEATH OF YOUR DAUGHTER CORNELIA FORT ON SUNDAY MARCH 21 1943

Cornelia's remains were shipped home by train, and the notice of her death was posted on FERD bulletin boards across the country. Nancy Love and Betty Gillies flew to Nashville for the funeral, and Christ Episcopal Church was filled with flowers, including yellow roses from the governor of Tennessee. The city and the state mourned with the Fort family.

A few weeks after her close call at Pearl Harbor, Cornelia had mailed her mother a letter from Hawaii, musing about the possibility of violent death in the skies: "I was happiest in the sky—at dawn when the quietness of the air was like a caress, when the noon sun beat down and at dusk when the sky was drenched with the fading light. Think of me there and remember me, I hope as I shall you, with love."

Nancy Love, who could never think of the right words in public, wrote to Mrs. Fort later from California. The letter said she had loved Cornelia—and that Cornelia had died as she wanted to, in an army plane in the service of her country.

With her death at twenty-four, Cornelia Fort reaped the uneasy honor of being the first woman pilot in the nation's history to die on active duty. More deaths would follow. However, except for one minor incident, hers was the first accident of any kind for the WAFS since the women's ferrying squadron had begun six months before. Cornelia was one of the most experienced WAFS in the squadron and had had over 1,100 hours' flying time when she was killed. The AAF accident inquiry found no pilot error on her part.

Nonetheless, on March 25, 1943, four days after Cornelia's accident, the WAFS at Romulus AAFB were permanently restricted to primary trainers. They were told to forget about transition. Also they would not be allowed to fly as copilots or ferry in flights with the men. And whenever possible WAFS would make deliveries on alternate days from male pilots, in order to keep them totally separate. Since their future flying duties would be so limited, one officer suggested the women pilots ought do some of the ferrying group's clerical work—typing and so forth.

A file copy of the Romulus orders at FERD headquarters had a penciled note in its margin: *Mrs. Love objected to this directive.* Actually Nancy hit the roof when she found out what was going on at Romulus. She went over Colonel Tunner's head and requested that Air Transport Command headquarters in Washington take a stand on the WAFS issue.

Before the ATC could get back to her, Nancy was forced to go outside of channels again. Four days after the Romulus restrictions went into effect, all ferrying-group commanders received a letter from the army with instructions that no woman would be allowed to fly during pregnancy—or from one day prior to her menstrual period to two days after the last day of the period. In effect this ruling grounded every WAFS for six to eight days *each month!*

This time Nancy consulted the Air Transport Command flight surgeon for an alternate opinion. He agreed pregnancy should be a disqualification, but said whether or not a woman ought to fly during her period was an individual problem. Let the WAFS squadron leaders or the doctors at the various bases make this decision. In any case, he asked, how could such a ban be enforced without the intimate cooperation of the women? How were the commanding officers to obtain this? On the other hand, the flight surgeon ruled that any delay on a cross-country ferrying trip due to a menstrual period shouldn't result in an official reprimand.

BETTY GILLIES had a notion of her own about how to calm the jitters following Cornelia's death. She took on a ferry mission that would test the limits of her WAFS and remind the Ferry Division of just what they were capable.

Three weeks after Cornelia's accident Betty led a flight of four primary trainers from Hagerstown, Maryland, to Calgary, Canada, a distance of 2,500 miles, for delivery to the Royal Air Force. The flight left at dawn on Sunday, April 18, and with a cruising speed of only a hundred miles per hour, the planes landed at Joliet, Illinois, just before dark. In spite of time-consuming fuel stops, the WAFS had covered seven hundred miles the first day.

The four were airborne again at daybreak and spent the next night at North Platte, Nebraska, after flying six hundred miles. By this time the haggard women with Betty suspected their determined squadron leader had a goal in mind, but wondered if they could continue to keep up the pace.

The third day out they landed at Great Falls, Montana, a large ferry base near the Canadian border where aircraft bound for Canada and Russia were processed through customs. No one at Great Falls could believe the women had flown 850 miles since sunrise.

On Thursday morning the WAFS flew across the border and delivered the trainers to the RAF in Calgary. All four pilots were back at the 2nd Ferrying Group by Friday evening, April 23. Colonel Baker wrote a letter to headquarters commending their record-breaking performance and the fine work of the entire Women's Auxiliary Ferrying Squadron. The outstanding mission was not only a boost to WAFS morale but a tribute to Cornelia from the women who had served with her.

ON APRIL 26 Nancy got the support she was asking for from the Air Transport Command. The deputy chief of staff, C. R. Smith, sent a letter to Ferry Division headquarters: "It is the desire of this command that all pilots, regardless of sex, be privileged to advance to the extent of their ability." This policy was to apply to all ferrying assignments within the United States.

Actually Colonel William Tunner had decided even before Smith's letter that he must adopt a more liberal policy for the WAFS. At any time he was expecting the first of Cochran's graduates. Even if Tunner succeeded in keeping the number of women in his division under three hundred, this many pilots in Class I would clog up the beginning level of training used to upgrade green ferry pilots into multiengine planes. The women would have to advance from primary trainers through the various levels of aircraft just like the men.

Tunner drew up a revised set of rules for WAFS operations that allowed the women under his command to transition into high-powered and multiengine aircraft under the same standard as "any other pilot." Still, no WAFS was to fly as pilot or copilot with a man, except during training missions, and no flights of aircraft piloted by both sexes could have the same clearance unless they were training flights. Under no circumstances were WAFS to fly in a close formation. They must stay at least five hundred feet away from any other plane.

This change of policy on the WAFS caused consternation at Tunner's staff meetings for weeks. One angry officer asked if Tunner was even going to let the women fly the P-51 Mustang, the hot pursuit just heading for combat. "Yes," the colonel replied, "they will fly everything they are capable of flying. In fact, as matters stand, they have to."

LELA LOUDDER went to Corpus Christi, Texas, in August 1942 to be a Link trainer instructor for the navy. She was a twenty-year-old cattleman's daughter from the Texas Panhandle, and this was the first time she had ever been away from home. She had enrolled in the Civilian Pilot Training at West Texas State College in her hometown of Canyon and had whizzed through the course. Then she sweet-talked her daddy, over her mother's objections, into paying for advanced training.

When Lela graduated from college in May 1941, she got a job as a music teacher near home. Much to her mother's horror, Lela used her salary to buy part interest in an airplane. She flew as much as her five partners and the weather allowed, and the hours started to mount up in her pilot's log book.

One of her partners, a local doctor, heard the navy was hiring women to be Link trainer operators, teaching instrument flying to Naval Aviation cadets. He encouraged Lela to apply. After all, she was a pilot *and* a teacher. Lela wasn't so sure.

Not very long afterward she received orders from the United States Navy assigning her to the naval air station at Corpus Christi, down on the Texas coast. The doctor had liked his idea so much he had filled out an application for her. Why not? thought Lela. Why? asked her mother.

Corpus Christi was sure different from her hometown of Canyon, even if they were both in Texas. Corpus was at least twenty times bigger, and, it seemed to Lela, everybody was young. The Gulf Coast city was bursting with people—naval aviation cadets, defense workers, fishermen, merchant seamen, and oil field hands. Corpus was built on the beach and had seawalls, bath houses, and palm trees. Canyon had prairie grass, tumbleweed, and cows.

The docks and the naval air station were jumping with activity. Corpus Christi was a major port, ringed with oil fields producing a quarter of a million barrels a year. Freighters from all over the world jammed the turning basin and the channel to the open sea. Navy planes and navy talk filled the air and navy uniforms filled the streets. Lela never knew there could be so much excitement.

At first she lived in a female boardinghouse, but within a few weeks she hooked up with six other girls working at the naval air station. They rented a house in town, 118 Maple Street, from a lieutenant commander in the navy, and they settled down to have an adventure and some good times.

During the day Lela taught naval aviation cadets instrument flying in the Link trainer. They were boys, nineteen and twenty, some twenty-one. Instrument training was critical for them. Navy pilots

[93]

couldn't use landmarks to navigate by. At sea these boys would have to get back to their carriers with dials and radio signals.

The Link trainer was a ridiculous-looking contraption, a toy airplane, with stubby wings, that turned and bobbed on a pedestal in simulated flight. With the cockpit closed, the Link had no ventilation, and in the humid Gulf Coast climate, it richly deserved the nickname Sweatbox.

Lela sat at a table loaded with electronic equipment and talked to her student in the trainer through his earphones. The navy had taught her what to do, and as a bonus she got three hours of flying time a month in a basic trainer. Lela thought Corpus and the navy were wonderful, and she would never forget them.

One of the girls Lela shared the house on Maple Street with told her that Jackie Cochran was training women to be ferry pilots over at an airport in Houston. You needed seventy-five hours' flying time to get into the program, she said, and they would teach you to fly all kinds of stuff. On top of that the graduates were supposed to get commissions in the Army Air Force.

Lela thought this sounded great, but her boss at the naval air station didn't. No, ma'am, he needed her right where she was—in Corpus. She had signed a contract. Forget Houston.

Two of Lela's roommates were accepted into Cochran's school. That did it. She told her boss she was leaving, going to Houston. Just what was he going to do about that? Lela knew she was only bluffing, but it worked. He let her out of the contract.

Cochran's office scheduled Lela's physical at the naval air station's hospital. She checked out fine, and so did her other credentials, because she got a letter of acceptance right away. All she needed, it said, was written permission from her parents since she was a minor.

Lela went home to Canyon the next week. But she was pretty sure neither of her parents was going to like her plans.

BY LATE SPRING of 1943 questions surfaced again about the status of both the WAFS and Cochran's WFTD in Texas. After several months both groups were still part of the civil service, although this arrangement was supposed to have been temporary. Now the first of Cochran's girls were about to report to duty with the WAFS, and there were four hundred more women in training.

The Women's Flying Training Detachment had been equipped and staffed almost by sleight of hand through an authorization to use civilian pilots in military aircraft. Congress had never specifically approved funds to teach women to fly the army way. Also, as under the current arrangement, there was nothing to prevent these women, who were getting the best and most expensive flight training, from resigning at any time.

While they didn't have to obey military regulations, they also did not have the protection of military benefits. Two women—Margaret Oldenburg, a student, and Cornelia Fort—had already been killed. Neither of them had been entitled to burial expenses or survivor's benefits. On top of this, medical care for sick or injured girls was piecemeal, up to the good graces of base commanders.

The proposal to put the women pilots into the WAC had been off-again, on-again during the fall of 1942. The WAC was still an auxiliary military corps, and the Ferry Division decided the WAC, in its present legislative form, wouldn't do.

Jackie Cochran had never wanted anything to do with the WAC. She made no secret of her disdain for Mrs. Hobby, whom she loved to refer to as a housewife. What did she know about flyers? Cochran planned a separate women's pilot corps in the Army Air Force.

In the spring of 1943 Hap Arnold called Jackie to Washington, and she had a hunch what he wanted. Before she flew east, Jackie assured the fourth WFTD class, 43-W-4, she had no intention of being a major to Ovetta Culp Hobby's colonel.

When she reached Arnold's office, her hunch proved correct. The Ferry Division had come up with a new proposal for militarizing the women pilots: While there were no provisions in the current WAC legislation for female flying officers, its staff found nothing in the Articles of War specifically saying that women could not be commissioned directly into the army. On the other hand, the army chief of staff, General George C. Marshall, had introduced in Congress a bill to grant the WAC full military status. What would Jackie think about making her girls part of the WAC if the bill passed?

Jackie replied tartly that her girls were flyers and they ought to be part of the Army Air Force. Pilots were different, special. Besides, consider what Mrs. Hobby was allowing to happen to her women's corps. For weeks nasty gossip and downright lies had been circulating among civilians and soldiers alike about the WAC. They were drunk all the time. The Army gave them contraceptives, just like the men, but still hundreds of them were pregnant. Some of the women not only slept with the soldiers but with each other. Jackie intended to make sure the women's air corps got a better deal than the WAC.

Regardless of what General Arnold thought about Cochran's attempts to discredit Hobby, he would never argue the point that pilots were a breed apart. He gave Jackie more time to work on a scheme of her own for militarizing the women pilots.

Meanwhile in April, just as the first class was graduating in Houston, Jackie lowered the requirements for WFTD candidates to thirty-five hours of flying time and a private pilot's license. This step made flying for the Army Air Force a thrilling possibility for young women who had only had a dream before. All over America girls who had taken a Civilian Pilot Training course in college rushed to apply. Others who had no experience at all enrolled in flying classes. During the next months thousands of young women applied to Cochran's Women's Flying Training Detachment.

RUTH CRAIG JONES heard about Jacqueline Cochran's flying school from a former college classmate. Ruth was teaching girls' gym classes at Central High School in Oklahoma City and worrying about her husband, Lee. They had been married the day after Pearl Harbor, when Lee enlisted in the navy. During the first long winter of the war he was a corpsman with the 2nd Marine Division in the South Pacific, and Ruth yearned to do her part as well.

She had wanted to fly for years, but lessons were expensive. Now Ruth was going to join the AAF women's program, no matter what. But first she had to have a pilot's license, so she sold her coin collection and with the profits, plus Lee's military allotment checks, began flying lessons.

Ruth and Ida "Skip" Carter had been friends since they had competed on girls' soccer teams and graduated together from the University of Oklahoma in 1934. (Skip, like Ruth, was now a high school gym teacher.) Before Ruth's wedding she and Skip bought a car together, the one they felt lucky still to share despite all the wartime shortages. Skip thought they should learn to fly together too.

[96]

They started ground-school classes in the evenings at the high school where Ruth taught during the day and they did their flying at a cold, windy airstrip on the outskirts of Oklahoma City. The instructor's house was perched at the edge of the runway. His wife passed the time watching the lessons and drinking water tumblers full of whiskey, while boozily herding her two small youngsters out from under the taxiing planes.

Ruth would never forget her first flight, a scant thirty minutes in the air. That night she went to a party, but she was still high in the sky. Ruth gazed at the other guests and felt so sorry for them because they had never flown.

Ruth and Skip soloed on a bright spring day. As they drove away from the airstrip in jubilation, the instructor's wife smashed a whiskey glass across their car bumper. She always celebrated by smashing glasses, so the two friends knew she was happy for them. They applied for the Women's Flying Training Detachment that same week and bought a thank-you gift for their flying instructor: a new set of water tumblers!

KAY D'AREZZO found a job at the state capitol in Austin as the secretary to the Texas judge advocate general; she also found a new friend, Mildred Davidson.

Millie, who also worked as a secretary, was married to an Army Air Force officer, and she lived with her mother—just like Kay. Millie was from a Texas ranching family that had a big spread west of Austin. Her father had died when Millie and her brother were children, and her mother had moved them into town. Millie and her mother were close, so living together right now was a comfort. Millie's brother was serving with the air force in Italy, and Bill Davidson was officially missing in action—just like Al D'Arezzo.

Kay worried about her new friend. In her heart she knew that Al was a prisoner of war in the Philippines, but Bill was probably dead. Millie and Bill had been sweethearts at the University of Texas, and they had married in June 1942, right after he graduated from AAF bomber school. Six months later, in January 1943, his B-17 was shot down over the North Sea while it was returning to England from a raid in Germany.

Mrs. McBride, Kay's mother, was a great cook, and she was always trying to feed Millie, fatten her up. Millie enjoyed the Mc-Brides' house. It was cheerful and full of Kay's younger sisters and all their friends.

Millie was the one who heard about Jacqueline Cochran's flight training and that the students were destined for the Army Air Force. Millie and her husband had flown together when they were in college, and she liked the sound of Cochran's program. She told Kay flying would be just right for her too.

Kay had only been in a plane once in her life. When she came back to Austin from the Philippines, a friend had taken her up. Al wasn't happy when she wrote him about her adventure. "Why did your mother let you do that?" he wrote back. What would Al think if he knew she was handling guns and jumping off fire towers during Women's Defense Corps drills?

Millie convinced her to try a flying lesson, and Kay liked it as much as Millie had promised, so they signed up for classes together. And flying was fun. They could both use some fun. When they finished their private licenses, they'd both apply to Cochran's school.

THE NUMBER OF LOSSES of American B-17 bombers and crews in Europe was appalling. Americans were flying daytime missions because they were equipped with the precise Norden bombsight that could "drop a bomb in a pickle barrel." However, there were no fighter planes with the range to protect the B-17s during raids deep into Germany. Over thirty percent of the bombers never returned from these missions.

By April 1943 the AAF commander in England suspended all attacks on the German homeland, hitting targets in France and Belgium instead. Within the month Arnold called him to Washington for "planning talks." In a letter to the army's European theater commander, Hap fumed about playing safe with flying missions. Had his flight leaders lost their dash? "I've been impatient all my life . . . that's my makeup and that's that."

On May 12 Arnold was rushed to Walter Reed Army Hospital with another heart attack. The doctors had to sit on the general to make him rest, just as they had three months before with his first attack. Arnold wrote to Marshall, the army chief of staff, saying how sorry he was. "This is one hell of a time to have this happen."

After ten days in the hospital Arnold was sent to the West Coast to rest and fish. This time his wife, Bee, went along. Ten days later the Arnolds were at the United States Military Academy, West Point, New York, where the general delivered the commencement address. Their second son, Bruce, was a member of the graduating class.

THE FERRY DIVISION finally received the first batches of Cochran's girls in May and June. Colonel Tunner was so angry because Cochran had lowered the requirements for her school again that he insisted, until almost the last minute, that he would not hire any of the graduates who could not pass the FERD's tests. When the Training Command requested permission for the trainees to buy WAFS uniforms before reporting, he refused. What if the women didn't qualify as ferry pilots?

At this point both the Army Air Force and the Air Transport Command ordered Colonel Tunner to accept the WFTD graduates per se. Barton Yount, commanding general of the Training Command, asked General George to give the girls a good break and let him know what Air Transport Command thought of their performance.

Next Tunner wanted to know, what if the new pilots actually couldn't do the job? He was instructed to give Cochran's girls at least a month, and then if they failed a second round of FERD tests, he could send them back to the Training Command.

The graduates were divided up equally among the four WAFS squadrons. Jane Straughan and Marie Muccie both went to the 2nd Ferrying Group at New Castle AAFB. Colonel Baker and Betty Gillies were leery at first. Baker complained to Tunner that the new women didn't know how to fill out the necessary paperwork and that most of them, against army policy, had homes in the immediate vicinity. Betty Gillies, an hour from her home by air, and the other originals from the East Coast laid low on this complaint.

Actually it didn't take long for Cochran's girls to prove themselves. By graduation they averaged well over five hundred hours of flying time and had checked out on several kinds of primary and basic trainers, as well as the AT-6 Texan and the twin-engine AT-17. Many of the originals still hadn't flown the Texan. Also every one of the WFTD pilots had soloed at night, and they had instrument training and Link trainer time.

Jane and Marie, along with the rest of the new women at New Castle, found themselves back in Cubs and PTs. They were assigned to ferry trainers south and barely got back to base before they were off on another delivery. They still didn't have uniforms and wore their general's pants and flight jackets when returning to Wilmington. If they had a break between missions, they were in class learning how to handle Ferry Division forms, or they went to the continuous ground school required of all ferry pilots. Even though Jane's husband was still in the States, they rarely had an opportunity to be together, and Marie's big family in New Jersey never got to see her at all. Soon the others at New Castle AAFB were saying Cochran's girls could fly all right and what's more, they were good kids.

The acceptance of the newcomers at Wilmington wasn't necessarily true at the other groups. Every one of their commanding officers agreed the pretty young women didn't always stick to proper military channels to get what they wanted, for example, assignment to certain aircraft or transition training. Cochran's girls knew sweet-talk worked better and faster than proper channels. However, in June the women pilots delivered 150 planes, three times the average for the first six months of WAFS operations. The women were also flying the same average number of hours as the men, but unlike the men their percentage of pilot error was zero!

By the end of June 1943 eighty-eight women, including originals and WFTD graduates, were on duty with the Women's Auxiliary Ferrying Squadron. General George reported back to Barton Yount at the FTC that Jackie's girls had adapted well to duty as ferry pilots and that their attitude and conduct were excellent. He suggested more emphasis on long, cross-country flying and additional practice in holding a loose formation. He also wanted Cochran to consult with the WAFS about a uniform. On the whole the Air Transport Command thought Jackie had done a good job.

As the ranks of women pilots grew in the Ferry Division, each group commander appointed a senior WAFS to maintain discipline and morale among the women and to act as liaison with operations. Betty Gillies's position as squadron leader at New Castle AAFB became an official slot in the chain of command. Florene Miller, the Texas beauty, was named squadron leader at Dallas Love Field.

B. J. Erickson, the assured young pilot who had become close to both Betty and Nancy Love, was awarded the leadership position she had already been occupying at Long Beach. Barbara Donahue was appointed the leader at Romulus, the toughest base.

BEFORE BETTY GILLIES had checked out in the P-47 Thunderbolt, it had taken her several weeks to complete transition in between regular ferry missions and her squadron responsibilities. Meanwhile several other originals also began transition on their own into pursuits. B. J. Erickson in California and Teresa James and Evelyn Sharp on the East Coast were using manufacturers' promotional films and hangar talk to learn how to fly the fast, high-performance "peashooters." The single-seat planes had no room for an instructor on board, and a pursuit was an unforgiving teacher. A beginning pilot only made one mistake.

In May 1943 these originals began ferrying P-47s from the Republic factory in Farmingdale, Long Island, to a modification center at Evansville, Indiana, or to docks at Newark, New Jersey, for transport overseas. They could make several trips a day to Newark, because Farmingdale and the port were only minutes apart by air. This was gear-up, gear-down flying as the women took off, circled the Statue of Liberty in New York Harbor, and landed. They were taken back to Long Island in a military-staff car. The women stayed at a hotel in Farmingdale, and Betty Gillies was able to see her children often because her house was nearby.

When she also began delivering P-47s to the West Coast for shipment to the Pacific, Betty was able to take transition on the P-51 at Long Beach in between missions. Most seasoned originals were right behind her. They soon checked out in the Mustang and before long they were qualified to fly the P-38 Lightning as well. These pursuit pilots had started to carve a special niche for the WAFS in the Ferry Division.

DURING THE SUMMER of 1943 Cochran moved her office back to Washington. General Arnold arranged a meeting between Jackie and Colonel Hobby to determine whether or not the two women could compromise on militarization, but the aviatrix and the housewife didn't get very far. "What kind of a person should be in charge of the women pilots?" Jackie asked. She emphasized that the administration of the women's pilot program should be handled by people who understood them and the kind of work they did.

"I don't know what you mean by *administration*," Colonel Ovetta Culp Hobby replied pointedly. Then she added that she didn't think it would be likely that women pilots who were members of the WAC would have anyone in charge who *didn't* understand them.

"Yes, I think so," Jackie retorted as she marched out of Hobby's office.

When he heard about their meeting, Arnold ordered the whole militarization matter shelved for sixty to ninety days.

THE FERRY DIVISION moved its headquarters to Cincinnati, Ohio. In May Nancy Love was appointed to the staff of Colonel William Tunner and ordered to leave Long Beach. Tunner needed Nancy to supervise the growing number of women in his division.

Nancy held on in California until June, getting in as much flying as she could before going back behind a desk. She had checked out in fourteen different kinds of military planes in just four months at Long Beach, proving what a competent woman pilot could do given the chance. En route to Cincinnati, Nancy Love delivered a B-25 Mitchell to Kansas City and added the celebrated bomber to the long list of planes she was the first woman to pilot.

Soon after Nancy reported to FERD headquarters, General Harold George made an inspection visit to Cincinnati, and in his speech he praised her work and the performance of the WAFS.

ON JULY 1, 1943, by an act of Congress, the Women's Army Corps received full military status. Four days later, on July 5, 1943, General Hap Arnold named Jacqueline Cochran director of women pilots within the Army Air Force. This was an AAF headquarters staff function, responsible for recommendations on everything from training standards to recruiting. Jackie was also responsible for liaison with AAF units who employed the women pilots and plans for eventual militarization.

This same day recently promoted Brigadier General William Tunner named Nancy Love the executive for the WAFS in the Ferry Division. Many of Love's responsibilities were parallel to Cochran's in order to block any interference from her in FERD matters. General Arnold's announcement seemed to give Jackie vague authority over all women pilots in the air force, no matter what command they were assigned to. This was the last thing Tunner wanted.

The newspapers and magazines had a field day with the shake-up in the women pilots' program, playing up the rivalry between Jackie and Nancy. They made Jackie's appointment seem like a victory in an ongoing war. Up until now this war had been undeclared, but from July 5, 1943, onward the careful guarding of command prerogatives versus the aggressive attempts for headquarters-staff control often overshadowed the accomplishments of the women pilots—and in the long run contributed to their doom.

On August 5, one month after Arnold made Jacqueline Cochran director of women pilots, the WAFS and the WFTD were officially merged and christened the Women Airforce Service Pilots (WASP) because the acronym sounded catchy for women flyers.

6.

Zoot Suits and Parachutes

JACQUELINE COCHRAN'S GOAL for the Women Airforce Service Pilots was to prove that any healthy, stable young American woman could learn to fly as well as her brothers. She hoped to justify a woman's auxiliary corps in the Army Air Force. Over 25,000 women applied to the WASP, approximately 2,000 were accepted, and slightly over 1,000 earned their wings. There were eighteen WASP classes. All but two trained at Avenger Field, Sweetwater, Texas.

When the trainees from 43-W-4, which had been in Houston, flew their PT-19s cross-country to join their classmates at Avenger, one member of the combined class stood out from the rest: Hazel Ah Ying Lee, a scrawny, boisterous, brown-skinned Chinese girl from Portland, Oregon. Her classmates agreed that Ah Ying was homely. She had buck teeth, flat features, and an even flatter chest. She wore her pitch-black hair yanked back or poked up under her cap, and from a distance it was hard to tell if Ah Ying was a man or a woman. But her handy, hearty laugh made her the favorite of everyone on the base. She also had an off-kilter brand of luck that could draw mishaps like a lightning rod.

AT THE BEGINNING of primary flight instruction Ah Ying and her classmates, with their instructors in the front seat of their PT-19 trainers, flew patterns, landings, and takeoffs. They also practiced loops and slow rolls, the air work that extended a student pilot's control of her plane—and herself. The tandem seat, open-cockpit, 175-horsepower PT-19 was rigged for communication with a gosport—a one-way speaking tube for the exclusive use of the instructor—and a rearview mirror.

Ah Ying's primary instructor was enamored with loops and vain about his ability to execute them to perfection. If one of his students could pull off a good loop, she was guaranteed to pass any flight test, whether it required loops or not. His standard procedure for introducing the loop was to surprise the student by flying through one of his own flawless maneuvers. As he pulled out, he would proclaim through the gosport, "That, Missy, is how a loop should be flown."

Even though the startled student had no means to reply, she was expected to nod and smile into the mirror with admiration. If she frantically grabbed the sides of the cockpit and hung on for dear life at the top of the loop—with the sky suddenly below, the earth above, and her stomach in her mouth—the instructor would inform her, "You must have confidence in your seat belt to do a decent loop. Next time at the top hold your arms over your head—out of the cockpit."

The morning he took Ah Ying up to acquaint her with the perfect loop, she didn't realize her seat belt hadn't latched properly. Without warning, the instructor lowered the trainer's nose to gain airspeed, then pulled up sharply and over. As he came out of the loop, he checked his cockpit mirror for her approval. No Ah Ying! The instructor landed and rushed into the office of the director of flight training, pale as a ghost and mumbling that he had lost his student. Before a search team could get airborne, a trainee on the flight line spotted Ah Ying trudging across an open field toward the hangars dragging her opened parachute.

Ah Ying's father fled from China at the beginning of the struggle between the Nationalist government and the Communists. He settled in Oregon, married, and had an American family.

In 1937, when Japanese troops marched down from Manchuria, Chinese-Americans rallied together to aid China. Hazel Ah Ying Lee and her older brother had logged a few hours of flying time, and they had an appetite for battle. With the financial backing of the Chinese-American community in Portland, both of them completed flight instructions and sailed to join the air forces of Chiang Kai-shek. But Hazel Ah Ying's patriotic mission was doomed. Despite a daily aerial onslaught by the Japanese, the Chinese military couldn't bring themselves to accept a woman pilot. While her brother flew combat missions, she taught school in the village where her father had been born.

Still, life in China, even in a traditional female role, was difficult for an American woman, so Ah Ying returned to the United States— but not to Portland. For a while she worked in New York City and then in the fall of 1942 she heard that Jacqueline Cochran was training women pilots for the Air Transport Command. At least, Ah Ying thought, she could ferry the aircraft that might fly in combat against the Japanese.

After Ah Ying and her classmates soloed in the PT-19, they concentrated on gaining experience and the required number of hours. She never learned to pick out landmarks in the flat, west Texas terrain, and as her class advanced to longer flights Ah Ying constantly got lost. A windmill was a windmill. One stock tank looked much like another. Unless she located a community she recognized by the name on its water tower, Ah Ying often meandered until her trainer ran out of gas and she was forced to land.

Scuttlebutt said she once put down in a field so small there was no room to take off again, so the plane had to be disassembled and returned to Avenger on a truck. Another time, after landing in a cotton patch, she was trapped inside the cockpit by a frightened farmer brandishing a hoe—even though she threw her hands up in a gesture of surrender and shouted at him, "Me Chinese! Me Chinese!"

Invariably when she made one of her emergency landings, Ah Ying had to do some fast talking before she could convince the locals to phone Avenger. She was always relieved to see her instructor's plane coming to fetch her. Ah Ying Lee was only half kidding when she told her classmates that before long some rancher would probably shoot her as a Japanese spy.

For nearly four weeks after Ah Ying and her classmates arrived at Avenger Field, they were the sole proprietors—except for the male AAF cadets who were on the base finishing primary flight instructions— and during this brief period in the spring of 1943 Avenger Field was the first coeducational air force flight school in history. Men and women sharing the same facility was slightly shocking even in wartime, and it worried Jacqueline Cochran.

The men and women trained at opposite ends of the field, but on the flight line and in the classrooms the two groups worked to chalk up the best record, to beat each other out. Although the WASP trainees were allowed late breakfast on Sunday, they still ate early, just as neatly turned out as the men, who were at the far end of the mess hall. The competition kept the student pilots' morale high. The men graduated in the middle of April, soon after the rest of Ah Ying's class flew up from Houston.

Overnight Avenger Field became the first all-female flight school in history. For several days dozens of eager cadets from neighboring AAF training facilities made "forced" landings at the base. In a single afternoon thirty-nine men taxied up to operations reporting mechanical difficulties with their aircraft. Within a week Avenger's commanding officer was obliged to close the field to all outside air traffic.

The trainees were forbidden to have social contact with the AAF staff or their civilian instructors. The student-instructor relationship was considered emotional enough without risking romance. The WASP students dubbed their new girls' school Cochran's Convent— but they weren't always kidding when they sang and moaned about loneliness.

> Girls, girls, is our middle name
> We are the girls of Sweetwater fame.
> We never neck and we never pet
> Give us a chance and we'll do it yet—
> Our instructors stay out late but we never get a date!

ON APRIL 5, 1943, when the Houston contingent landed at Avenger Field in high spirits, the reception from their classmates was chilly. One hundred and twenty-five rookies from 43-W-5 had arrived only two weeks before, and the number of trainees at Avenger had tripled. For a time the women who had been on the base since February seemed to regard the others as intruders.

Besides dealing with the cold shoulder, the Houston trainees faced other adjustments. They no longer lived in motels but in real army barracks, on a real army facility, with military discipline twenty-four hours a day. The long, one-story barracks were divided into bays, which had six cots and footlockers. A bathroom, with two sinks, two showers, and two toilet stalls, connected the adjoining bays. Reveille sounded at six fifteen each morning, with breakfast formation and roll call thirty minutes later. There were bed checks each night. They marched to meals, to classes, to the flight line, to physical training. "We'd probably march to the john, too," grumbled a foot-sore student fresh from Houston, "if we all had to go at the same time."

"Don't give 'em any ideas," muttered another.

The top-notch equipment at Avenger was a pleasure compared with the odds and ends at Howard Hughes Airport, but the runways were a mess. The existing runways were being lengthened, and a new one was under construction.

The Houston trainees were relieved to be free of the humidity and fog, but at Avenger the wind seemed to blow eternally, grinding the west Texas sand into their teeth, their skin, and their eyes—and a snatch from a marching song composed by the fourth class during the weeks they spent together in Sweetwater was adopted as the slogan of the women pilot's flight school:

> We live in the wind and the sand . . .
> And our eyes are on the stars.

SWEETWATER was a small west Texas town surrounded by ranches, cotton fields, and a few oil wells. The old, yellow Nolan County Courthouse sat in the town square that had one- and two-story businesses, a bank, and a couple of picture shows shuffling around its edges. The best hotel was the Blue Bonnet. Two blocks east of the square was the red-brick railway station, and two blocks west was the new Spanish-style civic auditorium. Ten or twelve churches crowded into town to tend Sweetwater's souls. Life was simple and sincere.

The citizens of Sweetwater didn't know what to make of the women at Avenger Field. One thing was sure, though: When the cadets left the training base, the social life of the local belles dropped off considerably. Now the town swarmed with pretty, self-assured girls on Saturday night, not handsome young fellows. Sweetwater families with marriageable daughters weren't happy about the situation. Who were these women anyway?

Mrs. Deaton wangled time on the local radio station to answer some of the town's questions before matters could get out of hand. Next Jackie Cochran flew in to see what she could do to quiet suspicions. Since Sweetwater was a churchgoing community, Jackie began by convincing the local Catholic priest to say Sunday Mass in Avenger Field's brand-new chapel—after all, her girls had souls too!—and the trainees were required to attend this service or one in town.

Then Cochran paid a call on the mayor. She assured His Honor that while their mission was still classified top secret, these were good, clean, all-American girls doing their bit to win the war. She suggested the two of them throw a party, a barbecue, so that the local folks and the trainees could get acquainted. For entertainment the WASP put on a talent show, and the ranchers staged a rodeo.

This get-together was so successful that after Cochran went public with the WASP at 43-W-1's commencement in April, Dedie invited the town out to Avenger to watch the second class graduate. The class arrived from Houston the evening before the ceremonies, roaring over Sweetwater in a spiffy formation of gleaming advanced trainers. Jackie landed right behind them, flying her hot Beechcraft Staggerwing from Fort Worth.

The next morning cars lined the road from Sweetwater to Avenger Field's main gate for two miles. Inside along the flight line there were a band and flags and a glittering array of army brass. The WASP trainees paraded smartly down the runway behind their own color guard while newspaper photographers and newsreel cameramen elbowed each other to catch the show. Sweetwater could see that something exciting was happening, and most people decided the WASP must be all right.

THE ROOKIES of the fifth WASP class, the first to complete all its training at Avenger, were required to have at least seventy-five hours of flying time, but the type and amount of experience varied enormously. For example Helen Dettweiler, a professional athlete and the 1938 women's open western golf champion, flew as a hobby, while Helen Richey, an airline pilot before the war, had just completed an eighteen-month contract with the British Air Transport Auxiliary.

As Jacqueline Cochran exhausted the supply of qualified women pilots, she began to emphasize geographical distribution for WASP candidates—a trick she learned from her generals to keep the congressmen happy. Because of this, Yvonne "Pat" Pateman became a member of 43-W-5.

Pat had a mere three hours' flying time when she wangled an interview with her heroine, Jackie Cochran, in late 1942. But she *was* from New Jersey. Jackie had just gotten off the phone with that state's senator, who had been insisting that more of his female constituents ought to be WASP. When she saw Pat's home address, Jackie immediately agreed to accept her—with the stipulation that she would earn seventy-five hours first.

Pat had read that Cochran picked her pilot candidates, gauged their caliber, "by the look in their eyes." Thrilled by Jackie's immediate, if conditional, acceptance and full of a new-born self-confidence, she talked her brothers into lending her enough money to wrap up the necessary hours before Christmas.

The four-month training program for the early classes proved to be inadequate for those following who had little previous flying experience, and during the first year at Avenger the curriculum was constantly modified as the scope of Cochran's experiment grew. Eventually the women received the same primary-through-advanced flight training as male Army Air Force cadets, with the exception of aerobatics and formation flying, which were only deemed necessary for combat. The expanded course included 400 hours of ground school, with technical classes ranging from the theory of flight to Morse code. The most important part of the training was 210 hours of flight instructions—learning to fly the army way.

Almost from the beginning Pat and her classmates knew that if they could learn to fly the army way in the severe conditions at Avenger Field, they could probably fly anywhere. After the class arrived in March, they were rousted out, day or night, whenever a spring thunderstorm raced toward the field, to lend a hand holding the trainers down on the flight line. By the end of the summer they were dodging dust devils and tumbleweeds on takeoff and landing. And the daytime temperatures hung at 100 degrees for the entire five months they were in training.

By August 1943 there were regularly four to five WASP classes at Avenger at one time, as many as six hundred women at various stages of training. Each class was split into two flights, with their day divided between classroom and cockpit. And while male cadets moved from one field to another as they progressed from primary to basic to advanced training, the women stayed at Avenger for all phases of their instruction. A sky full of student pilots, in everything from pokey primary trainers to 600-horsepower AT-6s, kept the instructors sweating and the controllers in the tower hopping. On a clear day the traffic pattern over the field held as many as forty planes, flying stacked four or five levels high, waiting for their turn to land.

MEANWHILE 250 miles north of Sweetwater in Canyon, Texas, Lela Loudder's mother finally signed a waiver allowing her daughter to join the Women Airforce Service Pilots. Lela's parents had been staunch in their refusal throughout three days of tears, until her older sister came up with the winning argument. "After all, Lela has been on her own for months," her sister reasoned, "down in Corpus Christi—with the *navy!*"

That afternoon Lela ran into Nell Stevenson, who had been in Civilian Pilot Training with her during college. Lela could barely wait to tell her what she was up to, but Nell beat her to it. "I'm going to be one of Jackie Cochran's women pilots," she announced.

Nell was scheduled for the same class as Lela. Two hometown girls going into Army Air Force flight training was big news in Canyon, and the postmaster said that he had even been questioned about both of them by an FBI agent. A security check! That was *something*, Lela thought. She knew she was going to be involved in important work!

In the middle of June Lela and Nell wheedled a tank of gas at the Chevrolet dealership and drove from Canyon to Avenger Field. They stopped on the outskirts of Sweetwater to ask directions to the airfield. About three miles the other side of town, they were told, and then up a gravel road another mile or so. Before they reached the turnoff, they could see the planes and hear the engines roar.

Lela and Nell slipped into the air base's administrative offices to join the flock of frightened girls, disguised like themselves in hats, gloves, and high heels, warily eyeing one another and waiting for something to happen. Some had their sophisticated finery rumpled by long journeys across the prairie, while others looked fresher than they felt after spending a tense, sleepless night at the Blue Bonnet Hotel in town—but they were all doing their best to seem nonchalant and knowing. Lela thought a cigarette would have helped, but a sign read NO SMOKING.

Before long a stern Army Air Force officer in starched khakis greeted the new class with a list of rules and warnings, and handed out printed copies. Then a small, dark-haired woman, who spoke with homey authority and introduced herself as Mrs. Deaton, assured the rookies that their families would be notified they had reached Sweetwater safe and sound. Eyeing the mound of suitcases and trunks surrounding the girls, she added, "Since there is only one footlocker per girl in each bay, you will be allowed to store surplus baggage here in the office—until arrangements are made to ship it home."

This caused a scramble. What ought to stay? Yes, one night a week they'd need a dress for dinner.

What could they do without? "Large musical instruments and golf clubs might not be appropriate—under the circumstances."

Deaton told them to form groups of six, pick up their bed linens at the laundry, and find a bay in the barracks. The one hundred girls in Lela's class devoted the next couple of hours to getting acquainted with each other—and their new living quarters.

Two showers—two mirrors—for twelve of us? They've got to be kidding! Sweetie, would you mind switching cots with me? . . . hey, well, you can't shoot a gal for trying! My God, I didn't know this was what she meant by a footlocker. She's got to be kidding! A friend in 43-4 told me a girl got killed last week with her instructor—night flying. No, I am not kidding. The plane burned! They didn't find the bodies until the next morning. The plane burned? Her name was Jane Champlin. She was in my friend's class.

Besides Nell, Lela's baymates included Micky Axton, a cheerful girl from Kansas; Tommy Tompkins, a dark-haired looker from California who was married to an RAF pilot; and Jo Naphen, a savvy New York City gal.

[112]

Across the hall, Caro Baley, one of the smallest in the class, waddled off to supply to exchange a zoot suit with the crotch hanging down to her knees, "I can't wear this thing," she declared. When supply said switching was no good since the overalls only came in size 42-44 extra large, Caro waddled back again and stood under a hot shower hoping to shrink her gigantic flight gear. "I don't think it's going to help much," she sputtered.

An upper class trainee, who was their senior squadron leader, assembled the class and then divided it into two flights. She told them to pick a squadron commander for administrative duties and two flight lieutenants, to call breakfast formation and marching cadence. She gave them a tour of Avenger and a sample of the songs that were the spirit of the WASP.

> Along came a pilot, ferrying a plane,
> He asked me to go fly with him down in lovers' lane.
> And I, like a silly fool, thinking it no harm
> Cuddled in the cockpit to the pilot warm.
>
> Singing zoot suit and parachutes and wings of silver, too
> He'll ferry airplanes as his mama used to do.
>
> Early in the morning before the break of day
> He handed me a short-snort bill and this I heard him say,
> Take this, my darling, for the damage I have done.
> You may have a daughter or you may have a son;
> If you have a daughter, teach her how to fly,
> If you have a son, put the bastard in the sky.
>
> Singing zoot suit and parachutes and wings of silver, too
> He'll ferry airplanes as his mama used to do.
>
> The moral of this story as you can plainly see
> Is never trust a pilot an inch above the knee.
> He'll kiss you and caress you and promise to be true
> And have a girl at every field as all the pilots do.
>
> Singing zoot suit and parachutes and wings of silver, too
> He'll ferry airplanes as his mama used to do.

The senior squadron leader marched the formation past the hangars and the long, low building next to the runways that held the classrooms and the student pilots' ready room. Flying was over for the afternoon, and as the recruits passed the flight line, Lela and her classmates itched to touch the planes—the PT-19s and the big, powerful Texan trainers, silent for the first time that day and parked wingtip to wingtip.

Just before chow they met Avenger Field's drill instructor, Lieutenant La Rue, who was also in charge of physical training and calisthenics. As he described what lay in store, someone in ranks whispered, "He looks like he's getting a kick out of this."

As they marched into the mess hall, the rookies were amazed to see food—steak, ice cream, butter—that civilians hadn't tasted in months. After they had eaten, some of the upperclassmen wandered through the rookies' barracks, making cracks, bragging, and teasing.

Just flew a long cross-country today. That T-6 is sure a honey.

I passed my pattern work check ride . . . flew the smoothest lazy-eights and chandelles you ever saw.

Did you ever put a plane into a spin? Ever make a forced landing?

To hear it, they were hot pilots, each and every one, but this was as close as they could come to hazing. The welcome for the sixth class had been so rough, some of them had gotten hurt during a melee in the showers. After that, the upperclassmen were ordered to keep their hands to themselves.

The cocky visitors also filled the newcomers in on the gossip. Nancy Love had made her first visit to Avenger the week before. She told the trainees the women pilots would soon have uniforms almost like Army Air Force officers, complete with insignia and wings. Also Avenger had just gotten a new commanding officer and a completely fresh cadre of army officers. Jackie got the last bunch fired. She didn't like the way they ran *her* operation.

Long after dark at the end of their first day, the six girls in Lela's bay undressed, with backs turned to one another and shoulders hunched. They fell exhausted onto their cots and fitfully tried to sleep in a room full of strangers.

AFTER ARRIVING at Avenger, the recruits had to pass a swimming test that required them to get from one end of Sweetwater's public swimming pool to the other—wearing their flying gear. When Lela learned about this, she figured she was finished as a WASP before she had even begun. She couldn't swim a lick. Why did a pilot, she thought glumly, *especially* a WASP, need to know how to swim? Women ferry pilots were confined to the continental United States. All Lela had to do was not land in any lakes.

Jo Naphen, Lela's baymate from New York, was a strong swimmer, and she came up with a scheme. But if it backfired, both of them would be through. When their class went into town for the swim test, Jo planned to go first while Lela waited at the back of the line. "After I finish," said Jo, "we'll switch zoot suits and name tags, and I'll take the test again—as *you!*"

Her plan worked, and a few weeks later Lela's guilty conscience got a reprieve when the swimming requirement was dropped.

After the new students were scorched and blown in an open PT-19 for several hours each day, the demand for a mirror in the morning dropped off dramatically. In any case most of the women were too exhausted to primp. When reveille sounded, they stayed on their cots until the last minute and then made a split-second dash for breakfast formation, zipping up their zoot suits on the run.

The constant sound of flying—engines warming up, testing, taking off, landing—was fundamental to the environment at Avenger from the first full light until evening. And once the upperclassmen advanced to night flying, the trainees were lulled to sleep by the roar of engines as well. Aircraft noise was a backdrop for every activity on the field.

The students waited their turn to fly in the ready room in a hangar next to the flight line. They drank sodas, smoked, studied, or slept hunched in a corner. By midsummer, with six hundred women in training, some had to be diverted to auxiliary fields a few miles away. These were dirt airstrips, with a rickety staging shack, where students who had already soloed could practice during daylight hours. Part of the group flew the trainers out to the auxiliary fields, while the others rode in "cattle cars," trailers with canvas flaps, pulled behind an army truck. They spent the next several hours sitting on the ground, in a scrap of shade if they could find one, waiting to fly, kibitzing each other's performance. And singing. More than one WASP song rose out of the dust during the hours spent on the auxiliary fields.

Oh, I'm far from home
Where the wild Texans roam
Where the snakes and tarantulas play
Where seldom is heard
An encouraging word
And we never have time to make hay.

A WASP trainee am I—
All sunburned and dusty and dry.
There's no time to play,
They work us all day,
Volunteers, but we'll never know why!

If I graduate
I'll get out of this state
And never see Texas no more—
We'll ferry their planes
Through the wind and the rains
And help all our boys win the war.

LELA SOLOED in the PT-19 with ease, but during the final stage of primary she got into a scrape that landed her in the base hospital—for psychiatric observation. At the end of each phase of training the WASP students had to show they could use the navigation skills the ground-school staff had been hammering into their heads by plotting and flying a long, cross-country trip of approximately two hundred miles. First they went on a practice jaunt with their instructors to study the terrain. These excursions were uneventful, although one instructor let his student overshoot their destination by fifty miles before mentioning they were completely off course. However, on the solo flights PT-19s were scattered far and wide. One girl in Lela's class flew the entire round trip from Avenger without ever laying eyes on her destination, and another landed to ask for directions.

Lela hit the destination right on the mark, but after she entered the traffic pattern to land west, she saw that the wind tee had switched to the east. She made a perfect three-point landing all right—but heading in the wrong direction! The bellowing from the control pilot on the field made her ears ring. "Don't ever let this happen again," he warned.

Lela took off for the return trip to Avenger, where she was careful to check the wind tee before entering the pattern. She made another perfect landing only to find, as her wheels hit the ground, all the other trainers landing from the *opposite* direction. The tee had suddenly switched *again* just as she turned on the base leg.

When she taxied up to her instructor, he howled, "What the hell is the matter with you?" For some reason landing downwind—twice in the same day—struck Lela as hilarious, and she grinned. He grounded her for two days and confined her to the base hospital for pilot fatigue.

The doctor decided the backward landings weren't symptoms of a psychiatric disorder. But he advised Lela to land in the same direction as the rest of her flight in the future.

AT THE END of each phase of flight training, the women had to pass a check ride, a test of their ability, first with their civilian instructor and then with an AAF check pilot. These army pilots circulated among several training fields, and their arrival at Avenger gave the trainees a general case of the jitters. Every student had more than one chance to pass, but the army pilots were tough, and several made no secret of how they felt about women in the cockpit of military aircraft. One had washed out so many WASP trainees he was known as Captain Maytag.

The trainees developed a ritual to beseech fate for a successful ride. A small, native stone fountain on the base was proclaimed a wishing well, and the students treated an attack of "check-its"—a queasy condition brought on by impending check rides—by tossing in a coin with a fervent wish for good luck! As the wishing-well ritual evolved, the first girl to solo in each flight was dunked in the fountain, flight suit and all, by her classmates. Before climbing out, she was allowed to retrieve two lucky coins, one for herself and one for her instructor.

Each WASP class got one weekend pass. The rest of the time the women had to be on the base every night. If their bays passed inspection and they hadn't piled up too many demerits during the week, the trainees got from noon on Saturday and all day Sunday off to sleep, do their wash, write letters, or go into Sweetwater to shop or see a movie.

Lela's class got a forty-eight-hour pass after successfully completing primary training. Those who could headed for a taste of civilian living, but Dallas, 250 miles distant, was the nearest city. Lela and Nell loaded up the car with friends and drove to Canyon for some home cooking, good whiskey, and a couple of mornings devoted to sleeping late. This lively crew of young women, high with their up checks, were a hit in Canyon. Lela thought she even caught a glimmer of excitement in her mother's eye.

After returning to Avenger 43-W-7 took on the cumbersome 450-horsepower BT-13. The trainer had an enclosed cockpit, fixed landing gear, and three pages of procedures that had to become second nature to its pilot. Students needed eight hours of dual instruction before they could solo, and were only permitted to execute spins with their instructors on board because the ponderous, 185-mile-per-hour BT-13 had a nasty tendency to oscillate in a spin and crash.

Basic trainers were equipped with radios, and now the women had to notify the tower prior to every maneuver—taxiing, taking off, entering the traffic pattern, and landing. Learning radio jargon and the switches, plus handling a microphone, brought on some severe cases of stage fright at first. However, identifying voices on the airways got to be a game.

And the trainees caught on quickly to the advantages of talking—even talking back—to their instructors, particularly the few who acted as if they had invented profanity. "You jackass," Tommy Tompkins's instructor screamed into the radio during the first week of basic, "get the goddamned nose down! Do you want to spin this crate in?"

Pressing the mike button, Tommy replied, "Hey, bud, take it easy—and watch your language!"

After several minutes of silence Tommy's instructor continued in a calm, careful tone that lasted for days.

Shooting landings in a BT-13 was like dropping a Mack truck on the runway. One morning Lela's trainer got away from her and smacked into a plane sitting on the flight line. Emergency vehicles surrounded the wreckage, and someone plucked her out of the cockpit by her parachute straps, shouting a warning about fire.

Lela put up a good front because her classmates all knew she had flown BT-13s in Corpus, but the accident rattled her. That night she called home for solace. Once her dad heard no one had been hurt, he demanded, "And how much is this going to cost me?" Lela laughed out loud for the first time that day.

THE CLASS SETTLED DOWN to serious work, trying to harness the BT-13, and the women discovered the more they could make a plane do, the more experience they got, the more flying became a natural physical response, like walking or running. As time passed, they began to have a feeling for the movement of the plane, a sense of affinity between their body and the aircraft. They understood what was meant by flying by the seat of your pants. Gradually they were becoming at ease in the sky flying upside-down, climbing, rolling, or spinning.

However, instrument hops threw a kink into this new self-confidence. A canvas curtain was drawn between the student and the outside world, leaving only the instruments, altimeter, airspeed indicator, and turn-and-bank dials to rely on while she flew "under the hood." There were no natural points of reference. Dials, not the pilot's body, decided up and down, direction, and distances. A trainee had to learn to trust her instruments without question, fly patterns following radio-range signals, and make landing approaches without seeing the field if she was to stay out of trouble in the clouds or at night.

For Lela Loudder the open plains, flat and barren, were home. To others west Texas was like the backside of the moon. No buildings, no traffic, no sounds or lights at night, just silent stars stretching from horizon to horizon. This was the breaking point for some of the big-city girls, such as Lela's baymate, Jo Naphen.

In any case, Jo failed to pass her check ride following basic, and her baymates were grief stricken. After intense weeks together, learning as much about themselves as about flying, Jo's departure was like a death in their family.

The washout rate in the early classes varied mysteriously from twenty to forty percent. By the late summer of 1943 Avenger was hit with a storm of pink slips, and the washout rate zoomed to over fifty percent. The effects on morale were devastating. Check rides had became such arbitrary procedures that Leni Deaton was alarmed. After one girl with excellent credentials was failed by an instructor who had made several unsuccessful passes at her, Deaton requested a review board. This board, composed of the AAF staff and the civilian director of flight training, with Deaton in an advisory position, had the last word on all eliminated students.

THE WAR DEPARTMENT installed a cinematographer at Avenger to produce charming stills and reels of glamorous documentary film for the Army Signal Corps and for distribution to the major newsreel services. For the camera the whole school was turned out for calisthenics—in matching blue physical-training shorts. The photographer went everywhere the trainees went, and he even persuaded an army pilot to take him up so that he could snap a student flying solo in a PT-19 with her long red hair flowing free.

The cameraman's taste ran to petite, winsome blondes with pigtails. Shirley Slade, a member of the fifth class who hailed from south Texas, was picked for the cover of *Life* magazine in July 1943. She posed on the tail of a Texan trainer in her zoot suit, a pencil in her delicate hands and an intent look in her eye. Leonora Horton, another New York City native in Lela's class, who had heart-stopping dimples, was featured on the *Army-Navy Screen Magazine*.

The filming of this short almost caused a disaster. The cameraman set up halfway down the runway to catch a group of trainees, bunched up wingtip-to-wingtip in BT-13s and Texans, who had orders to take off as fast as they could get onto the runway. Normally they were spaced in long intervals by the tower, so they responded with enthusiasm. Since the Texans were much faster than the BT-13s, the flock of trainers dodging each other while trying to get airborne hardly fit the announcer's dialogue: "brave, sunbrowned lassies soaring into the air." On the second take, two instructors in AT-6s led off and set the pace.

IN AUGUST Grace Stevenson came home from England. She had renewed her Air Transport Auxiliary contract for another eighteen months, even before it expired, because the Brits offered a reward of a month's leave. A bleak Christmas in a war-ravaged England, where there were no decorations, no gifts, and only a flicker of holiday spirit, had added infinitely to her homesickness. Even though she was proud of her role in a famous allied force of women pilots, Grace ached to see her family.

When she arrived in Holdenville, Oklahoma, her little sister,

Marge, was home from college for the summer, breaking horses for local ranchers and flying. Marge was determined to be a pilot too. When she returned to Linwood College for sophomore year, she started flying lessons on the sly. Before dawn she would sneak out of the dorm through a window to take classes at a nearby airfield. Marge paid for flying with the money her father was sending to properly outfit his cowgirl for Linwood's equestrian team. When he figured out what she was up to, her father offered to pay for the rest of the course. He reasoned, "Any woman who would spend clothes money for flying lessons must be serious."

Grace remembered guiding a sixteen-year-old Marge through her first landing two summers before, with the little 50-horsepower Piper Cub hippity-hopping down the runway at Spartan Aviation. Marge had come a long way since that time, but Grace had known even then that her little sister had the potential to be a better pilot than she ever would.

While she was stateside, Grace wanted to see Jackie Cochran's flying school. Rumors had flown for months among the members of the 15th Ferry Pool about the U.S. Army Air Force women's training detachment and when the first class graduated in Houston, the folks back home bombarded the American ATA-girls with news clippings. Some of them felt double-crossed, and now that Cochran's school had moved to Sweetwater, scuttlebutt said it was equipped with nothing but the best. A friend of Grace's from Spartan Aviation was at Avenger, and one of the first American ATA-girls, Helen Richey, was there too. Grace decided to find out for herself if she was missing something by staying in England.

Grace arrived at Avenger in her handsome, blue Air Transport Auxiliary uniform, the fine English wool uniform that proclaimed she was serving as near to the war as any woman pilot could get. She was a star, a visiting dignitary. And so hot she thought she'd die! It was 110 degrees in Sweetwater.

Just before Grace had left for the States, all the American ATA-girls had received a letter from Cochran announcing her appointment as director of all women pilots in the Army Air Force. She wrote that over five hundred women were training in the Women Airforce Service Pilots, and if any of the women in England decided to fly for their own country, there would immediately be a place for them in the WASP. She added in closing, "I feel that I should warn you, it is just a matter of weeks before it will be militarized, which will mean if you come home you will have to join the army."

Scouting around Avenger Field, Grace wasn't sure all the marching was for her. She was sure about the planes, though—those beautiful advanced Army trainers, the Texan and the twin-engine AT-17. And the WASP had use of Link trainers. Grace wished she would have had the opportunity to learn with equipment of this caliber.

Grace suffered from envy, at least until the next morning. Because of the heat, she slept outside on the porch of a barracks. When she awoke, Grace was covered by a blanket of crickets, and so was everything in sight. The WASP trainees seemed to take the noisy, wiggling bugs in stride, sweeping them out of their way, but they gave Grace the creeps.

She headed back to Holdenville with news that was going to thrill Marge: Cochran had lowered the WASP age requirement to eighteen. She had been bending this rule all along, but now Air Force research had proved that youngsters ages eighteen to twenty made the best pilots.

At the end of her month's leave Grace hitched a ride across the Atlantic on a cargo plane. The most important item she took back to England with her was a supply of stockings.

THE AMERICAN ATA-GIRLS weren't the only ones who had heard that Avenger Field was equipped with the best. During the summer of 1943, eighteen months into the war, the House Committee on the Civil Service, under the chairmanship of Robert Ramspeck, undertook an inquiry into civilian employment in the government. The committee soon zeroed in on Jacqueline Cochran's Women Airforce Service Pilots and their training program.

At the same time the Ramspeck investigation was beginning, the women in Pat Pateman's class, 43-W-5, were completing the advanced phase of instruction. At this point, the class trained in pairs in the twin engine AT-17 Bobcat, with the emphasis on cross-country navigation and instrument flying, by day and by night.

By night the cockpit of an advanced trainer was a murky cave, full of dim, green instrument dials and hidden switches. The aircraft exhausts spit fire and flames into the black sky. The horizon was barely discernible. The surrounding darkness masked hazards and havens alike. Landing between two rows of flickering lights on a black runway was an act of blind faith. But flying on instruments, under the hood, was an act of faith as well.

After lunch on August 30, 1943, just ten days before graduation, Helen Jo Severson and Peggy Seip took off with their instructor in an AT-17 Bobcat on a course they had plotted to Big Spring AAFB, some sixty miles away, and back. Helen Jo was flying under the hood. The AT-17 had two front seats, with dual controls, and space for three passengers in the rear of the cabin. The trainees twenty-five hours' flying time in the Bobcat not only gave them multiengine experience but a chance to find out how well their classmates could handle a plane.

Severson and Seip had divergent aviation backgrounds. Helen Jo Severson had studied to be a librarian and had learned to fly in her spare time. Peggy Seip had graduated from Sarah Lawrence in 1938, a year ahead of Cornelia Fort, and she had qualified for a private license in the fall of 1940, piloting seaplanes off Lake Michigan near Milwaukee, Wisconsin. In 1942, she was one of the first women to join the Wisconsin Civil Air Patrol. That fall, both she and Cornelia had enrolled at the Link Instructor's Training School in upstate New York. When she joined class 43-W-5, Peggy was teaching instruments to AAF pilots. The trip to Big Spring was the first time the two women had flown together.

They had spent the morning sweating on their cots, inside the long, wooden barracks and nervously reviewing their flight plan. When they completed the cockpit check and took off, the air cooled pleasantly as the Bobcat gained altitude. The sky was clear and the sun was bright.

In addition to Severson and Seip, eight other student teams were on cross-country, instrument flights. Their planes landed, one by one, just before three, and as the trainees reported to operations, they learned that Helen Jo and Peggy's Bobcat was missing. Avenger's army cadre took off to search for them, but it was long after dark when the wreckage of their plane was reported in a farmer's field near Big Spring. Both women and their instructor were dead.

Before lights out word of the disaster had spread across the entire base. The trainees were in shcok. Death revealed itself in stages to fledgling pilots. At first, it was something that happned to strangers, but eventually death confronted the novice—on a runway or in a spiral of smoke and flame on the horizon—and they realized that some of those they trained with would be killed by planes, by bad luck, or by their own errors. Finally this recognition had to be followed by acceptance, as well as a certain sense of immunity, if these youngsters were to earn their wings.

The official report of Severson and Seip's accident faulted the aircraft's structure, not pilot error. During the first twelve months of the women's pilot program, seven had been killed, two on operational flights and five in training mishaps. Death was becoming an eminent member of the Women Airforce Service Pilots.

As she arranged to have the bodies of Helen Jo and Peggy shipped to their families, Dedie Deaton discovered that the local undertaker had put their remains in rough pine boxes, paupers' coffins, because the government allowed no funds for burying civilians. She squeezed money for caskets and train transportation out of Avenger Field's administrative budget. She also bought two train tickets, so that a classmate could escort each of the dead women to their homes. The trainees and staff chipped in for a casket blanket of yellow flowers with WASP written in blue blossoms.

ORDERS HAD COME DOWN from Washington that Lela Loudder's class would be the last to fly the AT-17 Bobcats. Henceforth, the graduates of Avenger Field would take twin engine transition after reporting for operational duty.

One of Lela's roommates from the house on Maple Street in Corpus Christi was in a later class, and she craved to get her hands on a Bobcat before it was too late. "Come on," she urged Lela, "take me up with you."

One night Lela and a classmate acting as copilot were scheduled for a solo training mission. Their Bobcat paused at the end of the dark runway before takeoff—where an unauthorized passenger scrambled out of the weeds and into the cockpit. Once airborne, all three of the women on board, bouyant and laughing and unafraid of the perils lurking in the night, took turns as pilot.

But as Lela landed, the twin-engine trainer blew a tire. "Quick, out!" shouted the copilot, shoving their passenger through the door as the AT-17 rattled to a stop. She hit the ground running as all three prayed she wouldn't be picked out of the night by the headlights of the emergency vehicles speeding toward them.

DEDIE DEATON threw a Halloween party for the trainees, with a band, at the Avengerette Club, a gathering place the citizens of Sweetwater had set up for the trainees. Cadets were bussed in from Big Spring AAFB and Ballinger Field for dance partners. Cute, dimpled Leonore Horton, the star of the *Army-Navy Screen Magazine* segment on the WASP, stole the talent show with a spoof of Lieutenant La Rue's physical-training exercises. The audience howled with appreciation as the victims of Leonore's workout were hauled away on stretchers. The cadets from Ballinger Field stayed overnight, and many trainees—who usually slept in on Sunday— showed up at the mess hall for breakfast to see the men off.

LELA AND HER COLLEGE FRIEND, Nell Stevenson, were scheduled to make their cross-country flight at the end of advanced training on the same day. Their course took them right over Canyon. As the pair flew north over the winter-dry prairie cut with red arroyos, they decided to treat the hometown folks to a demonstration of their skill. Coming in at treetop level, their AT-6s zoomed right down the center of main street.

But as the trainers regained altitude, fear—and *reality*—set in. Buzzing was absolutely forbidden. What if someone from Canyon complained to the air force? "Nobody will know it was us," Lela and Nell assured one another.

That night, back at Avenger Field, Lela had an unexpected phone call from her dad. "If you are going to fly those damned planes, at least keep 'em in the air," he warned.

ONLY HALF the members of Lela's class who had reported in June remained to graduate. Mrs. Barton Yount delivered the principal address and presented the silver pilot's wings, a gift from Jackie Cochran, to the class at the ceremonies on November 13, 1943.

When 43-W-7 received their duty assignments from Air Staff, they felt let down, hurt. Not one of them had been posted to the Ferry Division. The originals were transitioning into pursuits, and every one of Lela's classmates had dreamed of ferrying P-47 Thunderbolts or some other hot fighter. Instead, they were posted to a variety of other flying jobs at air bases scattered all over the United States.

Unknown to Lela or her classmates, members of previous WASP classes had already been assigned to other Army Air Force commands because Jackie was experimenting to find out what else her girls could do—and because General Tunner had been complaining to both the Air Transport Command and AAF headquarters in Washington that Cochran's most recent graduates lacked the experience to be ferry pilots. He charged they were poorly trained and called them airport pilots. To make matters worse, the week before Lela's class graduated, one of Jackie's girls stationed at the 5th Ferrying Group, Dallas Love Field, had been killed in a buzzing incident.

THE DAY AFTER 43-W-7 graduation, Sweetwater celebrated the Women Airforce Service Pilot's first birthday with a parade and brass band. The parade came to a halt in front of the Nolan County Courthouse where the mayor and Ethel Sheehy, standing in for Jackie, made speeches. Mrs. Deaton cut a four-layer birthday cake topped by wings and decorated with stars. And the Texas theater held the premiere of Paramount's technicolor short about the WASP, which was filmed as part of their Unusual Occupations series.

7.

For God, Country, and the Thrill of It!

IN JULY 1943 thirty-eight green pilots, fresh from Avenger Field, had reported for work with the Ferry Division. Before they had time to be flight-checked or to pick up their equipment, over half of these 43-W-3 graduates received orders to report immediately to Jacqueline Cochran at her suite in the Mayflower Hotel in Washington, D.C.

When they reached the capital, Jackie told the group she had personally picked them for an important secret mission, a challenging experiment that would expand flying jobs for women in the air force beyond the limits of the Ferry Division. They were going to have the opportunity to fly bigger and better airplanes than women

[127]

had ever flown before rather than just ferrying trainers, like their classmates. Then Jackie asked, "Is there anyone here who doesn't want to be assigned to this mission?"

Before dispatching them on their mysterious mission, Jackie took the women to the Pentagon, where four-star General H. H. Arnold congratulated them on being chosen for such vital work. They had yet to hear a single detail about this "vital work," but Cochran said their performance was critical to the future of the women pilots' program. She also told them this was temporary duty, just a two-week stint away from their ferrying groups. Brimming with excitement and expectation, the young women climbed aboard a C-47 Gooney Bird, outfitted as a cushy airliner for Air Staff, and flew off for the unknown.

They were on their way to Camp Davis, North Carolina, the army's largest antiaircraft and aerial-gunner training school, to join the more than five hundred pilots in the Third Tow Target Squadron. Camp Davis was built in a swamp, adjacent to the Atlantic Ocean and a long, white-sand beach. Antiaircraft batteries lined the beach, and pilots flew set patterns above them, towing a canvas sleeve at the end of a long cable, while guns of all types and calibers attacked the billowing fabric as if it were an enemy aircraft—and while artillery officers stalked up and down the beach shouting to the gunners, "More lead! More lead!"

Jackie had decided that target towing was another type of useful, noncombat flying job a women's air corps could undertake. However, she neglected to inform the Third Tow Target Squadron of her decision. Her girls were a shock to the squadron's commanding officer, and his men were horrified by the idea of working with them. Until he figured out what he was supposed to do with them, the squadron commander gave the women minimal flying duties in Cubs and other light trainers.

Within the week Jackie showed up, unannounced, at Camp Davis. With her clout at AAF headquarters she demanded that the WASP fly the same equipment as the men—and she promptly extended their training experiment from two weeks to the entire six-week course for tow-target pilots.

The A-24 Douglas Dauntless dive bombers used by the Third Tow Target Squadron were worn-out survivors of months in combat, and after training in the best at Avenger the planes seemed marginal to Jackie's girls. Because all new parts went to the front, the squadron mechanics barely kept the A-24s in the air. After each flight the pilot made note of problems, and the mechanics drew a red line on the aircraft's Form I to alert the next pilot, who decided for himself if he was capable of flying the A-24 target tug under those conditions. Before long the women pilots were calling the dive bombers the Douglas Doubtful.

A towing run started at one end of the long beach. A Dauntless, a target sleeve flowing behind, flew at an altitude specified by the officer in charge of the large gun emplacements, and then swooped down lower for small arms. At intervals the training officers on the ground would radio for the planes to dive, to attack the guns and their greenhorn crews. In the fall of 1943 one of the artillery training officers instructing at Camp Davis was a May graduate of West Point, Second Lieutenant Bruce Arnold, the son of the commanding general of the Army Air Force.

When the gunners trained at night, the target tugs were highlighted against the back swamp and sea by spotlights. The pilots could see fire spewing from the mouth of the guns and the bullet tracers rocketing toward them.

Many of the pilots with the Third Tow Target Squadron had just returned from combat and were as war weary as the unit's dive bombers. Most considered target towing a dull and tiresome chore. On the other hand the women were eager and keen and were soon requested by the gunnery instructors over the male pilots because of their enthusiastic flying.

UNTIL FALL 1943 the object of the 318th Training Detachment at Avenger Field was to qualify the women pilots to ferry army training aircraft. Three hundred ninety-five WASPs had graduated, and up through Class 43-W-5 nearly all were assigned to the Ferry Division. When General Barton Yount of the Training Command asked for an evaluation of their work and suggestions to improve their training, Nancy Love replied that they were "well adapted to their duties as ferrying pilots. Their attitude and conduct have been generally excellent." However, Nancy added, as deliveries were often made in flights of five-to-nine airplanes, practicing how to assemble after takeoff and hold a loose formation might eliminate a few hair-raising experiences later on.

In a short time the attitude of the Ferry Division changed. On August 5, when the Army Air Force created the Women Airforce Service Pilots out of what had been two separate outfits, Tunner and Jacqueline Cochran interpreted this action somewhat differently. He viewed Cochran as an advisor to Air Staff whose job was to recruit and train women pilots. Jackie saw this new organization and the additional vague authority it vested in her as the director of women pilots, as another step—a giant step—on the way to a women's air corps under her leadership.

She moved into an office at the Pentagon where she had an opportunity to study firsthand how the AAF commanding general wheeled around, issuing verbal orders and going directly for his objectives. Hap's methods suited Jackie perfectly! During her campaign to gain control of all the women pilots, she repeatedly tried to use her headquarters-staff function to override customary command prerogatives. Within months of her appointment there was no longer any room for accommodation between Jackie and General William Tunner.

In July 1943 the total strength of the women pilots in the Ferry Division was 88; in August, 120; in September, 192; and in October, 275. On August 7 the fourth WASP class graduated 112 women, and 87 went to the Ferry Division, with 25 others assigned to Camp Davis.

When Cochran's graduates reported to the Ferry Division, they became Nancy Love's responsibility. She allocated them to the ferrying groups and arranged for further training. When Love was ordered without explanation to turn twenty-five recent Avenger graduates over to Jackie for temporary duty, she had no idea what had happened to them for almost three weeks—until a bill arrived from Air Staff for several thousand dollars' worth of airline transportation from Washington to Camp Davis, North Carolina. Outraged, General William Tunner absolutely refused to pay this unauthorized expenditure.

On August 19 the Ferry Division received orders to loan an additional twenty-five women to Cochran for an experiment "to test women pilots' adaptability for duties other than ferry pilots." But the division was to continue paying their salaries! Tunner was fuming over the transfer of personnel that belonged to his command without being privy to their mission, and he questioned the legality of paying the women for duty they were not performing. He suggested it could be embarrassing if Congressman Ramspeck's Civil Service Committee looked into the matter.

Two months after the first batch of WASP arrived at Camp Davis, Mabel Rawlinson was killed on a night check ride when her dive bomber clipped a stand of trees and stalled. The aircraft broke apart on impact, throwing her instructor clear, but Mabel was trapped by a faulty cockpit latch and burned to death in the flaming wreckage. Less than two weeks later Joyce Sherwood cracked up her Dauntless and fractured her skull.

After the second accident, Jackie felt the women at Camp Davis were near panic. She flew to North Carolina to calm them. The future of the women pilots' program was at stake.

The WASP claimed the A-24s were faulty and certainly not fit for night training. Jackie flew several of them and examined the mechanics' squawk sheets. The planes had a myriad of small problems, but she asked the girls, "What plane being flown in these days doesn't?"

Soon after Cochran's visit, Betty Taylor Wood died when she overshot a landing and as she tried to go around, her engine failed. Her aircraft cartwheeled off the end of the runway.

Jackie was shaken to discover evidence of sabotage—traces of sugar in the gasoline tank of Wood's plane. "Enough to stop an engine in no time at all," she said privately, although she knew the information must not reach the public.

Frightening rumors drifted through Camp Davis, and two of the women pilots wanted to resign from the Third Tow Target Squadron. They had joined the WASP to be ferry pilots, not to get shot at! Cochran squashed their request and confined them to quarters. The rattled women then asked to transfer back to the Ferry Division. Again Jackie said no. The squadron commander suggested they be relieved from the tow-target experiment and assigned to other flying duties. Nonetheless Jacqueline Cochran dismissed the pair two days after Wood's crash, without preferring formal charges, and blocked their attempts to appeal through the FERD on the grounds that no one could override an Air Staff decision. These rebels threatened the WASP program.

Jackie got another scolding from General Tunner, but she had put an end to a rebellion in the WASP that might have otherwise ruined her plans to expand the organization and its mission. Instead more than three hundred women pilots eventually towed targets for air force and army training programs during World War II.

The Ferry Division wasn't finished with the Camp Davis affair. The 2nd Ferrying Group sent a representative to check up on their missing personnel. He was outraged to discover there had been several accidents, none of which had been reported to FERD headquarters. Some of the women had been sent to Camp Stewart, while others were taking radio training at Savannah, again without notifying the Ferry Division. They were being carried on four separate payrolls—none of which were correct—and their paychecks had yet to catch up to them. But the WASPs told him they liked their work, and besides, they were getting in a lot of flying.

Meanwhile the ferrying groups were complaining about the abilities of the recent Sweetwater graduates. The WASP accident rate more than doubled during the first month the largest class, 43-W-4, went on duty. Tunner was appalled by the novices' apparent lack of experience and poor judgment. The mission of his command was to deliver aircraft intact. He ordered a thorough flight check for these women and a board of review in the case of any WASP who had repeated mishaps—with the idea of discharging her.

Because of their numbers the WASP rookies had an impact at all the ferrying groups, but they were particularly a jolt at Love Field. A block of twenty-seven had been posted to the Fifth Ferrying Group, Dallas, Texas, and now more than half of the women stationed there were beginners from the fourth class. Young and self-confident, almost cheeky, they were full of the director of women pilots' lofty notions and her worthy vision for women in military aviation. Two of them, Elizabeth Mitchell and Dwight Hildinger, failed to pass the Ferry Division flight check on three separate occasions with three different instructors, and when a board of review ruled they were not capable of being ferry pilots, they called Jackie at the Pentagon—who went across the hall to plead their case to Arnold and his staff.

Tunner was so irritated by this time that on September 10 he wrote to AAF headquarters declaring that unless the Sweetwater graduates were better prepared, the Ferry Division did not want them. He returned to his original demand that the women must have a minimum of three hundred hours' flying time to be hired as ferry pilots. And he strongly recommended a cross-country trip of two thousand miles prior to graduation, with several landings at strange fields and at least two nights spent away from home base.

When, after three weeks, he received no reply, Tunner formally requested the Air Transport Command to reduce the quota of WASP assigned to him to *no more* than fifteen per month for the rest of 1943 and throughout 1944.

On October 6, 1944, General Tunner and Colonel Bob Love, assistant deputy chief of staff of the ATC, met with the Training Command. Tunner had a list of seventeen WASPs he wanted returned to Sweetwater immediately for at least fifty hours of additional instructions. The next day Air Staff informed Tunner that he could not discharge any WASP for lack of flying proficiency and that he must retain these women on his payroll until further notice.

IN THE OPINION of the men Nancy Love worked with, she was a G.I. She was a top pilot and had a no-nonsense way of handling business.

However, since the shake-up in the women pilots' program had hit the papers and stories about her rivalry with Jacqueline Cochran started popping up in national magazines, they both looked like cats fighting over shining trinkets. Nancy was embarrassed and angry. She was also fed up with Cochran's meddling.

She flared up on a trip to Air Transport Command headquarters in Washington, and the next day her husband, Bob, sent a letter to her, delivered by the hand of General Barney F. Giles. Bob apologized for what he had said the night before—because he hadn't gotten his meaning across to Nancy. "Sweetie, you must listen. None of us here feel any differently about 'that bitch' than you do. The thing that hits me, however, is that your background and her 'grossness' are now sharply contrasted in everybody's mind." He urged Nancy not to lose her composure and play into the neat trap being set by the tabloids and cheap reporters.

ON NOVEMBER 5 a telegram from Miss Jacqueline Cochran, signing for General Arnold, sent to the commanding general of the First Air Force, suggested that he transfer the Camp Davis WASP to his jurisdiction—and payroll. General Tunner agreed to this arrangement, but he heard at New Year's that the women at Camp Davis still had not been picked up on the proper payroll. They had spent a sparse Christmas without enough money to see a movie or pay their barracks bills. Tunner immediately wrote Cochran a lecture on how to execute a personnel transfer correctly, so that these WASPs could finally get a paycheck.

Meanwhile Jackie was driving the commanders of the ferrying groups nuts by showing up on their bases unannounced. She ignored normal military courtesy by going directly to the WASP alert room, taking care of her business, and leaving without informing the proper chain of command.

Then there was the WASP uniform. Once the first Sweetwater graduates went to work, General Tunner wrote to the secretary of war about a proper uniform. The eighty-eight new women pilots on the job in July were wearing "attire dictated by individual tastes," and he knew that sooner or later one of them was bound to show up in a costume that her commanding officer would find objectionable. General Tunner suggested a uniform that was slightly different from the one being worn by the WAFS. He proposed that the originals continue wearing their grays due to replacement costs.

Three weeks later Tunner also sent a description of this uniform to Avenger Field—only to find out that General Arnold had given personal instructions to hold any decision on uniforms for the women pilots for thirty days.

Jacqueline Cochran thought the WAFS' gray gabardine uniform was dull. And the army's suggestion for a uniform was even worse: cast-off, poorly tailored WAC suits. She hired Bergdorf Goodman in Manhattan to design a uniform, and the minute she was named director of women pilots, Jackie dressed two WASPs for a Pentagon fashion show.

The most striking girl she could find in Washington modeled the Bergdorf creation. She paraded the models through Arnold's office—and that of General George C. Marshall, army chief of staff. Both generals approved Jackie's choice, a distinctive suit in fine Santiago-blue wool with silver wings and a saucy beret, to make her girls look young and fresh.

General Tunner resented the Santiago-blue uniform, not only because his command had no say in its selection but because his WAFS were being forced out of their grays.

The new uniforms would not be ready for months, and as the

fall weather turned nippy, the Women Airforce Service Pilots switched out of their general's pants and into the khaki woolen shirts and pants, the "pinks," worn by male AAF flyers.

EVEN THOUGH he couldn't fire any Sweetwater graduates for flying deficiencies, Tunner still insisted on flight-checking each of them, and if a new WASP was found not qualified, she was ordered to attend her ferrying group's school.

Cochran was furious. She retaliated by asking the air inspector to investigate why the Ferry Division was not making better use of its women pilots—and the 5th Ferrying Group, Dallas Love Field, was a special target.

The air inspector ruled in favor of the WASP. In his judgment there was wide resentment at Love Field toward the women pilots and they were not being treated fairly. He formally admonished the commander of the group.

Actually many of Jackie's girls at the 5th Ferrying Group were wangling their way into heavier, faster aircraft—without taking the time to really learn the planes. The increase in the WASP accident rate was most pronounced at Dallas Love Field.

Jackie had encouraged them to use their wiles to sway and persuade at any level. She told them if a man wanted to put their parachute in the airplane and take it out, let him. "That's what men are for: to be nice to us. If we run around trying to act like men, they are going to treat us like men." In her view she was not delivering a mixed message, she was simply teaching the WASP how to use the weapons at hand to win.

To make the situation in Dallas worse, on November 7, Mary Trebing of 43-W-4 was killed when she buzzed a farmhouse south of Norman, Oklahoma, and was unable to pull up before hitting nearby powerlines. Both the mission leader and another WASP who was part of the flight faced a court-martial.

Then on Sunday, November 28, Florene Miller, the WASP squadron leader, was involved in an accident that made headlines in both Dallas papers: WASP LEADER KO'S LOVE FIELD LIGHTS, LANDS BIG FIGHTER BY EMERGENCY BEAMS and WOMAN PILOT LANDS IN DARK.

Florene was in a P-47 Thunderbolt practicing takeoffs and landings when the weather closed in, and she knew it was time to quit for the day. As she dropped down on final approach, trying to look

over the Thunderbolt's big nose for obstacles, Florene caught a large
and *significant* utility pole, ripping open the pursuit's undercar-
riage. She wrestled the damaged plane back into the air, but both
the lights *and* all the radio communications for Love Field had been
entirely knocked out.

The city completely surrounded Love Field, so she circled the
P-47 over a large lake to the north in case she had to bail out. Just as
darkness fell, the base operations officer, Captain L. H. Pickens,
established contact with Florene through a radio at the Lockheed
Aircraft plant. She said the Thunderbolt's fuel was running low.
Pickens instructed Florene to make a pass over the tower, and relayed the message that the Thunderbolt's gear was down. They
both knew Florene had never made a night landing at Love Field
before. The captain's instructions were clear and his voice steady.
The Air Force commandeered cars, jeeps, and even a truck from
the Dallas Fire Department and beamed their headlights along the
dark runway. Florene lined the P-47 up, using the rows of headlights, and brought the crippled pursuit in safely.

"Miss Miller stepped out," the papers said, "unharmed, just a
little pale." Actually, Florene nearly passed out when she saw the
damage to the plane. There had been nothing left between her feet
and the open air but the floorboard of the cockpit.

Nancy Love flew to Dallas that week. In addition to the unac-
ceptable accident rate and the air inspector's negative report, the
explosive growth in the number of WASPs had bred a string of
administrative difficulties, and the women's morale was poor. These
findings, coupled with the flashy headlines about the P-47 accident,
forced Love to relieve Florene of her duties. However, in her report
to General Tunner, Nancy observed that the overall policies and
procedures at Dallas seemed to affect every pilot in the 5th Ferrying
Group, not just the women's squadron.

BY AUGUST women pilots in the Ferry Division were officially allowed to transition into multiengine aircraft. Several of the originals at the 2nd Ferrying Group were flying P-47s from the factory
on Long Island to the docks in New Jersey. The most experienced
women pilots at Love Field were delivering AT-6s and twin-engine
advanced trainers, and the women at Long Beach flew everything
from basic trainers to P-51s.

Love ruled that the WASP administrative staff at each ferrying group, the squadron leader and her assistants, must also take turns ferrying planes, in order to maintain their flying proficiency. This was a rule Nancy applied to herself as often as possible.

In the late summer, B. J. Erickson, the young squadron commander at the 6th Ferrying Group, Long Beach, California, made four two thousand–mile deliveries in slightly more than five days of actual flying. She left Long Beach on the morning of July 29, 1943, and delivered a P-51 Mustang to Evansville, Indiana, before dark that night. The following day, she flew a P-47 back from Evansville to San Pedro, resting overnight on the way. On August 2, B.J. ferried a C-47 from Long Beach to Fort Wayne, Indiana, and then took care of business at Ferry Division headquarters in Cincinnati until August 6, when she returned to California in a P-47 Thunderbolt. Due to her multiengine rating, B.J. was at the top of the pilot roster at each stop and made incredible time.

Even though chance had played a role, hers was an unusual feat, and it was noted in a routine weekly report sent to the Air Transport Command. Ferry pilots often flew a series of missions, picking up a new aircraft through operations at each destination, and they preferred to make a delivery when returning to home base, rather then waiting for a commercial airliner. Still the process usually took a month or six weeks, not a few days. To the astonishment of both B.J. and FERD, when Air Staff in Washington got word of this string of snappy deliveries, the ATC was directed to recommend B.J. for the Air Medal.

AS THE SECOND YEAR of the war came to an end, American aircraft factories cut back production of trainers and workers set about building record numbers of fighters and bombers. As soon as a new bomber rolled off the assembly line, the Ferry Division had to get it to the front. There were never enough experienced pilots to handle the job. War-weary veteran pilots were rotated back home and assigned to ferrying, but for every one of these General William Tunner had to exchange a Class V ferry pilot as a combat replacement. The Training Command was graduating fresh pilots by the thousands, and while Tunner was entitled to a percentage of these youngsters, months of additional training lay between flight-school graduation and piloting multiengine combat aircraft.

During 1943 the loss of B-17s over Europe was staggering. One out of every ten never returned from a bombing raid, and at least thirty percent sustained severe damage. On the bloody Regensburg mission, twenty-four Fortresses, each with a ten-man crew, were demolished on a single day.

In August Tunner's command was given a big job: to deliver a hundred Flying Fortresses, in a blitz movement, to the Eighth Army Air Force in England for a major offensive. To make this assignment even more difficult, many of the Class V pilots who had recently checked out in the B-17 were griping about the long, dangerous haul across the North Atlantic during the upcoming winter.

Tunner had several women in his command who could qualify as Class V pilots immediately. He also had orders to allow them to advance to their capabilities. Tunner believed that his WAFS executive, Nancy Love, and her most experienced squadron leader, Betty Gillies, were ready for the sophisticated, powerful B-17, and he suggested they ought to ferry a Flying Fortress "over the pond"—to prove it was a simple task, just a regular ferrying assignment.

Love and Gillies were secretly working toward a transatlantic mission scheduled for early September. Meanwhile Tunner sent a memo to all ferrying groups: "There will be absolutely no publicity put out about WAFS ferrying four-engine airplanes."

The two women practiced for hours hauling the heavy plane around the sky with their hands and feet, testing their endurance and strength against the yoke and the rudder pedals, until their uniform shirts were plastered to their backs with sweat. Nancy briskly refused offers of help from the instructor. "We have to find out if we can fly this plane by ourselves."

At the end of a letter to Nancy, Bob Love added an encouraging P.S.: "As to your ability to do this thing, you both are so much better qualified than I was that I could hardly draw any sound conclusions—think for your whole crew!"

The team went through thirty-two hours of intensive training, including night landings, instrument operation, cross-country, and full-load operations. On August 15, 1943, Nancy Love and Betty Gillies qualified as pilots on the Flying Fortress. Three days later, with Love as first pilot and Gillies as copilot, they became the first women to deliver a Fortress when they flew from Cheyenne, Wyoming, to Great Falls, Montana. The following day they delivered another B-17 from the Boeing factory in Seattle to Cheyenne, and on August 22 they took a third bomber from Seattle to Dallas Love Field.

Love and Gillies received a blanket travel order, good for ninety days, to deliver a B-17, #4230624, from Cincinnati, Ohio, to the Eighth AAFTSC in Prestwick, Scotland. General Tunner assigned his personal navigator, Lieutenant R. O. "Pappy" Fraser, to the flight. There were five crew members in all, including T/Sgt L. S. Hall, who had flown with the two women on the initial B-17 deliveries.

On September 1, 1943, while Hap Arnold was out of the country, General William Tunner cleared their mission through the AAF staff in Washington, and Love and Gillies took off from Ferry Division headquarters in Cincinnati.

All four engines on #4230624 sounded good, and the two women kidded their crew over the interphone about the whiskey bottles they'd heard clinking in the men's flight bags. Would they need a few stiff drinks to get through the trip?

In her B-4 bag Nancy carried a letter of introduction, written on Air Transport Command letterhead, to Major Roy Atwood, the executive officer of the ATC European Wing in London. It asked him to do what he could for a couple of pilots who were bringing a B-17 over from the States.

> They should arrive in Prestwick presently and due to the shortness of time will bring this letter. I have known these people for a good while and they are thoroughly competent as pilots, as well as having a background of aviation activities. They are being sent to perform a certain amount of liaison with the ATA and other agencies interested in the ferrying of aircraft to the UK.
>
> I am sure you will find these two personalities pleasant, if not unusual, in that they arrive as they did, and sincerely hope you will give them your highly accredited effort in showing them around.
>
> Very sincerely yours,
>
> Robert M. Love
> Colonel, G.S.C.
> Deputy Chief of Staff
>
> P.S. Incidentally one of them is my wife and the other a good friend.

Another B-17, piloted by a full colonel, with the director of FERD personnel as a passenger, flew not far off #4230624's port wingtip. At 10:30 P.M. the pair of Flying Fortresses touched down at New Castle AAFB, where the crews spent the night and picked up the fleece-lined flight suits and oxygen masks required for the North Atlantic air route. They flew on to New York's La Guardia Airport for overnight briefing, proper clearance, and the application of appropriate nose art to Love and Gillies's ship. On the port side of the nose, just under the pilot's window, in a flowery, feminine script, was written *Queen Bee*, accompanied by "WAFS" painted in a stern, no-nonsense block print. The bombers then continued to Presque Isle, Maine, and, on September 4, landed at Goose Bay, Labrador. All the way up the coast the two bombers had encountered considerable instrument weather and the mission took a slight delay at Goose Bay due to fog.

Meanwhile, back in Cincinnati, at what he had planned to be the last minute, Tunner wired Colonel C. R. Smith at the Air Transport Command headquarters that the *Queen Bee* was on her historic way. Smith relayed the message to the commander of the ATC European Wing in England. It arrived during a dinner party at the officer's London home—where the guest of honor was AAF Commanding General Hap Arnold. Military courtesy required that the telegram be given to Arnold and when he read it, he hit the ceiling.

Fifteen minutes prior to the *Queen Bee*'s scheduled takeoff time from Goose Bay for Prestwick, a radiogram arrived from General Arnold, via the North Atlantic Wing. He ordered Love and Gillies out of the *Queen Bee* and back to the United States—at once. On September 6, 1943, the two women were among fifty passengers on a C-54 Skymaster transport to New York as a male crew completed the delivery of B-17 #4230624 to the 8th ASFTSC.

Six weeks later Nancy got a letter from Pappy Fraser telling her that Sergeant Hall had rescued her shoes and papers from the *Queen Bee* and that he was also going to send her copies of the photographs taken of the crew at Goose Bay. Fraser closed his letter with a proposition for Nancy: "How about cooking up a deal to deliver the first B-29?"

JACKIE COCHRAN was fuming when she found out about the Love and Gillies undertaking. The woman who made her mark with individual aviation records and who was forever proud of being the first—and only—woman to deliver a bomber to England during World War II, reported on her agenda for the WASP, "Individual cometlike achievements should be avoided, graduation into important new assignments should be not by exceptional individuals but by groups."

Some of the originals accused Jacqueline Cochran of having sabotaged the *Queen Bee* endeavor in a fit of jealousy. They contended she got wind of the mission when the bomber stopped at La Guardia Airport and tattled to Hap Arnold in England. If so, she couldn't have been pleased by the result. Within days AAF headquarters at the Pentagon issued a directive confining women pilots to the continental United States.

THE FIRST COSTELLO BILL was introduced into the House at the end of September and proposed to commission the WASP directly into the Army Air Force, just like medical personnel, with the same privileges and benefits as reserve officers. There were mixed feelings about militarization among the WASP already on duty, particularly among the originals and the first graduating classes. In fact Jackie had told the 43-W-1 trainees at Houston in the fall of 1942 that there was no hope of militarization. Those who were married worried because they would no longer be free to resign when their husbands came home. There were others who had children younger than eighteen, which was in violation of the Women's Army Corps regulations.

Cochran made the rounds of the WASP ferry squadrons stumping for the Costello Bill. Jane Straughan, who was stationed at the 2nd Ferrying Group in Wilmington, reminded Jackie of her remarks about military status during her welcoming speech at the Shamrock Hotel. Cochran told Jane she had it wrong and if she wasn't careful, she'd be on her way to Camp Davis. "I'll quit first!" Jane replied.

"We'll see about that," Jackie threatened.

Later that week orders transferring Jane to Camp Davis were presented to Betty Gillies, who simply ignored them.

BEGINNING with the sixth Avenger class in October 1943, the Army Air Force launched a planned diversification of assignments for women pilots. The next three classes were sent to the Training

Command, and General Barton Yount took over the responsibility not only of training the WASP but of employing a large percentage of them after graduation. His command put the women to work in target towing, radar calibration, engine testing and copiloting slots at training bases. And a few were selected to go to operational training schools to test the further capabilities of women pilots.

Shortly after Nancy Love and Betty Gillies's aborted transatlantic mission, Jacqueline Cochran wrote to the commanding officer at Avenger asking him for a list of trainees he judged to be the most mature and who had the best scores during the two weeks of twin-engine training in the AT-17. These girls also had to meet certain height and weight limits. "Send me a list of the best and the biggest," she requested.

After careful study, Cochran picked seventeen of his nominees and ordered them to report to B-17 Bomber Transition Training at Lockbourne AAFB outside Columbus, Ohio, by October 15, 1943. Jackie planned to put these women through the same bomber transition program that the AAF used for men and to qualify each of them as first pilots on the Flying Fortress.

Nine of Jackie's choices were members of the sixth WASP class, scheduled to graduate on October 9. The rest were from the previous class, 43-W-5, which had been assigned to the Ferry Division only two weeks before. When their orders arrived at the ferrying groups, no one could believe that Air Staff actually intended to train women to fly the Fortress—after Arnold's reaction to Nancy Love and Betty Gillies's attempt.

The WASP assigned to Lockbourne were stunned, overwhelmed by their good fortune. The women were turned over to three of the training squadron's most experienced instructors, all of them also happily married men, and the course was enlarged from nine to twelve weeks, with an additional twenty-five hours of flying time to compensate for their sparse multiengine experience.

They had their own Flying Fortresses, each aircraft with a playful name, such as *Pistol Packin' Mama*, painted on its nose. Four women could easily train at once. There was ample room in the cockpit for those not flying to observe from behind the pilot and copilot seats, standing erect at the turret gunner's position, while their instructor bobbed between the student pilots in a swing seat. The giant ship made the AT-17s at Avenger seem frivolous. Each time it lumbered down the runway, with all four throttles pushed forward and its four huge engines thundering, everyone on board strained to get the bomber airborne.

Nearly all of the Lockbourne WASP soloed within forty hours. They learned to synchronize the Fortress's engines and to tell from their sound if all was well. They flew with instruments and in three-plane V-formations, keeping their aircraft's wingtips level with the leader's waist-gun positions. The women demonstrated they had the stamina for five-hour training flights. They learned to fly and land with two engines shut down. Even though the B-17 was equipped with a hydraulic system and trim tabs, the WASP had to prove they had the upper-body strength to control the 65,000-pound bomber manually. And these B-17 WASP became the first women to fly above 25,000 feet in an unpressurized cabin. Bundled up within the cold-weather flying suits and breathing with the aid of oxygen masks, they watched while ice formed on their ship's wings and the earth's horizon curved dreamily off into the distance.

In November Ann Waldner from 43-W-6 wrote to Mrs. Deaton after she soloed in the Flying Fortress with a WASP crew—only six weeks after graduating from Avenger:

> And what a thrill! There we were all alone, except for a crew chief, who was right on his toes, chewin' his nails to the bone, and I believe a bit frightened.
>
> We've completed the rigid ground-school course for the second time. They don't miss a thing, and that doesn't make me a bit angry. I love every minute of it here.
>
> It certainly is fun marching to the flight line and ground school with captains, majors, and especially a full colonel, who was our flight leader. And, don't laugh now, but we can talk and even go out with them without getting a demerit!

Air Staff gave the WASP at Lockbourne ample publicity, in contrast to the Ferry Division's policy for the women ferry pilots. On November 20 General Tunner testily wrote the War Department's Bureau of Public Relations and copied the director of women pilots:

> It has been brought to the attention of this Headquarters that statements have been made to the effect that the first WASPs to fly four-engine aircraft are at present being trained at Lockbourne. . . . This Command wishes to state that two of the women pilots employed by

the Ferrying Division have been qualified as first pilots on B-17 aircraft since 15 August. . . . It is requested that prior to release of news stories involving the WASPs of the Ferrying Division, the accuracy of statements be checked with this Command.

After the New Year one of the B-17 WASP, Lucille Friesen, married Lockbourne's training inspector, Major John McVey. The romance had been developing for weeks and had even survived several tense check rides. The training squadron's CO gave the bride away, and the photographers from Chicago and New York swamped the base chapel to record the wedding of two bomber pilots.

After logging 145 hours in the Fortress and successfully completing a cross-country flight of several thousand miles, thirteen of the WASP assigned to B-17 transition at Lockbourne remained to graduate on January 15, 1944. The training-squadron staff celebrated with a champagne dinner dance. Four of the women were retained at Lockbourne, including Helen Dettweiler, the women's golfing champion who would later be assigned to Cochran's staff, and Lucy Friesen McVey, the new bride. There were rumors that they might be used as instructors, but instead they flew engine tests on repaired Flying Fortresses.

Nine of the B-17 graduates were sent to Buckingham AAFB, Florida, where they acted as copilots on B-17 gunnery training missions over the Gulf of Mexico. These flights lasted four to five hours and began at high altitudes to give student gunners—who swiveled around enthusiastically in the bomber's gun turrets—an opportunity to fire at a target sleeve towed behind a B-26. Then the Fortress climbed even higher, above 25,000 feet, so that the gunners could practice firing while wearing oxygen bottles. Finally the pilots took the bomber down on the deck and skimmed across the Gulf, and the students fired into splashes of seawater thrown in the air from previous rounds.

The gunners trained every day the weather permitted. They were young, mostly teenagers, and small in order to fit into the the snug Plexiglas gun turrets. They looked like bantams next to the strapping WASP pilots.

SIXTEEN OTHER WASP from the sixth class were ordered to South Plains AAFB, Lubbock, Texas, to learn to tow gliders with the twin-engine C-60 Lockheed Lodestar. Their experiences were quite different from those of the Lockbourne WASP. This group ran head-on into a wall of negative attitudes.

Because of their meager twin-engine experience, the women were required to take two months of transition in the C-60, including ninety-six hours as copilot, before beginning glider-pilot towing school in January 1944. Only six of these women graduated from the course, and they were rated with minimum skills—under ideal conditions.

In his report to the Training Command, the commander at South Plains wrote that the women's judgment was not developed enough to fly heavy airplanes, in spite of the excellent instruction they had received. They did not have the strength or stamina required and could not seem to handle the nervous strain of a five-hour towing mission or the exacting nature of the work. Some were overconfident, while others were too unsure of themselves even to solo. The only reason there were no accidents was because of precautions taken by their instructors. In fact the women were often not even aware of their danger. He recommended a less strenuous assignment for them—such as the Ferry Division.

THE FIRST WOMEN to graduate from B-26 transition at Dodge City were also hand picked from 43-W-5 and 43-W-6. The twin-engine B-26 Marauder was slightly larger and faster than the C-60 used to tow gliders, and the plane had an appalling reputation. Its stubby wings made the bomber skittish to handle. Crews joked the B-26 had no visible means of support and nicknamed it the Flying Prostitute—or, more grimly, the Widow Maker, in black tribute to all the flyers it had killed.

Many of the B-26's problems were cured when the wingspan was increased by six feet, but the stigma lingered on, so Jackie talked General Arnold into letting her girls try the dangerous Marauder—for the effect! On top of this, she suggested, the women could be preparing to pilot a variant of the bomber used as a target tug in gunner training.

Jackie selected the candidates for Dodge City herself, and since these greenhorns had never heard the deadly scuttlebutt about the Widow Maker, she requested separate classes so that they wouldn't pick up any fear from the men. Of the seventeen women who began

[145]

training, eleven graduated from the nine-week course. While they had less technical background, the women's average ground-school grades equaled those of their male classmates. The school's commanding officer reported that, "they displayed a most cooperative attitude and were enthusiastic and tried harder than the normal student."

After this first class of WASP successfully completed B-26 Transition, two more groups of women were trained at Dodge City—fifty-seven in all, with thirty-nine graduating.

Over one hundred WASP eventually checked out in the Marauder, upgrading to the aircraft through transition taken at their home bases. Most were stationed on the Texas border as tow-target pilots, and Jackie Cochran received a letter of commendation from the Training Command about the contributions of these women.

THE DUTY ASSIGNMENTS for Lela Loudder's class, 43-W-7, were reshuffled several times before and after their November 13 graduation. Only one thing remained constant: Not a single member of the seventh class was going to work for the Ferry Division. After months of dreaming, they knew it would be a long time, if ever, before any of them got a crack at a P-47.

Twice on graduation day Air Staff sent changes in orders to Avenger. Some of the class had already gone on leave when the last change arrived. Eventually most were scattered through various AAF commands and flying jobs, usually in twos and threes, and the whole class envied a group of twelve chosen for a B-25 bomber training squadron in California.

Lela Loudder was assigned to production-line maintenance at Williams AAFB, Arizona, where she would test-hop patched-up planes. At the train station on the morning she left for Arizona, Lela admitted to her sister that she was nervous. She had never been out of Texas before—and she had never ridden a train before. "I don't know how to act. What to do!" Lela whispered.

"Oh, just ask the conductor," her sister replied. "That's what they do in the movies."

When Lela arrived at Williams Field, dressed in a fashionable traveling suit, the guard at the front gate was sure she must be a spy. He called the colonel, who seemed to agree, because he dispatched the provost marshall to fetch Lela to his office. Once he

23. *Above*: Trainee Joan Garrett, 43-W-6, in the front seat of an AT-6 with her instructor, Elmo Hatcher, riding behind.

24. *Below*: Hazel Ah Ying Lee practicing in the Link trainer.

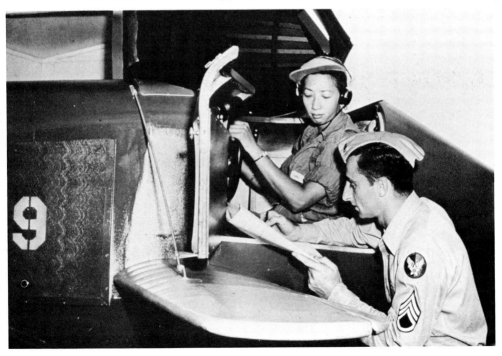

25. *Above*: A rancher assists a trainee as she mounts her horse during a party given in Sweetwater for the women pilots.

26. *Below*: Mrs. Leoti Deaton, the Chief Establishment Officer, sitting at the wishing well.

Airplanes must fly — accidents will happen, but those caused by foolish, careless, disobedient, cocky or grandstand pilots can and must be stopped.
Save the cockiness for combat.

27. *Above*: Trainees learning some extra maneuvers from an instructor during a coffee break.

WOMEN ... ÉES
— ONLY —
IN THIS AREA

28. *Right*: No Man's Land: Cochran's Convent.

29. A WASP graduation parade on the flight line at Avenger Field with AT-6's in the background.

30. *Opposite page above*: Class 44-W-2 graduation—Jacqueline Cochran, Ethel Sheehy, Mrs. Leoti Deaton, General H. H. Arnold.

31. *Opposite page below*: H. H. Arnold and B. J. Erickson on the reviewing stand at Avenger Field just after the general presented her with the Air Medal.

32. A-24 Dauntless flying a target sleeve for gunnery practice.

33. WASP who fly target tugs at Camp Davis get a close look at an anti-aircraft gun used to fire at the target sleeves.

34. Three WASPs checking their route before takeoff.

35. *Opposite page above*: WASP Elsie Dyer discussing a tow target mission with an AAF officer.

36. *Opposite page below*: *Pistol Packin' Mama*. Four of the WASP selected for B-17 transition: Frances Green, Margaret Kirchner, Ann Waldner, and Blanch Osborn.

37. The B-17 WASP standing under the wings of a Flying Fortress at Lockbourne AAFB.

38. WASP Joanne Trebtoske, pilot, and Marjorie Logan, copilot, preparing to ferry a C-47 transport from Romulus, Michigan, to Canada.

39. B-26 bomber pilot Velma Saunders.

40. B-26 bomber pilot Libby Gardner, Harlingen AAFB, Texas.

41. DeDe Johnson and Dora Dougherty with Colonel Paul Tibbets, who taught them how to fly a B-29 with their Superfortress, *Ladybird*.

42. *Opposite page above*: Tommy Thompkins (back) with friends Audry Tardy (front) and Micky Axton (center) on the wing of an AT-6 at Pecos AAFB.

43. *Opposite page below*: Teresa James with the ten-thousandth P-47 manufactured by Republic during World War II. During a gala celebration, the plane was christened 10 Grand by Jackie Cochran and then delivered to the docks at Newark by Teresa.

44. B. J. Erickson, squadron leader at Long Beach, California, and Betty Thackaberry, who was in the first class in Houston, lead the parade in their Women's Auxiliary Ferrying Squadron grays.

saw her, the colonel vaguely recalled receiving a letter about the WASP. On the other hand, he was absolutely crystal clear about neither wanting nor needing any women pilots on his airfield.

Nevertheless Lela had her AAF orders in her hand. There were civilian quarters, about two miles from the flight line, the colonel told her, where she could stay. On the jeep ride from the gate Lela had spotted an empty BOQ near the hangars and stated that she preferred to live there. "You can't," he replied emphatically.

"You can't stop me," she countered, certain of Jackie's backing. The colonel argued that the BOQ was too far from the civilian mess, and he had no intention of allowing her into the Officers' Club.

"I'll eat there tonight," Lela assured him.

Later that day one of Lela's classmates also reported into Williams and joined her in the forbidden BOQ. When the army nurses and WAC officers heard the two WASP were planning to have dinner at the Officers' Club—where they had never been, even once—they excitedly tagged along. As the group of women walked into the club, the colonel stomped out in a helpless rage.

The women pilots' work at the Williams maintenance facility was routine but necessary. And occasionally they found a mistake. Within the first month Lela brought a repaired BT-13 back from a test hop after a wing split entirely in two.

Still, the colonel never softened. Over the holidays Lela and her classmate went into Phoenix with a group of junior officers to celebrate. A few of the guys, who were very drunk, kept suggesting the whole gang ought to check into a motel room together. Later one apologized to Lela and admitted the colonel had put him up to the idea—to get enough on the two women to have them kicked off the base.

The elated group from 43-W-7 who were heading for the West Coast to learn to fly the B-25 Mitchell bomber faced a big comedown. Nowhere along the way did they find a single soul who had even heard of the WASP! At a café in New Mexico the women carefully explained who and what they were, only to be asked afterward, "Do they ever let you go up in a plane alone?"

Just outside of Mather Field, east of Sacramento, they spied a large formation of the famous twin-tailed bombers flying overhead, each ship neatly in place. The women stood in joyful wonder—like a bunch of bobby-soxers who had just spotted Frank Sinatra. And when they discovered the massive stockpile of young air force officers on the base, a feast of available men after a six months' fast at Sweetwater, the women were even more dizzy and dazed.

Within a month one of them married and resigned to follow her new husband, who had just completed B-25 transition, to his next posting. The others reveled in flirting with the officers, but they were head-over-heels in love with the powerful, thrilling Mitchell bomber.

Transition required 110 hours of flying, and a WASP had to log 15 hours before she could take the bomber's controls as first pilot. The instructors at Mather acted as if they believed a women could be taught to fly a Mitchell, just like a man—and their women students learned to believe, more than before, that they, too, could fly the celebrated B-25.

During the winter the California fog rolled over the top of the Sacramento Mountains, blanketing the valley below. Low visibility caused endless delays in training, and the WASP wasted many days in the ready room, knitting Christmas gifts, reading tech orders, and singing songs from Avenger Field, while waiting for the weather to clear. When a break came, they scrambled into the cockpit, stashing their knitting bags under the pilots' seats, ready to fly.

Before graduation the women had to make a cross-country flight at night. They felt more at ease up in the dark with a Mitchell bomber than in the trainers at Avenger, but the California airspace was packed with large aircraft—day and night. Even with the red-and-green navigation lights blinking on their ship's wingtips, the WASP flicked their recognition lights every so often to make sure the other pilots knew they were there.

The night flight was taken in a formation of five B-25s, with two women in each bomber as pilot and copilot. Looking like plump teddy bears in their AAF winter flight suits, the WASP toddled out to their planes with maps, a log, a computer, and a good supply of cigarettes and candy bars. Since it was impossible for a short girl to swing herself up into the aircraft in this heavy gear, the smaller women had to wait under the open bomb bay doors for a male crew member to hoist them inside.

The WASP flight went east, away from the unreliable weather near the Pacific Ocean and over the soaring Sierra Nevadas. As their Mitchells climbed to 14,000 feet, the women put on oxygen masks and communicated with each other and the ground through throat mikes. Beneath them was a black unknown, without a sign of habitation. Once over the mountains and out in the desert, the women picked out random patches of light, isolated dwellings, before sighting the glitter of Reno and turning back toward the coast. The five B-25s touched down on Mather's runway, in perfect intervals, two hours later.

Every one of the women at Mather successfully completed transition—with the exception of the girl who quit to get married—and graduated with their ground-school class. Afterward they were assigned to tow-target squadrons in California and Texas.

MEANWHILE Nancy Love oversaw the transition of the women ferry pilots through the regular training sequence at the ferrying groups. The veteran members of the WASP squadron at the 2nd Ferrying Group, New Castle AAFB, were piloting a variety of advanced aircraft—and they were issued automatic pistols to protect the secret instruments in them. If threatened, they had orders to destroy the devices and disable the plane—not the menacing thieves or spies! Tiny Marie Muccie often carried a pistol on missions but hadn't any idea how to use it. The WASP were never given small arms instructions. If Jane Straughan was ordered to draw a pistol from inventory, she always removed the ammunition clip and left it behind at New Castle. When she turned in the pistol at her final destination, Jane had a stock alibi for the missing clip. "I don't know," she would sweetly say, "it was like that when I got it."

Helen Richey, the former British Air Transport Auxiliary pilot, was assigned to the 2nd Ferrying Group after completing an abbreviated course at Sweetwater and immediately checked out as first pilot on the B-25 Mitchell bomber. Richey was appointed squadron leader for a group of Ferry Division WASP posted to the North American aircraft plant in Kansas City. They would be trained to deliver Mitchell bombers from the factory to AAF operational schools around the country.

Marie Muccie went with the Kansas City squadron. She could

see that Helen Richey deserved the laurels of a famous, first-rate pilot, but she seemed fidgety, wound tight. She needed pills, and sometimes booze, to sleep at night.

Although the Air Transport Command permitted women to transition in multiengine planes, General Tunner insisted that his pilots be flight-checked by another woman who had already qualified in that class of aircraft. He wasn't comfortable with mixed crews. However, this process of training for Class IV and V was cumbersome and slow, and eventually the demand for experienced pilots forced Tunner to alter this rule.

To speed upgrading, a man could flight-check a WASP, and ferry missions could be considered training flight, so long as they had been planned as such and *some* instruction was actually taking place.

Marie regularly received orders as copilot for missions with a handsome captain from Texas. Too regularly, she suspected, but it was a chance to fly, and he was qualified for instrument checks. Soon orders, with her name on them, materialized for every one of the captain's ferry assignments. They were married in the summer, and Marie retired from the WASP after eighteen months in service.

IN NOVEMBER Army Air Force headquarters announced a series of proposals to clarify the vague powers given to Jacqueline Cochran when she was appointed director of women pilots and to solidify her authority. Nancy Love was in Washington visiting her husband when the announcement came, and she telephoned General Tunner to warn him: Cochran was on the prowl again!

From the Pentagon Jackie directed that the WASP squadron leaders would be chosen by Air Staff, not the commanding officer where the women were stationed. She also intended to have a representative, a nonflying WASP executive officer under her control, stationed at each base—a plan that bypassed Nancy Love and effectively eliminated her position as executive for the women pilots within the Ferry Division. Also, all reports of accidents involving women pilots must be sent directly to the director of women pilots. And she would issue duty assignments for the Avenger graduates from her office.

Tunner was indignant. Cochran was walking roughshod over the functions of his command—again! From his point of view these proposals not only violated the proper chain of command but constituted special treatment for the women pilots. Tunner insisted that in the Ferry Division men and women pilots were treated much alike.

This time, General Harold George backed Tunner all the way. He stated, "Any system which directs administration control from headquarters AAF directly into the squadron is intolerable. A commanding officer has a mission to perform and he must have full and complete responsibility." He demanded the right to handle the women pilots in the Air Transport Command on exactly the same basis as men pilots.

Two weeks later, just before Christmas, AAF headquarters supported General George's stand and issued a new AAF regulation on the WASP preserving hallowed command prerogatives. Furthermore, each AAF command employing the WASP was to have a female staff director, a position very like Nancy Love's with Ferry Division, to act as an executive layer, a shield between Air Staff and the women's operational units. And headquarters assured the Air Transport Command that no graduates of Avenger Field would be assigned as ferry pilots until Class 44-W-1 completed an improved curriculum in February 1944.

8.

Silver Wings and Santiago Blue

BEFORE THEY COULD FINISH their flying lessons, Ruth Craig Jones and her friend, Skip Carter, were notified to report for their AAF physicals at Tinker Field, just south of Oklahoma City. Ruth started to worry as soon as she opened the envelope. She missed the five feet four inches required by the Women Airforce Service Pilots by about half an inch.

During her free periods at the high school where she taught physical education, Ruth hung by her heels from an overhead beam in the gym, hoping to stretch her bones out. The morning of the physical, she hung upside down as long as she could manage without passing out and then rode to Tinker lying flat in the backseat of the car to keep her skeleton from squeezing back together. "Let's measure first," she suggested hopefully to the AAF doctor. He wrote "five feet four inches" on her file, and Ruth was surprised to find that every time she was measured later on, the additional half an inch apparently was hers to keep.

Ruth's father didn't approve of the WASP, and the principal of her high school warned her not to expect him to save her job. "You know why the Army Air Force wants women—*young women*—on their bases with all those men, don't you? What would your husband think if he knew?" Ruth looked down at the principal, a man so small he had to crook his neck and peer upward to see, and replied, "My husband knows what I'm trying to do. He has always told me I could do anything I felt big enough to do."

The day Ruth and Skip drove out of Oklahoma City across the summer-brown prairie toward Sweetwater they received notice in the mail that they had passed the written portion of the test for their private pilot's license. They hadn't had time to complete the flying tests.

All the women reporting for Class 44-W-1 were dressed to the hilt. This was an important day for them. They had come to dusty west Texas from every corner of the nation and every walk of life chasing a common dream: to fly! "When you wish upon a star, your dreams come true," the good fairy sang to Pinocchio in Walt Disney's 1940 film. Jacqueline Cochran, with a vision of a women's air corps, was the bright star every WASP trainee wished upon.

Cochran had been director of women pilots for two months, and she was pushing the WASP program to full throttle. By the time Class 44-W-1 graduated, women would be trying their hand at a variety of noncombat flying jobs and accomplishing transition into most of the aircraft flown by the AAF. Congressman John Costello would have introduced into the House a revamped WASP bill, and Cochran would have arranged to send her girls to a short course in Orlando, Florida, to familiarize them with military customs and procedures prior to their commissioning as officers in the Army Air Force.

But on this hot, windy August day, the 101 rookies in Ruth's class, feeling proud and lucky, folded their chic clothes away in footlockers, put on their government-issue overalls, and prepared to learn to fly the army way. Like Ruth and Skip, the majority of this class met the WASP flying requirements by the skin of their teeth. Marie Mountain played first-chair flute in a symphony orchestra. Marge Harper, a stunning twenty-three-year-old brunette from New Castle, Pennsylvania, wanted to help fill the shoes of her brother Edwin, a marine pilot, who had been killed in the South Pacific. Both women held private pilot's licenses but had less than fifty hours. Katherine (Kay) Dussaq, a court examiner from Chicago, was a rare exception to the class norm. She had logged four hundred hours of flying time and held an instructor's rating. Poised and sure of herself at thirty-three, Kay was one of the oldest members of the class and was married to her second husband, Rene A. Dussaq, a lieutenant in the military's secret service.

"Unload your gear and find someplace in town to leave this car," the officer of the day told Ruth. Trainees were no longer allowed to keep cars on base. Ruth found a space to store the Ford at Pop and Ollie's Garage south of the Sweetwater square and took a taxi back to Avenger.

The class was assigned to bays in alphabetical order, just like real army rookies. During an introductory briefing, their senior squadron leader introduced a safety precaution designed for them by the commanding officer, Major Robert Urban. To keep the students' hair out of the machinery, he ordered them to wear it wrapped up, swamilike, in a piece of white cotton—dubbed an Urban's Turban. Each trainee gassed her own plane. Army regulations forbade drinking on post. Drinking within twenty-four hours of a scheduled flight meant an automatic washout. Finally she warned about loose talk and military security. "Be careful what you write home about our planes and training."

Next Captain Nels Monserud, the army flight surgeon at Avenger, made complete dental records of each of the recruits to keep on file in order to identify their bodies in case of a crash. He vaccinated them for smallpox and gave them the first in a series of three shots for typhoid and tetanus. By the next morning most of the class had sore arms and queasy stomachs, and several passed out during breakfast formation.

On the flight line the women were assigned to their primary-phase flight instructor according to height. Zoot suits could bag, but for safety, parachute straps needed to be snug. Two or three

trainees the same size could share a single parachute without remembering to adjust the shoulder and groin straps.

The air force furnished all pilots, whether a two-hundred-pound
man or a hundred-and-ten-pound girl, with a standard parachute,
but the trainees got almost no parachuting instructions, except for
a skimpy booklet with cartoon how-to illustrations.

Slender Marie Mountain got the opportunity to test her parachute knowledge during the first weeks of primary. On a blustery
afternoon she was up with her instructor at 3,000 feet practicing
tailspin recoveries in a PT-19. Marie executed a flawless right-wing
spin but on the recovery, her seat belt unsnapped, and she went
soaring out of the cockpit—over the head of her amazed instructor.
He righted the trainer, banked, and found Marie floating toward
earth, bobbing and waving merrily from under her parachute canopy. He radioed Avenger to pick her up, but lightweight Marie
blew for miles, skimming along with an army jeep bouncing behind
her, before she finally settled to earth.

When Marie got back to the field, she was inducted into the
Caterpillar Club—that fraternity of unflappable pilots who in a
jam not only manage to pull the rip cord on their parachutes but
still have the handle when they land—and a lucky keepsake for life.

At this stage the women's training detachment was getting new
equipment weekly, and the control tower had just been brought up
to army standard, including a red beacon light on top that auto-
matically turned off and on at sunrise and sunset. The tower operators finally had an unobstructed view of the runways and the
traffic pattern in every direction, and all aircraft, especially primary trainers, were warned to keep an eye out for signal lights.

One rookie attempting to land after practicing at an auxiliary got
seven red lights in a row from the tower. Finally she flew back to
the auxiliary to ask the flight commander what to do. When he
called Avenger asking why this student had gotten so many red
lights, the operator informed him that *none* had been given all
afternoon. "She must have been flying by the new tower beacon,"
he said.

Mrs. Deaton gave the new class permission to move their cots
outdoors at night to escape the stuffy barracks—until rattlesnakes
were spotted cuddling up to some of the sleeping girls. The August

[155]

heat, combined with the endless runway construction, had stirred up the rattlesnake population around Avenger and made them more of a menace than usual.

During the daytime the rattlers usually stayed out of sight, hiding in a cool spot. At night they were on the prowl, hunting for food and another place to hole up before sunrise. Occasionally they chose an airplane. Early one morning a terrified 44-W-1 rookie discovered, following takeoff, that she had a rattlesnake for a passenger. The snake wiggled out of a flap joint on the trainer's wing and was crawling with determination toward the cockpit. The trainee jerked the stick from side to side, tossing the trainer about until the propwash dumped the varmint. From then on all the trainees checked their planes carefully before climbing inside.

Even though Avenger was closed to outside traffic, wandering male pilots still dropped in, particularly on Sunday afternoons when the field was not in use. On Navy Day, Sunday, October 25, fourteen navy aircraft—ten Stearmans headed for the naval air station at Memphis, two Vultees up from Corpus Christi, a Hellcat, and a Corsair—made emergency landings. Only the Hellcat's pilot actually had a girlfriend at Avenger. The other navy aviators were merely scouts.

As the weeks passed, Ruth Craig Jones proved herself outstanding in every area of training: the classroom work, military drills and procedures, and flying. The minute her class began flying, Ruth knew that the teacher she and Skip had had at the little dirt airstrip in Oklahoma City had been top-notch, for she knew so much more of the basics than did the majority of her classmates. At the end of primary she was appointed senior squadron leader for an incoming class. "You're just a superstar," Skip kidded her.

Ruth knew luck played a part too. The hottest pilot in her flight was Lili Pearl, a deceivingly quiet, shy young woman who was a former navy flight instructor. But for some reason Lili Pearl didn't seem to be able to learn to fly the army way. She collected one pink slip after another. Ruth wondered, when she finally washed out, if Lili Pearl's trouble hadn't been that she was a better pilot than her teachers.

Ruth enjoyed Lili Pearl. She was not only a good pilot, she was a good companion. One Saturday after inspection they had ridden the trolley into Sweetwater together. Lili Pearl was going to the movies—the thing she loved best, next to flying—while Ruth took care of errands.

Trainees customarily gave their flight instructors a present when they graduated to the next phase. Ruth thought her primary instructor was tops, and that Saturday she was determined to buy him a pint of whiskey in return for his patient, good-natured efforts. Since the entire Texas Panhandle was dry, she asked a connection on the air base staff to call his bootlegger in Sweetwater. A pint was ready and waiting when she arrived. But what to do with it while she took care of her other business? Lili Pearl never touched whiskey. The pint would be safe with her at the picture show. Lili Pearl took the bottle, tucked it inside the waistband of her slacks, and gave it a pat before stepping on line to buy her ticket.

Ruth wound up her Saturday liberty with a juicy steak at the Lone Star Café, but when she met Lili Pearl at the trolley stop, she knew tragedy had struck. Lili Pearl could barely meet Ruth's eyes as she described how the pint had slid down her pants leg when she stood up to leave the theater. She had forgotten she had the bottle, and it skidded under several rows of seats, picking up speed before smashing against the stage in a hundred aromatic pieces.

THE MAJORITY of the thirty to forty civilian instructors at Avenger were competent, although they took pride in being extremely profane and completely unmilitary. On the whole they asked only that a trainee do nothing to get them or herself killed while learning to fly.

Some of the army check pilots were another matter. They had graduated from flight school, been commissioned, and then, instead of going on to operational flying, these men had been sent back to instruct novices. They hated their work, particularly giving check rides at Avenger, and they could be sadistically demanding. One evening at a party off base Ruth bumped into one of these disgruntled army pilots, who was exceedingly drunk and morose. She asked him what his trouble was. He glared back. "What am I going to tell my little boy when he asks, 'What did you do in the big war, Daddy?'—that I taught a bunch of *women* to fly?"

Check rides were often the source of lyrics for the trainees' songs.

Some were sung with spirit and spunk, some with the women thumbing their noses in the face of their fears, and others were tongue-in-cheek washout dirges.

I'm a flying wreck, a riskin' my neck and a helluva pilot too!
A helluva, helluva, helluva, helluva, helluva pilot, too!

If I had a civilian check, I'll tell you what I'd do,
I'd pop the stick and break his neck and probably get a "U"
If I had an Army ride, I'd take off without any flaps,
And show him that an easier job would be over fighting Japs!

Clothes packed, I'm leaving, my flying days are done.
Home to raise babies, the army says it's fun,
Making tiny garments, luck to you, you varmints.
Check-flight instructor has washed me out today!

DEDIE DEATON did her best to comfort the trainees who washed out, and she had a compassionate assistant in Dr. Nels Monserud, the army flight surgeon, who acted as a father figure, consoling the heartbroken girls. Monserud had arrived at Avenger Field on August 25, 1943, five months after the first trainees, and had been promoted to captain and commanding officer of the local medical detachment. He was in charge of the medical needs of all personnel on the base. He airlifted serious medical problems to the bombardier's hospital in Big Spring and delivered the babies of officers' wives at the civilian hospital in Sweetwater. However, his real job was a formal medical study of women flyers.

As part of the Women Airforce Service Pilots experiment, Jacqueline Cochran not only tinkered constantly with training and assignments, she directed Dr. Monserud to thoroughly research and record every one of the students' physical and emotional responses. During almost two years of study Dr. Monserud had ample opportunity to examine the two thousand young women who entered WASP training and to analyze the results. He collected data on height and weight, strength, concentration, illness, and particularly on menstrual cycles.

EVERY MONTH the trainees had to report to the medical office when they had their periods. They were positive the purpose of this embarrassment was to find out if any of them had gotten pregnant, but much more was at stake than their good names. Cochran wanted to put to rest the enduring suspicion that women were especially fragile and, worse yet, unreliable during their periods.

Dr. Monserud's research findings were precisely what Cochran had hoped for. Not only did the doctor give a positive report about every aspect of the women's flying ability, he declared that their overall performance was actually better around the first day of their periods and that they lost less time per month due to physiological reasons, both during training and operational flying, than men.

THE WOMEN'S TRAINING DETACHMENT published a weekly newspaper, *The Avenger*—"News from the Mother Hive of the Army WASPs." During the last two months of 1943 Anne Berry, a student librarian from Martha's Vineyard, was editor and Kay Dussaq was one of the reporters. The paper carried an eclectic assortment of stories and was supported by ads from local merchants. The Sears Roebuck store on Pecan advertised every week. So did J. C. Penney and the drugstore on the ground floor of the Blue Bonnet Hotel. *The Avenger* carried a column on flying technique, "Airbella Advises," written by an anonymous instructor, and ran a box score of AAF kills "American Combat Aircraft." The paper also discussed the movies showing each weekend at the three theaters in Sweetwater and filled the trainees in on gossip about the stars. In November 1943 *The Immortal Sergeant*, with Henry Fonda and Maureen O'Hara, played at the Texas movie house on the town square. The Tinsel Town chatter was slanted toward leading men—"Swooncrooner Frank Sinatra classified 1A in the draft," and "Captain Clark Gable escapes injury in an automobile accident in Hollywood."

WHEN THE RECREATION CENTER and gym were finished, physical training moved indoors from the windy, sand-swept athletic field. The gym was open until 11:00 P.M., except for two hours in the afternoon, which were restricted for the use of officers and enlisted men. The rec center had a jukebox, a movie projector, and a reading room with a fake fireplace.

After the army announced that the regular AAF physical fitness test would be required of all trainees and would include pull-ups, sit-ups, and the hundred-yard dash, these new facilities got extra traffic. While the army's decision brought moans and groans from the trainees, Lieutenant W. H. La Rue, the physical training officer, saluted this step and said he also intended to enforce stricter rules in formation. "Bad formations show a lack of discipline," he declared.

ON NOVEMBER 5, 1943, Kay D'Arezzo and Millie Davidson drove up from Austin to Sweetwater. The previous weeks had been chaotic for both of them. Colonel McBride thoroughly disapproved of the Women Airforce Service Pilots, and as always, his wife agreed. They felt an obligation to reason with their oldest daughter. Eventually Kay's mother conceded, "Since you're a married woman, we really can't stop you." Millie still needed to gain weight to pass the AAF physical, and Mrs. McBride stuffed her with delectable treats several times a week—while Kay struggled to lose a few pounds. Then the Red Cross delivered a letter from Al, Kay's first words from her husband since December 1941. Nearly two years with nothing but his name on a list of prisoners, first at camps in the Philippines and then in Japan. She rushed to buy Christmas gifts for the Red Cross to ship to him. Millie's husband, Captain Bill Davidson, was still missing in action.

When Kay spotted the ten-foot-tall imp, Fifinella, with her red boots and flaring blue wings, on top of the administration building, she knew Avenger was going to be different from any army post where she had ever lived. She and Millie were assigned to the same bay. D'Arezzo and Davidson both began with a *D*. Because of her rank in the Women's Defense Corps and her tall, commanding appearance, Kay was appointed squadron commander of Flight One. She picked Millie as one of her two flight lieutenants.

November 1943 was the first time most of the young women at Avenger had been away from home at Thanksgiving. The army officers and instructors went duck hunting for two days, and the mess hall did its best with a traditional feast. Thanksgiving night the trainees marched to the new gym through a downpour. Marie Mountain played a flute solo, and Hazel Raines, a former British ATA who was in Kay's class, told tales about flying Spitfires.

SHORTLY AFTER Kay and Millie began training, the PT-19 primary trainers were replaced by the Stearman, a 225-horsepower, open-cockpit, biwing trainer. "It's a swell little airplane," said Elmer Riley, the director of flying training, in an interview in *The Avenger*. "Safe, maneuverable, sturdy. On the ground or in the air, it is one of the finest training ships made." Painted canary yellow, the Stearman could do acrobatics that would disintegrate a pursuit or be dropped to a landing from a stall twenty feet in the air—with barely a scratch to show for it.

To the delight of the students their new yellow trainers were ferried to the field by WASP, who then flew out the Fairchild PT-19s. The Stearmans ushered in the beefed-up curriculum that had been demanded by the Ferry Division. The course was extended by three weeks, and flying instruction increased from 180 to 210 hours. Two separate thousand-mile solo cross-countries were required during the final phase, which kept the women away from base for three or four nights.

A trainee normally needed six to eight hours of dual instruction in the Stearman before the first solo flight. The instructor decided when each student was ready. Afterward there were long hours of intense solo practice to perfect loops, spins, and chandelles before the army check ride.

Millie and half of Flight One flew to a practice area about forty miles from Avenger to work on aerobatics. Since the Stearmans had no navigational equipment or radios, the trainees had used the "iron compass," railroad tracks, to find their assigned area. The sky was cold and gray, and snowflakes started to fall. Even in their fleece-lined flying suits, the women were freezing, and by the time the practice session was over, all trace of the railroad tracks had vanished under a layer of snow. All that was visible were a few poles in the section line fences. Cold and afraid, the trainees flew in circles, waving their arms and wondering how to find the main field.

Meanwhile one of Avenger's AAF cadre set out in search of the missing group. When the lost trainees spied his plane, they flew straight for him. Millie tucked right up under his wing, all the way back to Avenger. Their rescuer was a veteran of fifty combat missions in Europe, but he swore, after landing, that he had never been more frightened than when he was trying to evade the bevy of yellow biwing trainers coming at him from every direction.

THE FIRST WEEK in December Sears Roebuck held a Christmas shopping night for Avenger's personnel. The store stayed open until nine o'clock and offered to wrap gifts and mail them anywhere in the United States without charge. Gift suggestions ranged from a Crash Bracelet, an identification bracelet for flyers marked with the army, navy, or Marine Corps insignia, to a genuine aviator scarf, twelve by seventy-two inches, in white rayon crepe with self-fringed ends, for $1.98.

To raise Christmas money while waiting around the ready room, Marie Mountain came up with an idea for a handmade gift. She offered to knit Dog Tag Mittens, in a choice of colors, with a draw-string at the top where the tag met the chain, to ward off the chill of the cold metal on winter mornings.

Just before Christmas the furniture Mrs. Deaton had ordered for the Avengerette Club in downtown Sweetwater was delivered, and 43-W-8 held their graduation dance there. The next day Jackie Cochran missed WASP graduation ceremonies for the second time in as many months. She was recuperating from an operation at Johns Hopkins Hospital in Baltimore. Jackie was plagued by poor health, a legacy from her hard-knock childhood. She had had several surgeries and had suffered two miscarriages. This time she would take nearly three months to recover fully.

When Bing Crosby sang "White Christmas," a hit song of the season, he expressed the fond wishes of thousands of young Americans in military uniforms with the line, "I'll be home for Christmas, if only in my dreams." The trainees got a three-day leave for Christmas, but discretionary travel was still nearly impossible. Many of the women pilots were too far away from home in any case.

Mrs. Deaton put in an order for a twelve-foot tree, a Santa Claus, flight officer candidates, mistletoe, and an orchestra for a Christmas Eve party in the gymnasium. Kay Dussaq headed the student planning committee. The Avenger Women's Chorus rehearsed favorite carols, and the price limit for the gift exchange was set at fifty cents.

Marge Harper's mother somehow managed to travel all the way from Philadelphia to spend the holidays with her only living child. She took a room at the Blue Bonnet Hotel and put up a tree in her daughter's bay. Kay D'Arezzo's mother and sisters drove up from Austin to celebrate Christmas. The colonel was away on duty, and Kay's only brother was a cadet at West Point.

Ruth Craig Jones and her friend, Skip, planned to drive to Oklahoma City to be with their families, and their Ford was booked full. They were taking three other women home with them, one of whom was meeting her fiancé. He was stationed in Nebraska, and the couple had picked Oklahoma City as a midpoint and the location for a Christmas wedding.

In the afternoon as Ruth rode the trolley into Sweetwater to pick up the Ford at Pop and Ollie's Garage, it started sleeting. Pop wouldn't let her have the car. It was too dangerous for a bunch of women to be on the roads. Ruth wanted to go home in the worst way. She wanted to be with her parents, and she didn't want to spend her second wedding anniversary in a barracks. She even tried tears on Pop. But Ruth was never very good at crying, and besides, the brass at Avenger agreed with Pop: all Christmas leaves were canceled.

The bride tried frantically to reach her fiancé. But wartime, the Christmas holidays, and the weather conspired to keep the two lovers apart. The poor girl cried for a month, unfortunately with cause. Her handsome bridegroom did reach Oklahoma City, and when his bride didn't show up, he furthermore reached the conclusion that he had been jilted!

Avenger's CO and Pop did what they could to cheer up all the girls who were stranded at Christmas on the west Texas prairie. The commander called nearby AAF training facilities and invited the fellows over to celebrate Christmas—so long as they brought some of their Benny Goodman records and some liquid cheer. The results were vivid. Ruth could tell it took some people four days to get over being drunk.

Pop and his wife did their share by inviting all of the girls who had wanted to hitch a ride in Ruth and Skip's car to their house for Christmas dinner. And the following summer the poor abandoned bride married her boss at Eagle Pass AAFB, El Paso, Texas.

New Year's Eve, long after hours, Kay was in a hot poker game in the latrine between two bays. Playing cards for money, at any time, was forbidden, so when the establishment officers pulled a surprise bed check, Kay and her gambling partners scrambled for cover. The inspection was still in the next bay when Kay jumped under the blankets on her bed, but two of the others got caught hiding under cots down the hall. And two members of Flight One were sent home for keeping liquor in the barracks.

The week before, Kay had been instructed to check up on rumors about drinking on post, but she had come up empty-handed. The establishment officers were more canny and found a bottle of whiskey hidden in the tank of one of the toilets. "I never would have thought to look there!" Kay admitted to Millie.

After the holidays their class completed primary, and the revised WASP training put them directly into AT-6s. Going from primary trainers to the 650-horsepower Texan was nerve-racking. However, during this intermediate phase of training, the class learned all the maneuvers previously taught in basic, including spins, in the hot AT-6. Then they were returned to the BT-15 for instrument training, which consisted of thirty-five hours of instruction, all taught at one time, in one airplane.

In the meantime Ruth's class began advanced training—also in the powerful AT-6 Texan. A merciless army check pilot was dogging the class, arriving unexpectedly at auxiliary fields to give random check rides. When he showed up, the trainees escaped to the outhouse set up behind the staging shack, and it was a contest to see how many could squeeze inside at once.

Days of cold, pelting rain left the auxiliary fields so muddy that all aircraft had to land and take off on the gravel runway at Avenger. The student pilots flew in rectangular patterns near the main field so that they could beat it home as soon as storm clouds blew up. The tee switched every quarter of an hour in the reckless wind, and cross-wind landings became normal procedure. A coffee and doughnut bar was set up on the flight line for trainees after frosty night flights.

> We damn near freeze
> In these open PTs
> Deep in the heart of Texas
> We're never at our ease

In these big BTs
Deep in the heart of Texas
If you don't lock the latch
You'll fall out of the hatch
Deep in the heart of Texas
If you don't relax
You'll be in Air Facts
Deep in the heart of Texas.

These WASP songs became even more important to the training program. They built spirit, even though Cochran still fussed about the often earthy rhymes. One of the trainees' favorites was so obnoxious to Jackie that she had it banned from the post:

I just called up to tell you that I'm rugged but right!
A rambling woman, a gambling woman, drunk every night.
A porterhouse steak three times a day for my board,
That's more than any decent gal in town can afford!

I've got a big electric fan to keep me cool while I eat,
A tall and handsome man to keep me warm while I sleep!
I'm a rambling woman, a gambling woman and BOY am I tight!
I just called up to tell you that I'm rugged but right!
Ho-ho-ho—Rugged but right!

SKIRMISHES AND PRANKS between adjoining bays kept morale high when the weather caused training delays and boredom set in. Soap chips and nutshells scattered between the sheets or alarm clocks planted in enemy territory, set to go off at intervals during the night, erupted into rousing pillow fights. These antics helped burn energy on gray, drizzling afternoons when no one could face another hand of cards or there were no letters left to write—and thoughts of friends and lovers in harm's way loomed over the women's training detachment.

BY JANUARY 1, 1944, there were one thousand women in training or on active duty in the Women Airforce Service Pilots with various AAF commands. The Ferry Division maintained a moratorium on hiring, and the Training Command was having difficulty placing the women because the WASP graduates needed additional training after the six-month flight school to perform many duties—just as any AAF cadet did. The army's operational schools were used to prepare men for combat, so the majority of the WASP had to pick up supplementary flying skills on the job.

Recruiting was curtailed until the women's flying program absorbed those enrolled and those on the waiting list. The office of the director of women pilots was receiving eight hundred letters of inquiry every day. "All young women who wish to join the WASP may not have the opportunity to do so," Miss Cochran told the press, "because the army cannot train or utilize women pilots at the expense of training and experience needed for men pilots in the theaters of war." Privately Jackie said of the frantic response, "I'm sick and tired of seeing girls take their mother's insurance money to get thirty-five hours' flying time."

The first eyewitness accounts of the surrender of Bataan in April 1942 and the Death March on which eight thousand to ten thousand prisoners had died finally began to appear in the newspapers. The government had withheld information about this and Japanese atrocities for fear such stories would jeopardize those still being held captive.

The Avenger ran a profile of Kay D'Arezzo, Flight One squadron commander, 44-W-4, whose husband, Al, was a Japanese prisoner. She was touted as a pattern of the times—friendly, full of fun, and capable. In the same issue was a sidebar titled "Taps for Tokyo":

> Such a horror story was released January 27 by Army and Navy officials. It was documented by sworn statements of three officers who escaped from Japanese prison camps. The 4,000 word account described how the Japanese starved, tortured and in some cases wantonly murdered the defenders of Bataan—how 2,200 Americans died in two months in one of the prison camps.

These tales gave Kay nightmares. She knew Al was alive and that he had been moved to Japan. Through the Red Cross they could exchange brief messages, twenty-five words, on an irregular basis. She didn't tell Al what she was doing. Not only was the information restricted, it might worry him. She knew he couldn't tell her everything either. Kay let her husband assume she was still working as a secretary and living with her mother in Austin. But every day she was grateful for the chance to learn to fly army planes and for how busy she was, how tired each night.

AFTER A YEAR of clandestine planning, the Office of the Director of Women Pilots debuted the WASP uniforms. The well-cut skirt and suit jacket, as well as the slacks and waist-length jacket, were tailored from Santiago-blue wool gabardine. Both versions would be worn with a white cotton shirt and a black tie, in a four-hand knot. The insignia on the pert beret was a miniature of an army officer's, and the silver wings, with a diamond-shaped lozenge in the center, were smaller and more delicate than those of an AAF pilot. Hair was to be dressed no less than one-half inch above the collar, and no heavy or conspicuous makeup could be used. The uniform also included a putty-colored gabardine waterproof wool trench coat, black calfskin gloves, shoes, and bag. This official attire was to be worn in training and on active duty with the air forces. And the women were reminded, "WASP will at all times conduct themselves in a manner befitting the dignity of the uniform."

RUTH CRAIG JONES's CLASS was the first to wear the new silver wings and the stylish Santiago-blue uniforms when they graduated on Friday, February 11, 1944. Each of them had been measured by expert tailors dispatched to Sweetwater from Neiman Marcus in Dallas, but when the uniforms arrived on the day before the ceremonies, none of them fit. They were too long in the sleeve or too short in the skirt, too tight in the bust or too loose in the waist.

Skip Carter's parents had driven from Oklahoma City and brought Ruth's mother along with them. The two mothers stayed up all night altering, tucking, and basting, so that Class 44-W-1 would look its best.

Commencement exercises began Friday afternoon with a review and military inspection. Graduation was that night, and Universal Newsreel was on hand to film the smart new uniforms. However, Jackie was held up in Washington due to weather, so her dependable stand-in, Ethel Sheehy, took charge once again. Ruth and Skip's first flying instructor had come from Oklahoma City to see them get their WASP wings. Ruth didn't ask why her father wasn't there. She knew.

As a result of the beefed-up curriculum, 44-W-1 was the first WASP class to receive instrument flying cards. Five of the graduates, including Ruth Craig Jones of Oklahoma City, were presented the Bulova Watch Award for flying proficiency, ground-school grades, and student leadership. As she accepted the watch, Ruth thought of her husband serving as a navy corpsman in the South Pacific, slogging from one bloody island to the next with the marines toward Japan. Lee had always wanted to fly, but he was too tall.

The trainees sang at graduations when they were held outdoors, but Jackie had suspended the ditties when the formalities moved inside to the new gym. At Deaton's urging, the women began singing again at Ruth and Skip's graduation to see how the dignitaries would react. The opening song came from the graduating class, and then the others sang in order of seniority. Audience response was rousing.

> You'll go forth from here with your silver wings
> You'll go forth from here with your silver wings
> Santiago blue and a heart that sings—
> 'Cause you ain't gonna be here no longer.
>
> Leave your H.P. tricks to the babes in "6"
> Leave your H.P. tricks to the babes in "6"
> Leave your big-city tricks to the gals in the sticks—
> 'Cause you ain't gonna be here no longer.
>
> Leave your cross-country buzzin' to your W-2 cousin
> Leave your cross-country buzzin' to your W-2 cousin
> Leave the hedge hoppin' fun that was W-1
> 'Cause you ain't gonna be here no longer.

RUTH CRAIG JONES and Skip Carter were posted to the Las Vegas Army Air Force Base. Meanwhile women pilots already on duty with the Training Command were assigned to the Ferry Division rather than, as Air Staff had promised, members of 44-W-1 who had just finished the training demanded by General Tunner.

Through 1943 all WASP duty assignments were made by Air Staff. Early in 1944, Hap Arnold as a matter of air force policy, vested this authority in the commanding officer of Avenger Field. The trainees filled out preference sheets just before graduation about what they wanted to fly, where they wanted to fly it, and with whom from their class they wished to serve. They were also asked what factor they considered to be the most important in their choice. Almost always it was the type of aircraft. Rating sheets were gathered from the flight line, ground school, Link instructors, and the physical-training department, plus student officers and staff advisors. An overall rating was given to each graduate based on these ratings, their preference sheets, and the total number of disciplinary demerits. They were then given their choice, in order of class rank, as assignments came in from the Training Command.

The Santiago-blue wool uniforms were issued to the trainees at Avenger later in February. The women already on duty did not receive uniforms until April, when wool was uncomfortably warm. Their summer attire had yet to be completed, but the WASP didn't complain. They were sure their new WASP uniform was the snappiest-looking of any in the military.

JACKIE COCHRAN arrived at Avenger three days after Ruth's graduation, on Valentine's Day, flying a twin-engine military trainer and greeted by spirited cheers. She stayed overnight to discuss with Dedie Deaton her plans for the next WASP graduation in March, which was to be a special event for an array of potent brass and influential public media. Jackie told the trainees she was through recruiting for the time being, as classes were full until June. Also, she said, Congressman Costello was about to introduce a bill to commission the graduates of Avenger Field as officers in the Army Air Force. "I'm proud of the girls who graduate from here and of you," she told them. "Those graduates already at work are making a fine record for women as flyers. It's up to you to uphold it. Whatever you fly, you must perform your job to the very best of your ability, for you are making aviation history for women."

ON FEBRUARY 25, 1944, Betty Stine, 44-W-2, was on a long cross-country in an AT-6, her final requirement before graduation. She departed Blythe, California, just before 4:00 P.M. and headed toward Tucson. Fifteen minutes later a miner working ten miles northwest of Quartzite, Arizona, saw a smoking aircraft spiraling into the side of a mountain and a fluttering parachute bumping along the rocky ground.

After sunset a rescue party found Betty, battered and unconscious. She was placed in the back of a truck, wrapped in blankets, and taken into Quartzite, where an ambulance sent from Blythe AAF picked her up. Betty died in the base hospital a short time later. The AAF report said that sparks from the plane's exhaust had set fire to the plywood-and-fabric right horizontal stabilizer and tail. The pilot bailed out, but was dragged along by a gusty wind over rough, mountainous terrain. Betty Stine was a great-niece of humorist Will Rogers.

The next issue of *The Avenger* described a parachute harness designed for women who flew—the WASP, nurses, and others. An apparatus for parachute training was to be installed at Avenger and twelve hours of instruction added to the curriculum.

AT THE REQUEST of the War Department, on February 17, 1944, a WASP militarization bill was once again presented to the House Committee on Military Affairs by John Costello, a representative from California. To whip up enthusiasm, Jacqueline Cochran planned to make the graduation of Class 44-W-2 a star-studded occasion, showcasing the WASP training and the accomplishments of the women pilots on duty, with Henry H. Arnold, Army Air Force commanding general, in a leading role. And perhaps this production would also distract the Civil Service Committee, whose investigation was singling out the Women Airforce Service Pilots for special attention.

Dedie Deaton took charge of the details for the March 11, 1944, extravaganza. Hap Arnold headed the guest list and would deliver the commencement address. His high-ranking entourage included Barton Yount, commanding general of the Training Command; Harold George, commanding general of the Air Transport Command; and four other general officers from Air Staff. Nancy Love, who was allowed to visit Avenger only with Cochran's okay, would attend in her capacity as executive for the WASP in the Ferry Division. As part of the gala celebration Love's squadron commander at Long Beach, B. J. Erickson, was going to be presented with the Air Medal by General Arnold in recognition of her record ferrying mission in August 1943.

The graduating class was away on cross-country flights almost until the dignitaries arrived. The rest of the trainees were spending hours drilling to perfection for the graduation parade. Mrs. Deaton picked the six highest-ranking student officers to join Jackie and her glittering exhibition of military brass for lunch.

At Jackie's suggestion General Arnold handed the women their silver pilot's wings rather than trying to pin them on their chests. Then the AAF commanding general and B. J. Erickson, who looked tense and uncomfortable in the new Santiago-blue uniform, watched side by side from the speaker's platform as the trainees marched in review. Speaking directly to the newsreel cameras, General Arnold said during his address, "I am looking forward to the day when Women Airforce Service Pilots take the place of practically all AAF pilots in the United States for the duration. WASP are doing an effective job of delivering aircraft in the U.S., from the smallest planes to the big fighters, bombers, and transports. . . . Indeed, this organization has come to serve a variety of useful purposes in the AAF organization. We're proud of you, and welcome you as part of the AAF. We can use and probably will continue to use as many WASP as we can turn out for these non-combat flying duties."

The 44-W-2 graduation was a day of heady experiences, and as a reminder General Arnold presented the training detachment with a metal plaque engraved TO THE BEST WOMEN PILOTS IN THE WORLD. Mrs. Deaton had it installed on the fieldstone wishing well.

MILLIE DAVIDSON was going to dances at the USO Club near Sweetwater on the weekends. Her twenty-two-year-old husband had been missing for over a year.

With spring in the air Sylvia Miller married her high school sweetheart, a recently commissioned flying officer, at the Episcopal church in Sweetwater. Major Urban gave the bride away, Mrs. Deaton served as matron of honor, and Lieutenant La Rue acted as best man. Unlike most wartime brides, Sylvia had all the trimmings, including a long white satin gown and a veil.

On love's somber side, trainee Irene Raven, 44-W-5, a widow, got permission through the War Department Office of Public Relations to christen a naval destroyer escort vessel named for her late husband, Lieutenant Julius Raven, USNR, missing in action since August 1942—and presumed dead. And now that the year required by law and more had passed since Bill Davidson's Flying Fortress had disappeared over the North Sea, the government also declared Millie's husband presumed dead.

In spite of pressure brought to bear by her influential family, a classmate of Kay's from the East Coast washed out during basic. She had struggled with the Link trainer and lacked the concentration needed to fly under the hood. Her one and only buddy ride, when she went up with another trainee acting as lookout and flew with a blackout curtain pulled around her canopy, nearly ended in disaster. After this, no one else in the class wanted to be her partner.

The day she earned her final pink slip, the woman botched a suicide. Mrs. Deaton turned her over to Dr. Monserud for medical care and a big dose of fatherly sympathy until she had recovered enough to be packed off to her parents. Deaton enlisted the woman's baymates in an effort to keep the incident quiet, and in her report to Cochran she wrote that the suicide attempt seemed to be for the effect, a play for her classmates' sympathy.

The class went on to advanced training. Kay was flying an AT-6 dual with an instructor she admired—a young man everyone knew was a top pilot—when he took the controls and came in low and fast, right over the roof of a ranch house. People were outside waving and watching. Kay figured he was buzzing someone he knew, showing off a bit. But as he started to pull up, a stand of trees suddenly jumped in the way, and the trainer clipped the tops. Looking through the canopy, Kay saw that hunks two or three feet across and a foot deep had been torn out of the leading edge of each wing. The instructor radioed an SOS, "Mayday! Sweetwater Tower, Mayday!"

They were cleared for emergency landing, and as the instructor turned the Texan directly into the wind on final approach, Kay's heart squeezed up into her throat, throbbing, blocking her breathing. Once the battered aircraft was safely on the ground, Kay asked what he was going to tell operations. "I'm going to say we were practicing forced landings," he replied.

They were both taken away for questioning. She was asked if the trainer had hit a row of mesquites. Kay wasn't sure what a mesquite tree looked like, but she wanted to help her instructor. Whether she answered yes or no, she was in trouble, so Kay tried to hedge—and failed. The instructor was fired for not owning up immediately, and Kay was confined to the base until further notice.

Dedie Deaton used her clout to protect Kay's position as squadron commander. And without Kay catching on, Millie and several other classmates took turns giving up their liberty to keep her company on the weekends.

Six weeks later Millie telephoned Mrs. McBride and invited her to drive up from Austin for a visit. Kay hadn't told her parents about her difficulties, but Millie thought it was time they knew. Mrs. McBride pulled rank to get her daughter released so that they could have lunch at the Blue Bonnet Hotel, and the next week Kay was reprieved. Her mother had sent Major Urban a note saying she felt Kay had been confined sufficiently—and that if the major didn't agree, she would have to write to Kay's father, Colonel McBride, about the matter. Kay was floored when she found out *her mother* had taken a hand.

In April 1944 the women's training detachment got a new commanding officer, Lieutenant Colonel George F. Keene. He was married, as Avenger's staff officers always were, and replaced Major Robert Urban, who had been on the job for a year. Before long Keene replaced Urban's turbans as well. Not only were the turbans slightly absurd, they were too bulky to wear with radio headsets. They were replaced by neat billed caps. And getting into the spirit of his new command, Colonel Keene christened his AT-7 *Miss Fifinella* and painted Fifi on either side of the twin-engine aircraft's nose.

In April Kay's class moved up to senior position. Ground school was almost over, with nothing left but the best part—more and more flying! The last day of classes, when the teacher dismissed the trainees, they ran whooping with joy to ring the Avenger Field's old fire bell. Along with the tossing of coins—and other trainees—into the wishing well for luck, ringing the bell loud and long at the end of ground school was on the youthful training detachment's short list of traditions. The bell was retired from alarm duty and mounted on a pole behind the classrooms. A red siren took its place sounding the alert for fires and crack-ups on the field. Now the old bell only rang in glee.

The expanded curriculum demanded more hours, more night flying, and most important to the Ferry Division, more and longer cross-country trips. In addition to hops of two to three hundred miles and a cross-country of one thousand miles in a PT-17, an even longer flight in an AT-6, with several nights spent away from base, was necessary prior to graduation. These long flights brought a problem into sharp focus. The women had no way of going to the bathroom for several hours at a time. Males could use relief tubes installed in the cockpits, but the WASP had to develop their own system. They learned not to drink anything for hours prior to flying and hoped their bladders held out.

At first Mrs. Deaton accompanied the trainees who traveled in batches, to arrange for housing and meals en route. One group plotted their AT-6 flight via Little Rock and Greenwood, Mississippi, to Atlanta, where they were forced to lay over for two days due to rain and fog. They passed the time eating at a different restaurant for every meal and shopping. They were away from Sweetwater for almost ten days! Destinations where the weather was likely to turn sour zoomed to the top of the list for cross-country trips.

> Who's that flying hither and yon?
> They're here one day and the next they're gone.
> Its W-4 on their cross-country trips,
> Ask about their social life and they'll give you good tips.

THREE MEMBERS of the Women Airforce Service Pilots died on active duty during April 1944. On the third of the month Evelyn Sharp, one of the most experienced and well liked of the originals, was killed in Pennsylvania when the engine failed on a P-38 pursuit during takeoff. On the tenth, Marie Sharon cracked up attempting to land a B-25 bomber in bad weather in Nebraska. And on the twenty-fifth, Edith Keene, a 44-W-1 classmate of Ruth and Skip's, crashed at Mission, Texas, on a routine flight in an AT-6.

Then, on April 16, 1944, a midair collision took the lives of two trainees near Avenger Field. At sunrise on a day that was fair and turning warm, several pilots from Kay D'Arezzo's flight took off for cross-country navigation flights to Alamo Field in San Antonio, 250 miles away across a fair sea of spring bluebonnets and back. In the late afternoon as news of a midair flashed through the detachment, two of these women were overdue—Mary Howson and Millie Davidson.

Kay waited near the flight line watching the fading sky. At last she saw a single AT-6 turn on final approach and land. As the trainer taxied toward the hangar, she trotted along behind, trying to see who was at the controls. When Millie climbed out of the cockpit, Kay grabbed her small friend in an emotional bear hug. Millie was flabbergasted!

She had taken a happy detour, thirty miles off course, to her grandparents' ranch west of Austin. Inspired by the spring day and the blooming bluebonnets, she had called her grandparents from Alamo Field to let them know she was on the way. They were in the yard, waving, as she flew over their house. She wiggled her wings and flew on, only twenty minutes off her planned ETA—but enough to unnerve her friend badly and rescue Millie from a deadly situation.

An hour earlier Mary Howson, a Smith College alumna from Pennsylvania with fifty hours logged in the Texan and only a month of flight school left, entered traffic on a 45-degree leg to the downwind leg, from a westerly direction. At the same instant Elizabeth Erickson, 44-W-6, who had just begun the second phase of training and was on her first solo flight in the AT-6 out of the traffic pattern, started to enter traffic on a 45-degree leg to the downwind leg, from an *easterly* direction. The two trainers were flying directly toward each other at an altitude of approximately 800 feet. Howson tried desperately to turn away, but as her plane banked, Erickson's trainer slammed into the fuselage of the other AT-6. Elizabeth Erickson was trapped in the cockpit and died when her aircraft plowed into the ground. Mary Howson attempted to save herself by bailing out, but she lacked the altitude, and her parachute opened just as she hit the ground. Her body was found only thirty feet from the wreckage of her plane. "The parachute did not cushion the fall at all as evidenced by the depression in the ground where the pilot hit and by the physical condition of the pilot" (AAF Accident Investigation Report).

Mary Howson's parents were planning to make the trip from

[175]

Philadelphia to see their only daughter get her wings. Instead Kay D'Arezzo, as squadron leader, had to pick someone from the flight to accompany Mary home.

On April 21, at nine in the morning, a forty-five-minute memorial service was held in the gymnasium for Howson and Erickson. The new class, which had just reported, was in attendance, wide-eyed and stunned. One of this class was eighteen-year-old Marge Stevenson from Holdenville, Oklahoma. She had traveled by train to Sweetwater and spent the previous night at the Blue Bonnet Hotel. Later that day after the service the civilian director of flight training issued a reminder to the students that they were not allowed to land at an accident sight.

The Avenger advertised that the spring and summer catalogs were available at Sears Roebuck on the square and that the Blue Bonnet drugstore was getting a fresh shipment of gum on Saturday. Other ads suggested Mother's Day gifts—Elizabeth Arden and Dorothy Gray perfumes or a WASP mother's pin, a pair of miniature women's pilot wings. This issue also ran a photo of Jimmy Stewart receiving the Distinguished Flying Cross for leading a bombing raid on a German aircraft plant.

The first WASP selected for the officer training course in Orlando stopped by Avenger on their way. The establishment officers would be attending OTC in shifts, and a similar class for the trainees would start at Avenger within a month.

In May the trainees were designated an Army Air Force wing, consisting of two groups. Group I was composed of the two upper classes, and Group II, the three underclasses. Wing Review was planned for 44-W-4's commencement, and *The Avenger* said three prominent women aviation enthusiasts would join Miss Jacqueline Cochran at the ceremonies. One was Mrs. Henry H. Arnold, who would be the second member of her flying family to take part in a WASP graduation.

The Washington newspapers interviewed Secretary of War Henry L. Stimson concerning the Women Airforce Service Pilots, a program that had become very public and very controversial. The newspapers were having a field day as the WASP bill was debated in Congress and in print. Washington was buzzing about Jackie and a high-placed general. Stimson gallantly defended the women flyers, who were under heavy fire from the Civil Service Committee.

The secretary regretted that even though they were performing a valuable service in time of war, the rights, privileges, and benefits available to military personnel were denied to them.

FIFTY WOMEN survived in Class 44-W-4 to receive their silver pilot's wings from Jackie Cochran on May 23, 1944. Mrs. Hap Arnold was not in attendance. Millie Davidson was presented with Bill's Air Medal and the Purple Heart. Kay D'Arezzo was named outstanding graduate and awarded a War Bond—despite the buzzing incident! Afterward her mother asked Kay to please wear her WASP uniform when she came to Austin on graduation leave.

Millie was posted to the Training Command at Maxwell Field, Montgomery, Alabama, and Kay was assigned to the 5th Ferrying Group at Dallas Love Field. She reported for duty on June 6, 1944, the same day the Allied forces landed at Normandy.

9.

Into the Wild Blue Yonder

THE FIRST P-51 MUSTANGS arrived in the air over Europe during November 1943. With a speed of 430 miles per hour and un-matched maneuverability, the brilliant fighter also had the range to fly cover for the American Flying Fortresses on raids deep into the heart of Germany, to Berlin itself. The pilots of the United States Air Force 4th Fighter Group based in England were the first to pilot the P-51, and they had the phenomenal aircraft in combat within twenty-four hours of delivery. "You can learn to fly them on the way to the target," their squadron leader ordered.

Nancy Harkness Love had escaped her desk at FERD headquar-ters in Cincinnati and was ferrying one of these hot new air force pursuits from Long Beach to the East Coast. As she approached a military field and radioed for permission to land, a male voice, after a long pause, radioed back from the control tower, "Can't see you."

Nancy circled for several minutes in the pattern waiting to land. "Okay to come in now?" she requested.

"Where are you?" the control tower demanded. "Can't spot you at all."

Nancy was ready to play. She buzzed the tower, flying the P-51 directly under the nose of the astonished controller. "Okay?" she asked sweetly, as she pulled the Mustang up and around.

"Cleared to land," came the flabbergasted response. "I heard a woman's voice and I saw the plane, but I just couldn't figure a woman would be flying a Mustang!"

WHEN THE WASP was limited to domestic flying by General Arnold in September 1943, those who reached Class V in the Ferry Division were stuck at the top and clogged the training path for the men who had to deliver aircraft overseas. At this same time, because of the heavy demand for bombers, the division hit a crunch in upgrading pilots from primary trainers to four-engine aircraft, and General Tunner omitted Pursuit Class from the training to speed up the process.

His decision opened up a perfect niche for the Ferry Division's women pilots. Pursuits lacked the range to cross the ocean on their own. They went from production lines to transport ships. However, these powerful aircraft were fast and hot on takeoff and landing and threw the entire burden of flying onto the pilot. As a class, pursuits had three times the accident rate of heavy bombers.

At the start of 1944 there were 68 WASP at Wilmington, 71 at Love Field, 72 at Romulus, and 64 at Long Beach. With a total strength in the Ferry Division of 175, the women pilots were delivering forty-three different types of aircraft, from PT-17s to B-25s. During January they ferried 840 planes of twenty-nine different models and logged 6,382 hours. Nevertheless General William Tunner was beginning to wonder if the WASP would not have to become pursuit specialists if they were to continue to be of use.

In the fall of 1943 Nancy Love had given Tunner a list of fifty-six women who were qualified for pursuit transition—although at that time the Ferry Division did not have sufficient facilities to train them. He suggested, without success, that the Training Command provide these women and the top graduates from each class at Avenger Field twenty-five hours of additional instruction.

BEFORE THE AAF BEGAN employing women pilots, it had authorization to hire civilians to fly for the Air Transport Command. Almost a year later, on July 23, 1943, the secretary of war, Henry Stimson, requested that the Civil Service Commission amend this original authorization to cover the women training at Avenger Field, but the expense was neatly buried under the heading COST OF TUITION FOR TRAINING OF PILOTS. Nowhere in the Military Establishment Appropriation Act for 1943 is the existence of Avenger Field mentioned. The legality of this was never questioned until the House Committee on the Civil Service, under Chairman Robert Ramspeck, began investigating in late 1943 and zeroed in on Jackie's girls with a vengeance.

Air Staff knew they had nebulous authority for such extensive civilian training but, from the first, had been planning to make the WASP full-fledged members of the Army Air Force. As early as November 1942 General Arnold sought the opinion of Colonel Oveta Culp Hobby, head of the Women's Army Corps, on militarization procedures. Meanwhile word was leaked to Arnold's boss, George C. Marshall, army chief of staff, who penned a terse memo: "I don't like the tone of this at all." Marshall forbade any attempt to form a women's air corps in the air force—without getting his approval first!

For a brief time plans went forward to incorporate the women pilots into the WAC; however, General William Tunner and Jackie Cochran both objected and proposed their own solutions. Just before Christmas 1942 the whole question was put on hold. Months of petty arguments and bold power plays passed before the status of the women was considered again.

On September 30, 1943, after all the women pilots, both on duty and in training, had been merged into a single organization—the Women Airforce Service Pilots—under Jacqueline Cochran, the first Costello Bill was introduced into the House. This bill made the rounds at the Pentagon, and after analysis by Air Staff and the War Department, amendments were suggested to broaden the scope of the legislation. However, when it finally arrived at army head-quarters in December, Marshall again proposed that the women pilots be taken into the WAC. Air Staff, again, opposed this move, and more time was consumed working out a compromise.

In the meantime, on January 15 the Army Air Force announced that as of June, Civilian Pilot Training would end and many of the civilian-contract flying schools would be shut down. America's long-range plans for training pilots had been based on grim statistics from England's worst days. The RAF calculated that a beginning pilot would be dead within three months, and in 1940 and 1941 this figure was often too optimistic. Nevertheless American casualties never ran this high, and the Army Air Force began cutting back on personnel in early 1944. Young pilot candidates were switched to the infantry, while their civilian instructors went into the draft pool. Unless these instructors could dig up other essential flying jobs fast, they were going to end up in the walking man's army.

IN DECEMBER 1943, the Ferry Division finally opened a pursuit school of its own at Palm Springs, California. One of the fifty-six women pilots on Love's list for pursuit transition, Nancy Batson, a WAFS original, was in the first group of women selected to attend—along with four other originals, including Florene Miller, the recently displaced squadron leader at Love Field. Nancy had just received a letter of commendation from Colonel Robert Baker, the commander of the 2nd Ferrying Group at New Castle AAFB, for a record delivery of an AT-6 Texan despite rough weather.

Not only was Batson an able and serious flyer, she was also a stunning, photogenic southern belle with a lush accent, a superb asset to the women pilots' image! Even Colonel Bob Love was not immune and got a kick out of teasing his own beautiful Nancy about the marvelous Batson.

Fourteen WASP were in the first two classes at Palm Springs, and not one of them washed out of the four-week course. But Dorothy Scott, another of Love's twenty-five skilled originals, was killed the week before Christmas in a midair collision with a P-39 Aircobra.

The Aircobra had an unsavory reputation among ferry pilots. It regularly caught on fire. General Tunner suspected that part of the problem was that the men delivering the P-39s were such cowboys. "Let's have the girls try it," he suggested to Nancy Love as the first WASP finished at Palm Springs.

Nancy Batson and four others went to the Bell plant at Buffalo, New York. They proved Tunner was right. By watching the P-39's airspeed from the minute they took off and correctly breaking in the engines, the WASP never experienced a single incident of fire— and they set new standards for the plane.

A large percentage of Aircobras were destined for the Soviets and were turned over to them at the Canadian border. After delivering the aircraft at controlled speeds, the Americans watched as the Russians hopped into the cockpits and kicked the P-39s to full throttle all the way back to the motherland. A WASP who had just landed with a flight of P-39s was standing out on the flight line while they took off again. An AAF officer watching beside her shook his head in amazement as the young woman in a Soviet pilot's tunic and jodhpurs left in one of the planes. "Did you see that woman fly a P-39 out of here?" he asked.

"Why not?" the WASP replied. "*This* woman just flew that P-39 in here."

Two years into the war every kind of public transportation was still mobbed with military personnel holding priority travel orders. Returning to base was often more of a challenge than making a delivery. The army had requisitioned half the airline industry's fleet, so there was a strict pecking order, even among the military, for available seats. First in line were persons traveling on Priority 1, direct orders from the White House, and next came Priority 2, pilots traveling to ferry bases or military stations. This included the Ferry Division's women.

The ticket agents were tough when it came to enforcing these priorities, and important people were thrown off planes on a regular basis to make room for ferry pilots. Usually the bigger the VIP, the more understanding he was.

Eleanor Roosevelt was going to New York from the capital on personal business when an army pilot rushed up at the last minute clutching his travel orders. Since she was the only passenger on board *without* a Priority 1 or 2, the First Lady was told she must give up her seat. "My goodness, of course I'll get off," she said with her famous toothy smile. "There's no question those pilots should go ahead of me."

SEVERAL WOMEN in the WASP squadron at Long Beach had checked out in pursuits by the seat of their pants months before FERD opened a training facility. They were ferrying fighter-type aircraft from coast to coast on the same basis as men when the U.S. Navy called the Army Air Force with a serious emergency: They had to transport half a dozen feisty Hellcat fighters from the Grumman production line to San Diego, where a recently commissioned aircraft carrier was waiting to sail. The navy was short of flyers on the West Coast who could manage a Hellcat. Admiral Ernest J. King, chief of naval operations, phoned the Air Transport Command and asked to borrow some of the 6th Ferrying Group's pursuit pilots for the job. The CO at Long Beach offered to send the admiral his WASPs, but King irritably refused. "You're not going to palm those broads off on the navy!"

Scuttlebutt had the Hellcats sitting on the ground for another ten days waiting for the male pilots—much to the enjoyment of the women Admiral King had turned down.

AT THE OPENING of 1944, the graduates of Cochran's women flyers were at work in the air force as tow-target, engine-test, and utility pilots. They were instrument instructors and flew radio test control missions. They assisted in training aerial gunners, laid smoke screens, and helped mark gun sights and ranges.

After their graduation from Avenger, Ruth Craig Jones and Skip Carter reported to Las Vegas AAFB along with Marie Mountain, Marge Harper, and seven other 44-W-1 classmates. The base greeted the WASP with a parade, and gave them billets in the nurses' barracks. Within six months, thirty-six women would be on duty at Las Vegas, making this the largest WASP contingent in the Training Command. This squadron would also perform nearly every flying duty provided by the Women Airforce Service Pilots' experiment during the war. Ruth Craig Jones was appointed squadron leader.

The nurses at Las Vegas were glad to see the WASP because they brought welcome changes. Jackie's girls were accorded the privileges of an army second lieutenant and the nurses shared part of these comforts. For example, the nurses' barracks weren't air-conditioned, and the women woke up once or twice every night to shower off and cool down so that they could get back to sleep. When Jackie flew out from Washington to visit the new squadron, blueprinted to be a WASP showcase, she stepped into the barracks and immediately asked Ruth, "What's wrong with your air-conditioning?"

"We don't have any," she replied.

"Oh, yes, you do!" Jackie said. "Every pilot in this man's army sleeps in a cool room." That night Cochran took her girls out for dinner and some fun at a Las Vegas casino, and by the time she left the next afternoon, the nurses' barracks had air-conditioning, just like the pilots' quarters.

Both Ruth and Skip were instrument instructors, qualifying AAF pilots to fly and navigate by instruments. Marge and Marie began with gun-sighting missions. The air force had been losing a pilot on gun-sighting runs about once every two weeks. This was tedious work, looping over and around artillery emplacements while the crews set the sights on their huge weapons. At Las Vegas young men regularly became hypnotized by the desert terrain or got lost in dreams of a hot P-47 Thunderbolt and flew right into the ground. The WASP were eager for any piloting chore and did much better at this repetitive assignment. During their ten months in Las Vegas not one woman was lost on a gun-sighting mission.

The WASP at Las Vegas AAFB were lucky. The commanding officer liked them and he was impressed with Jacqueline Cochran's power and influence. Ruth realized that every time she went to the colonel's office, he would ask if she had talked to Miss Cochran. "Did she mention my name?" he usually asked. Ruth decided the answer was always, "Yes, sir." She guessed that the colonel was bucking to be a general, and if he thought looking after his WASP might help—well, just fine.

MEANWHILE the Ferry Division's pursuit school was moved to Brownsville, Texas, and became the 4th Operational Training Unit (OTU) of the Ferry Division. Pilots had to have at least five hundred hours in Class I before moving up to a Class II rating, and the women pilots were required to have fifty hours in Class II aircraft before they were eligible for pursuit school. A total of 153 women pilots attended pursuit school with 96 graduating. The Women Air-force Service Pilots had a 37% elimination rate compared with 12% of males during the same period. While their ground-school grades were above average, flying deficiencies or inaptitude for fighter air-craft knocked them out of training. The flying ability of those women who did graduate was about the same as that of the men, and their accident rate was much lower.

Not all of the women in the Ferry Division wanted to fly pursuits. They were hot, perilous aircraft that required an aggressive, ven-turesome spirit—even for a flyer. Nancy Love emphasized that while FERD would not compel its women pilots to go through tran-sition in Palm Springs, there was a definite need for pursuit pilots. And women who expressed a willingness to fly pursuit would have priority at all levels of training. On January 14, 1944, Love wrote to the ferrying groups employing women, "It is felt that it is of the utmost importance that WASP be made to understand the need for their services as pursuit pilots. . . . Those WASP who are capable of flying these types will be performing the greatest service for their country and for the Ferrying Division."

IN FEBRUARY 1944, at the request of Air Staff, the commander at Camp Davis gave a status report on his women pilots. He said the WASP were capable of flying all the planes used by the Third Tow Target Squadron, except the B-34 bomber and the P-47 Thunder-bolt, and that most of them would *eventually* become first pilots on the twin-engine medium bombers used for towing and tracking missions. This report was submitted without the signatures of the WASP squadron leader or the establishment officer assigned to the group.

After prodding from Washington, Squadron Leader Alia Corbett signed a statement calling the seven-month experiment at Camp Davis a test in which punches had been pulled and "a mock battle so that no one will get hurt." She charged that three of the camp's airfields were closed to the women and that they had little oppor-tunity for formation or instrument flying. The experiment did not truly determine the capabilities of women pilots for use in a tow-target squadron. "We have been spared responsibility and risks," she wrote.

The establishment officer supported this indictment and said that furthermore the two fatal accidents involving WASP seemed to have shattered the confidence of the tow-target squadron's staff in women pilots. The commander defended himself by saying that no facilities or personnel were available in his squadron for anything but normal operating missions. He couldn't supply the women with the additional training needed to expand their usefulness.

ARMY AIR FORCE aviators the same age as the WASP, their youthful contemporaries, had the least difficulty accepting women in the cockpits of military aircraft. These were good-looking, beguiling girls with magnetism and self-confidence, and—except for pangs of jealousy over the hot planes they flew in the Ferry Division—the young men admired the WASP's spunk and ability. In fact most thought they were dynamite.

This was not always the opinion of older, more senior officers. Once the women went on operational duty, the resentment of these men presented countless hurdles—and sometimes defeated them. The radio-control flight leader of the Seventh Tow Target Squadron, at March Field, California, reported that after the first three days of operations the contribution of the WASP just assigned to him was nil. They were insufficiently trained, didn't plan ahead, and the precise nature of flying was beyond their comprehension. The WASP simply were not on their toes. AAF headquarters immediately replied that any evaluation should be based on at least thirty days of observation, not a mere three.

In March Jackie came up with another idea: Why couldn't girls serve as flight instructors? Her suggestion was tried with very limited success at one or two schools. The majority of senior officers felt that a woman instructor would be a great blow to the morale of any AAF cadet. He was a member of the air force, and he expected to be instructed by an air force pilot.

On the other hand women seemed to be acceptable, even successful, teaching instruments. Soon after she began instructing at La Vegas AAFB, Ruth was selected by Air Staff to attend an advanced instrument course in Bryan, Texas. Many of her classmates were majors, so Ruth figured this must be an honor. What she learned made her a better teacher, but she was away from her squadron duties for three weeks.

[186]

During the first six months Ruth was away from base over six weeks—even though she was squadron commander. After the advanced instrument course in Bryan, she went to the officer training course in Orlando, Florida. Over half of the WASP on active duty by the summer of 1944 took this course in anticipation of being commissioned. And Cochran continued probing the capabilities and options of the best, carrying the women pilots' experiment forward, with specialized training that took many of them away from their regular operational duties. Even on the air bases where the WASP were welcome, this policy made the commanding officers unhappy. They could never be sure when, or if, some of their female personnel would show up for work.

WHEN THE REVAMPED Costello Bill went back to the House in February 1944, congressmen were deluged with outraged letters. How could Congress approve pilot training for women when men already trained to fly were out of work? These disfranchised men and veterans' groups, including the powerful American Legion, organized a campaign against the Women Airforce Service Pilots. A number of the most widely read columnists joined the fray. Congress was alarmed by this public outcry—1944 was an election year!! The whole militarization project turned into a political football.

When the battle over the WASP "glamour girls" spilled into the newspapers, insinuations about the relationship between Miss Jacqueline Cochran and General Hap Arnold—"the knight of olde, or is it the old knight?"—popped into print. These vicious articles were hard for the general's family to ignore. The lengthy war and the general's deteriorating health in the wake of two heart attacks had put a progressive strain on the Arnolds. Long before the gossip about Miss Jacqueline Cochran, Bee Arnold was showing signs of severe stress.

General H. H. "Hap" Arnold was well liked both at army headquarters and in the halls of Congress for his blistering energy and boyish good humor. His celebrated charm polished the rough edges off his hardheaded vision for the air force. For months the congressmen had given the popular general anything he asked for without question, and Cochran was counting on his tremendous pull in the

United States Congress to get the WASP bill passed. Jackie ordered the WASP to remain silent. No letters to their senators or representatives from the women or their families.

However, she mounted a painstaking publicity campaign. The Women Airforce Service Pilots were at a high point, with Avenger's curriculum fine-tuned to forge women pilots equal to the cadets graduating from AAF flight schools and with WASP successfully filling a growing number of essential noncombat flying jobs. The War Department's public relations staff placed upbeat articles everywhere from slick magazines to hometown newspapers. The women's natty new Santiago-blue uniforms made a stunning debut. And on March 11, 1944, to please Jackie and bolster her program, General Hap Arnold had delivered the commencement address at Avenger Field. He had presented B. J. Erickson with the Air Medal and praised the fine delivery record of all the women in the Ferry Division, telling reporters the reason why their on-time performance was usually better than the men's: "They don't carry an address book with them."

Arnold had arrived in Sweetwater at the tail end of a fact-finding trip to B-29 Superfortress training facilities in Kansas. It had been a distressing journey. Of the one hundred Superfortresses completed, less than two dozen were flyable, certainly not enough to train a meaningful number of crews. Arnold had put the full force of his prestige in Congress behind the Superfortress. He had faith that the B-29 would bring America victory in the Japanese homeland and he believed that the big bomber would found the next generation of aircraft. But in March 1944 the Superfortress operation was in shambles.

On March 22, 1944, General Arnold testified about the WASP before a friendly House Armed Services Committee, flanked by three lovely ladies in new Santiago-blue uniforms, Jackie Cochran, Ethel Sheehy—and Nancy Harkness Love. Nancy had become alarmed by the uproar in the press. No matter how she felt about Cochran, the entire AAF women's program might be in jeopardy if everyone didn't pull together.

During the Armed Services Committee hearings the general affirmed that there was still a serious manpower shortage and that the women pilots were replacing men who could be flying in combat. He added, "It is not beyond all reason to expect that some day all of our Air Transport Command ferrying within the United States will be done by women."

Arnold assured the committee that many of the men clamoring for WASP jobs were not even physically qualified for the air force. The women, on the other hand, met all the necessary military requirements. He said they should not be incorporated into the WAC because the best women trainees, like the males, were between the ages of eighteen and twenty, and WACs had to be over twenty years of age. And some of the WASP had children under the age of fourteen—this was also against WAC regulations. When asked how many women he intended to train, General Arnold replied that he expected to have "enough to replace every man qualified for overseas service whose permanent duty is flying in the United States." When pressed for an actual number, he suggested between 2,000 and 2,500. The Armed Services Committee went to private, executive session to allow the general to speak more freely, and afterward they reported the proposed WASP legislation favorably to the House.

Still the Army Air Force was closing schools at the same time General Arnold was saying he thought it would be necessary to enlarge the number of women pilots. This conflicting testimony did not help the WASP cause in the press—or with Ramspeck's Civil Service Committee. Also, by this time women pilots were being sent to the School of Applied Tactics at Orlando, Florida, for officer training. On April 29, 1944, the *Washington Daily News* cried out, "The action literally jumps the gun on Congress by anticipating passage of a bill permitting officer status for the WASP, although enactment of the legislation is unlikely without a fight on the House floor."

The Ramspeck committee stepped up its investigation. Where was the money coming from to enroll the women in OTC? Why didn't the navy need female pilots? Who authorized the smart blue uniforms that had just been issued to the WASP? Was the uniform contract awarded after open bidding? The investigators charged, "The War Department is presently encumbered with one-half million dollars for these ensembles."

In reply Air Staff had Nancy Love pose for the *Washington Post*, along with another WASP beauty, in the Santiago-blue uniforms. The photo caption gushed, "Perfect models for the natty uniform of the WASP." In an accompanying interview Nancy was credited as one of the few women holding a Flying Fortress rating. She also got in a plug for the contribution of all the women in the Ferry Division: "We fly anything that's built. Nothing is too hot."

GENERAL BARNEY GILES, AAF chief of staff, had arranged for the women pilots already on active duty to take the officer training course (OTC) in Orlando, Florida. "As Women Airforce Service Pilots are becoming an integral part of the Army Air Forces, it is desired that all personnel be given training similar to that of Army Air Force officers."

Those selected were to have been on operational duty for at least ninety days. The course was four weeks long, and a new class, with fifty students, began every first and third Wednesday of the month. Four hundred sixty women pilots graduated from OTC.

The first class began on April 19, 1944, and was made up of squadron leaders and the women pilots who had been on duty the longest. Twenty-four of them were from the Ferry Division, including Nancy Love and Betty Gillies. Jacqueline Cochran would not be required to attend OTC.

Because of her rank as executive officer—and because she was keenly competitive—Nancy was determined to do better than anyone else, and she had gotten a copy of the course material to study before arriving in Orlando. The women went to classes six days a week studying military discipline, courtesy, and customs. They learned about the organization of the army and staff procedures. They memorized aircraft silhouettes and practiced air-sea rescue and jungle survival—including catching, preparing, and eating an assortment of swamp creatures.

These weeks in Orlando were the first time the originals had all been together in over a year, and like carefree schoolgirls, they had fun. Their barracks were kept by maids, who also washed their shirts and polished their shoes. On Sundays the women took a bus to the beach or went to the movies. Universal had released *Ladies Courageous*, and they went in a group to Orlando to see how it had turned out. *Ladies Courageous* was a silly flying fairy tale, a disaster, with the stars always looking perfectly gorgeous—no matter how long they'd been gamely fighting the elements to complete their mission! After seeing the movie the women in the Ferry Division knew they were in for a thorough ribbing from the men they worked with.

Members of the House Civil Service Committee descended on Orlando so that they could talk to a large number of WASP at the same time. Did the women really want to be in the army? There were plenty of gripes. The originals were less than thrilled about militarization under *Colonel* Jacqueline Cochran, and several were furious about being forced to give up their treasured grays for the snazzy Santiago-blue WASP uniforms.

RUTH'S CLASS, 44-W-1, graduated from Avenger Field in February 1944. They were assigned to the Training Command, although the Ferry Division had agreed several months before to hire a limited number of them. This group had come through the beefed-up curriculum Tunner demanded; nevertheless Cochran sent women with operational experience in their stead.

At Williams Field in Arizona, Lela Loudder got orders to report to the 5th Ferrying Group, Dallas Love Field. She was surprised and elated. At last she would have a chance to do the work she had joined the Women Airforce Service Pilots for—and she was getting away from the spiteful commander at Williams.

The WASP squadron in Dallas was one hundred strong, and in addition to space in the nurses' quarters the women had a new barracks of their own. Delphine Bohn was squadron leader, and she was from Lela's neck of the woods, the Texas Panhandle. She was a local glamour puss, often written up in the papers for both her flying and her socializing. Delphine had lost a favorite boyfriend to Lela's big sister. From the look in her eye, Lela was sure her new boss hadn't forgotten.

The work at Love Field was long and hard. Half a dozen aircraft manufacturers were located around Dallas, and the women pilots flew constantly. Only a handful were on the base at any one time.

Lela had a regular delivery run. She picked up AT-6 Texan trainers at North American Aviation and ferried them to Stewart Field on the Hudson River just above West Point. This took two long days of flying, with one overnight stop. After signing off on the trainer, Lela hopped a ferry down the river to New York City,

catnapping on the way. With her Priority 2 travel orders she took
an American Airlines flight back to Dallas—where she started all
over again.

Lela was as eager to fly P-47s as she had been at Avenger, but
even though she had the experience and hours for pursuit school,
she was never able to get Delphine Bohn's approval—no matter
how many times she asked.

IN JUNE eight of the top graduates from Class 44-W-4, including
Kay D'Arezzo, were also assigned to Love Field and put to work
delivering training aircraft. The Women Airforce Service Pilots was
often in the newspapers as the House prepared to vote on militarization, but Kay and the others were unaware of the controversy.
They were on the go continuously. They traveled in pairs to the
factories to pick up their planes. Kay and her partners were delivering to both coasts. As soon as they returned to Love, they had
another set of orders waiting for them. Kay learned right away that
if she was ever going to have a chance to wash her hair or catch up
on her laundry—and sometimes, her rest—she had to take the latest
possible American flight back to Dallas. If the WASP arrived back
at operations after midnight, they were not scheduled to fly again
the next day.

With three hundred women ferrying on the Air Transport Command's domestic routes, there was usually a group of young pilots,
guys and gals, clustered around the bar in the Officers' Club at
AAF training fields, laughing and singing along with the piano
players. When she completed a trainer delivery, Kay stayed away
from the bar and instead passed time playing the slot machines at
the back of most of the clubs. She could never forget she was a
married woman. She never wanted to. These jolly crowds only
made her more lonely, so Kay made sure to always have a stash of
nickels and quarters in her B-4 bag to keep her occupied.

Millie was at Maxwell AAFB in Alabama flying engineering tests
on repaired B-24 bombers. She was also checking out on all sorts
of equipment through the repair and maintenance facility, and the
entries in her pilot's log book already covered a page and a half.
On the weekends she was even permitted to borrow a plane for her
own use. In her letters to Kay she admitted she put this stroke of

luck to good purpose: Millie had a boyfriend stationed in another state.

Kay picked up a basic trainer destined for flight school in Georgia and on the way decided to check up on Millie. When she got to Maxwell, she circled the field several times, signaling trouble. When the tower flashed a green light, Kay wagged her wings in response before setting down on the runway. Inside operations, she said, "There's something wrong with the radio. It doesn't always transmit." Kay knew an intermittent-radio problem would ground her overnight while a specialist tracked the problem. She and Millie needed to get caught up.

The congressional committee hearings focused the attention of major metropolitan newspapers on the Women Airforce Service Pilots. The media, which had aroused American women to answer their country's call to war, now began to swing public opinion against those who had done so. While *The Boston Globe*, New York's *Herald Tribune*, and *The New York Times* still favored militarization of the WASP, both of Washington's daily papers were sharply critical—even though the WASP were the only women's service subjected, in the line of duty, to the same hazards as men.

The *Washington Daily News* charged that not all of the women wanted to become part of the army and would resign if this came to pass, and on May 18 the paper ran a headline that declared the WASP program smelled like some kind of racket. The other capital newspaper, the *Washington Times-Herald*, claimed that male civilian instructors weren't getting a fair hearing from the House Armed Services Committee because the women pilots had the backing of Mrs. Franklin D. Roosevelt.

The May 29, 1944, issue of *Time* magazine battered the Costello Bill. In an article, "Unnecessary and Undesirable," *Time* reported that while the Ramspeck investigation found the WASP to be earnest, hardworking, and rule-abiding, they were nevertheless an expensive experiment in which *nineteen* women had been killed! And there was a sizable group of men—some six thousand instructors alone—who could be trained for the same work in half the time and at half the cost.

Air Staff requested General Harold George to answer some of these charges, particularly complaints that women pilots were grabbing the choice ferrying missions away from men. General George turned the request over to Tunner at the Ferry Division with his comment, "Make it thorough, and make it good."

Within three days Tunner replied. The resentments seemed to be confined to a loudmouthed minority of male ferry pilots, and anyone familiar with the WASP's work appreciated their contribution. Also, ferrying missions were routinely assigned to the individual who had the qualifications for the scheduled aircraft and who had been longest at a base. Several of the WASP, Tunner pointed out, were highly qualified indeed.

In the middle of May Hap Arnold suffered his third heart attack in fourteen months and was quietly shipped off to recuperate in Florida. His wife Bee accompanied him, although the gossip billowing out of the WASP hearings was burdensome.

On June 5 the Civil Service Committee brought in a majority report that concluded that the WASP experiment was "wasted time and wasted effort" and expressed the strong opinion that a program involving 2,500 trainees, at an approximate cost of *$50 million*, was important enough to have required specific legislative sanction. The committee alleged that an outlay of $12,150 per trainee only qualified the women to fly light ships, and the extra training necessary to make them more versatile would boost the price to $20,000. Even worse, those who failed to graduate were a total loss to the taxpayer because they did not have any sort of further military commitment. The majority report recommended that training be eliminated immediately, although graduate WASP could remain on duty as civilians, and that provisions ought to be made for hospitalization and insurance.

Five members of the committee signed a minority report expressing the opinion that the women's flying program was a matter for the AAF to determine.

As the Civil Service Committee was reporting to the House, a large contingent of Allied forces massed for an attack on the coast of France at Normandy the following morning, June 6, 1944. This would be the beginning of the end of the war in Europe. Shortly after the invasion a weary Hap Arnold, still weak from his most recent heart attack, left for meetings in London and to inspect the landing beaches in France. On the way he learned that a flight of B-29s had completed their first wartime mission, a raid on Japanese-held Bangkok. And on June 18 the bombers made their first attack on Japan, three thousand miles round trip, from their base in China. The Superfortress's chronic problem of engines overheating and catching fire plagued the mission, and worse yet, the few that actually reached Japan, missed almost all of their primary targets. Arnold's B-29 had yet to prove its worth. The general returned to Washington on June 21, the same day the WASP bill came to a vote in the House.

The War Department decided to bring H.R. 4219 to a vote and fight it out on the floor of the House. The secretary of war, Henry L. Stimson, wrote to the House Committee on Military Affairs expressing support for the Women Airforce Service Pilots on behalf of the president and his cabinet. Representative Costello pleaded for fairness. "If they are doing the work that calls for the grade and calls for the pay, they are entitled to it. . . . I do not think that a woman should be discriminated against." However, thousands of out-of-work male pilots and the veterans' groups were still bitterly opposing the measure and running a noisy, belligerent lobby against the women.

The Air Transport Command was not consulted before the Costello Bill went to Congress, and the primary using agency of the WASP, the Ferry Division, was never called to testify.

Several important newspapers continued to lambaste militarization, with personal attacks on Cochran. Rambunctious Jackie, with her clever, pushy ways, had particularly offended eminent newspaper columnist Drew Pearson and, with H.R. 4219 due for a House vote, he was hot for the kill. Pearson traveled to Orlando to interview the women pilots attending OTC. With so many WASP in one spot, he hoped to find vocal dissenters. Also, he knew gossips throughout the Ferry Division were snickering about Jacqueline Cochran's sugar daddy in D.C. and swearing she had Hap Arnold wrapped around her little finger.

On June 14, just one week before the House vote, Pearson's column in the *Washington Times-Herald* got in a final lick: "In the last week, the shapely pilot has seen her coveted commission come closer and closer. One of the highest placed generals, it seems, gazed into her eyes, and since then has taken her cause célèbre very much to heart. . . . She's such an attractive composition of windblown bob, smiling eyes, and outdoor skin, nobody blames him."

On June 21, 1944, the debate in the House of Representatives on

H.R. 4219 grew bitter as the afternoon wore on. Amendments to limit the size of the organization and to make the women's commanding officer a captain instead of a colonel both met defeat. When at last the vote was called, the bill to make the women pilots a part of the air force, which had been advocated by the administration, the secretary of war, and the commanding general of the Army Air Force, was defeated by only nineteen votes.

Without renewing the battle in Congress, the only military option still available to the women pilots seemed to be in the WAC. Cochran warned General Arnold she wouldn't cow before Colonel Hobby, a woman who had never piloted a plane and prattled about aircraft as if they were toys for her two kids. "She has bitched up her program," Jackie said, "and she is not going to bitch up mine!"

Five days later General Arnold announced that recruiting and training of additional Women Airforce Service Pilots would terminate at once, although the women already at Avenger would be allowed to finish flight school. Meanwhile forty-eight girls had already arrived in Sweetwater to start training as Class 45-W-1. Mrs. Deaton saw that they were fed and lodged until the Air Transport Command made arrangements to fly them home. And the trainees at Avenger made up a new song:

> Would you like to swing on a star
> Ferry ATs home from afar
> And be better off than you are,
> Or would you rather be a WAC?
>
> A WAC may be an officer
> With bright bars that shine
> Her olive green and everything looks fine
> She's very proud of the name she bears
> As for you you don't want her cares;
> Her olive green was never meant for you
> You want Santiago blue.

EVEN AFTER the Costello Bill was voted down, WASP were still sent to Orlando for officer training. In June Marge Harper arrived from Las Vegas Army Air Force Base at the same time Hazel Ah Ying Lee came from Romulus. The funny, friendly Chinese-American girl from Portland delighted Marge. By the time the two women began

OTC, the summer heat boiled thunderstorms, almost hourly, across central Florida and steam sizzled off the blacktop sidewalks winding through the facility. Marge and Hazel often sat on the patio outside the classrooms during breaks to catch a breeze and talk.

Hazel Lee had been on active duty five months longer than Marge. Working in the 3rd Ferrying Group was tough, she confirmed. The women got shoved around. Nancy Love was telling her women pilots to try pursuit class, but this wasn't going to be a snap at Romulus. Transition of any sort was hard to come by. And Hazel had another problem learning to fly peashooters; in April she had washed out of instrument school in Missouri. She shrugged. "But I gotta make it—next time!"

One muggy afternoon Hazel Lee told Marge that when she was in China, she had a head-on collision with the culture and her father's family. They couldn't seem to catch on to an American girl at all! However, now she was planning to marry an officer in the Chinese Nationalist Air Force—a colonel who was Chiang Kai-shek's personal pilot. Their lives were a hemisphere apart, and at first he hadn't wanted to be engaged. With a loud, braying laugh she recalled, "That's all right, I told him. I'll be engaged to you!"

ON JUNE 27, one week after the defeat of the Costello Bill in the House, Nancy Love wrote to General George at Air Transport Command headquarters in Washington. She advised that the women pilots in the Ferry Division be militarized as soon as possible. For weeks Nancy had gone against her instincts and backed Cochran's efforts, believing her rival had enough clout to get the necessary legislation passed—if anyone did! Now not only had Jackie failed, she had stirred up a storm that threatened the future of all the women working as military pilots. Nancy was going to try her own tactics.

The first step was to position all the Ferry Division's women in essential jobs. As many as possible would have to check out for pursuit delivery—or be transferred.

Forty-four of the women from the 2nd Ferrying Group at Wilmington were able to check out in pursuits and filled vital slots in the Ferry Division. A few joined the WASP who were already ferrying P-47s from Republic at Farmingdale, Long Island. They delivered Thunderbolts to modification centers inland or to the docks in New Jersey for shipment overseas. Eight women on a rotating schedule were billeted in the Huntington Hotel, about ten miles from the plant. They were picked up each morning and returned each evening by a shuttle bus. They ate breakfast and dinner at the hotel and lunch in the Republic cafeteria, and before long had exclusive use of a twin-engine transport, piloted by a WASP, that flew them back from the docks to the Republic's airfield. By the end of the summer these women were delivering every Thunderbolt rolling off the production lines.

By April 1944 the Ferry Division had reached a total of 303 women pilots on duty. General Tunner wanted to be rid of any who were not pursuit material. Less than half of the WASP who had been assigned to the Ferry Division during the past twelve months had the necessary qualifications. Early in the summer the Ferry Division began a long effort to transfer out all of those who lacked the experience or the temperament for pursuit training. By August, 125 WASP had been released. Afterward the average number of women pilots on duty with FERD was 140—and they continued to be paid fifty dollars a month less than male civilian Class I pilots, even though they were flying Class IV and V multiengine and pursuits.

More than half of the WASP at Dallas Love Field were transferred back to the Training Command. Kay went to Bryan AAFB, Texas, for an instrument instructor's course. Lela was sent to Lubbock Army Airfield near her home to work as a utility pilot. Shortly afterward she heard that one of her 43-W-7 baymates had realized all their dreams. Tommy Thompkins was in pursuit transition at Brownsville, Texas.

Meanwhile General William Tunner was posted to the command of the Air Transport Command's airlift operation over the Himalayas—the Hump—from India to China. He had hired Nancy Love and her twenty-five originals two years before, out of desperation, but they had bested his doubts time and again. He was the tough and gallant champion of the women pilots in his command, and now he was leaving the Ferry Division just when they faced their greatest peril.

FLYING TRAINING MISSIONS in the fierce skies over the desert at Las Vegas was brutal work most of the year, and the pilots swallowed handfuls of salt tablets to stave off dehydration. After several hours of target towing, Marge Harper was stunned to find rings of salt encrusting her body when she unzipped her flight suit.

Skip Carter got sick. Her weight and energy fell off drastically. But the doctors at the base hospital decided Skip's thyroid, not the blaring heat, was to blame and performed surgery. Afterward the colonel arranged for a flight of WASP to deliver repaired PT-19s to Tinker Field near Oklahoma City so that Skip's friends could fly her home to recover. And rather than force Skip into a medical discharge, Jackie Cochran put her on Ethel Sheehy's staff until she was back on her feet.

After Marge returned from Orlando, she completed transition in the B-26 Marauder. The twin-engine bomber was used as a target tug to train Flying Fortress gun crews, and Marge was keen to get to work. When she reported to the bomber group's commanding officer, twenty-four-year-old Major Elmer Watson, her new boss was dazzled by her sun-browned beauty framed with long ebony pigtails and launched an ardent courtship. He dated her every night, and they made a supremely handsome couple, even if their relationship was militarily irregular. After a month Marge came back to the barracks late one evening, bright-eyed and mussed. "He says he wants to marry me," she confided in Ruth.

The night before the wedding, Ruth had to pull the bride through a bout of prenuptial jitters, but Marge and her major were married at Las Vegas on September 6, 1944. When they returned from a brief four-day honeymoon, she was handed transfer orders to March Field, California. It was against army regulations for husband and wife to live together if both were in uniform.

Throughout the Training Command the WASP encountered mounting difficulties obtaining transition and work. Late in July the four domestic air forces were notified that as many as four hundred WASP might be assigned to tow-target work. The Fourth Air Force replied that it could only absorb ten women pilots a month, and the First and Fourth Air Forces answered that they would not be able to take any additional women pilots at all. The Second Air Force was willing to employ a large number of women, but in September it was relieved of the mission to train gunners.

EVEN AFTER H.R. 4219 failed on June 21, the press continued to print ugly stories about Jackie and her girls. In July columnist Al

Williams wrote a harsh indictment of the women pilots in the *Washington Daily News.* He even charged that B. J. Erickson's eight-thousand-mile ferry mission that won the Air Medal was nothing but a publicity stunt. Three weeks later Jackie's arch-enemy, Drew Pearson, wrote,

> Air Force commander General "Hap" Arnold may not know it, but he is facing a regular cloudburst from Capitol Hill as soon as Congress gets back to a full-time job. The Congressmen are up in arms over Arnold's effort to sidetrack the law by continuing to use the WASPs . . . the government has spent more than $21,000,000 training lady flyers, primarily at the behest of vivacious aviatrix Jacqueline Cochran, wife of financial magnate Floyd Oldum. Magnetic Miss Cochran seems to have quite a drag with the Brass Hats and has even persuaded the Air Forces' smiling commander to make several secret trips to Capitol Hill to lobby for continuation of her pets, the WASPs. . . . It was arranged to sign the WASPs up as WACs, then have them reassigned to the Air Forces, this despite Congress' clear ruling that the WASPs should not be taken into the regular Army. When Colonel Oveta Culp Hobby, head of the WACs, got wind of this deal, she sent emissaries on forced marches to Capitol Hill to have her rank raised from Colonel to Brigadier General. Oveta was afraid that Jacqueline Cochran would be made a colonel in the WACs and wanted to outrank her.

Two days after Pearson's attack, on August 8, 1944, Jackie Cochran sent an eleven-page, single-spaced report to General Arnold in which she spared neither words nor facts outlining the WASP's achievements, their training program, and their history, including the rocky congressional hearings—*and* her recommendations for their future. Cochran took the unprecedented step of releasing the report to the public at the same time it went to Arnold. Legislative action identical to the Costello Bill was lying dormant in the Senate, and she wanted the Army Air Force to press for passage. She requested "simple justice" for the WASP, who got "none of the rights of military status, not even a military funeral." Put the women pilots into the army, Cochran demanded, with commissions, or junk their organization completely.

10.

"They Taught Us How to Fly, Now They Send Us Home to Cry..."

THE B-29 SUPERFORTRESS could carry twice the weight of a B-17 and could carry it twice as far. The bomber had a 141-foot wingspan, stood almost three stories tall, and had an almost inconceivable range: 4,200 miles. This leviathan was destined to conquer the vast distances in the Pacific Ocean and vanquish the Japanese.

However, the B-29 was the most technically sophisticated aircraft ever designed and in early 1944, it continued to be plagued by mechanical bugs—especially with its four engines that persisted in overheating and bursting into flames. Meanwhile shakedown missions in Kansas proved that the crews were also far from ready as the hefty bombers made forced landings all over the prairie.

Finally the 21st Bomber Command's B-29 Wing left for Asia in

April but of this first group, five crashed within the first month of operation due to overheated engines. Stateside, word of the Super-fortress's ominous debut seeped through the bomber training bases.

Dorothea Johnson was one of the five WASP assigned to Eglin AAFB, Florida, as tow-target and radio control pilots. On a May evening in 1944, she was in the lounge of the nurses' barracks read-ing when a young air force colonel strode in. DeDe thought he had come to visit one of the nurses, but he stopped in front of her. "I want to see you," he said. "Do you have any four-engine time? I'm looking for two WASP to check out in the B-29."

Stunned, she replied, "I have a little time in a twin-engine trainer." The B-29! she thought. "That's all any of us have—except Dora. She's up right now in an A-20." Dora Dougherty was the most experienced of the women pilots stationed at Eglin, and the A-20 was a 1,600-horsepower, twin-engine attack plane.

"I'll take her," he said. "And you. Do you want to do this?"

The B-29! She nodded.

"Be ready in the morning," the colonel said as he left.

Lieutenant Colonel Paul W. Tibbets, Jr., who would pilot the *Enola Gay* over Hiroshima the following year, was based at the very-heavy bomber training school near Birmingham, Alabama, and he was in charge of introducing the Superfortress. He was also sick and tired of the men's complaints about the big bomber. He had witnessed the startling effect on apprehensive air force pilots of women at the controls of the B-26 Widow Maker, and he had set out in search of a pair of WASP to help prove the B-29 Superfor-tress.

Tibbets took DeDe Johnson and Dora Dougherty to Anniston, Alabama, and put them through three quick days of intense train-ing. Since the engines were more likely to explode in flames if they had been through the accepted warm-up stage, he taught the women to taxi up to the runway swiftly and take off. They prac-ticed stalls and emergency procedures, and each of them flew eight hours as first pilot. On a check flight, coming into Anniston, with the women in the pilot and copilot's seats and Tibbets crouched between them, DeDe Johnson called the tower for the first time.

The bewildered controller replied, "B-29 landing without a ra-dio. Signal if you can hear me."

DeDe clicked the switch on her microphone and acknowledged, "Anniston Tower, yes, I can hear you."

As their Superfortress settled toward the runway, they could see a crowd of men standing on the tower's rim. And on the flight line the entire crew of a B-24 Liberator was up on top of the wings, watching. Tibbets had a fit of laughing. "Bounce this thing and you're dead," he gasped to his lady pilots.

Tibbets planned a cross-country flying exhibition for DeDe and Dora. For maximum impact he named their B-29 *Ladybird* and selected the WASP gremlin, Fifinella, for nose art. They flew from Alabama to a very-heavy bomber base at Clovis, New Mexico, making several stops along the way. When DeDe climbed down from the huge bomber at Tinker Field in Oklahoma, an officer working in the tower kidded, "My, you're a little thing, aren't you?"

"That's why they put trim tabs in these planes, sir," she snapped back.

The two WASP only got to strut their stuff in the *Ladybird* for a short time, less than a month. Word of Tibbets's gambit got back to Washington, and the air force brass wired him to cut it out! Congressman John Rankin, chairman of the House Appropriations Committee, had called AAF headquarters in a rage. "Get those women out of *my* airplane!" he screamed.

ALTHOUGH the Civil Service Committee took pains to indicate that it was not attacking the women pilots already on duty (but, rather, objected to Cochran's extravagant flight school for inexperienced girls), the failure of the Costello Bill on June 21, 1944, was nevertheless a ruthless blow to those women. Afterward their archcritic, columnist Al Williams, displayed a slight change of heart toward the Ferry Division's women in the *Washington Daily News* of July 13, 1944. He summed up their situation: "The whole thing was unfortunate, because it brought undeserved discredit upon the little band of gallant, able women pilots who stepped into the breach when there was a shortage of men pilots and ferried thousands of trainers to Army and Navy training posts. These women were known as the WAFS, respected by all flying people and deserving of the gratitude of the nation."

While Nancy Love and General Tunner both backed militarization, the key officers in the Ferry Division had made no attempt to lobby for or against the Costello Bill. Because of his distaste for Jackie, the general was never eager to place his women pilots under her jurisdiction, and he seemed to consider this legislation to be her show. He was miffed because his staff was not consulted during the hearings by either of the House's investigating committees, so Nancy had to go it alone during the spring of 1944 in conveying support for Air Staff's militarization efforts.

After June 21, 1944, the Ferry Division abandoned independent efforts to gain military status for its women. Nancy turned to Air Transport Command headquarters for help and gambled that specializing in pursuit delivery would distinguish the female ferry pilots from the rest of the Women Airforce Service Pilots.

Jackie Cochran wasn't about to take the House's rejection lying down either. She was infuriated by their recommendation to preserve the women pilots on duty while denying them commissions and eliminating her own function. Mortified by the personal attacks on herself—and on General Arnold—she felt positive this official rebuff had also wounded the women pilots' spirit. In only two short weeks, from June 13 to June 29, at the peak of the controversy in Congress, five WASP had had fatal accidents. Jacqueline Cochran was bent on a last-ditch, make-it-or-break-it attempt to salvage the women's air corps she and Hap Arnold had envisioned.

She took steps to rouse women by way of the Ninety-Nines International Organizations of Women Pilots and the WASP and their families. She encouraged them to write to congressmen Ramspeck and Costello, as well as their own senators and representatives, for reinstatement of the training program. The editor of the Ninety-Nines newsletter urged every member to get involved in the battle for the WASP so that "we would have to worry no longer about women's place in aviation."

In spite of these renewed efforts, some of the WASP chose to quit. One wrote, "Last month, due to recent action of Congress and the opinions of such columnists as Drew Pearson, I concluded that my services were not essential and, giving the above reason, resigned." Jackie felt these women were, at best, ungrateful. Nothing was going right.

Over the next weeks she compiled the detailed status report on the WASP that she sent to both General Arnold and the press on

August 7, recommending that he disband the women pilots unless another wholehearted attempt was made for militarization. The newspapers, most of which remained hostile to WASP training, heralded her tactics as an ultimatum to the AAF commanding general. And the American Legion put forth a resolution that "the WASP be immediately and honorably disbanded."

The next day Nancy Love finally enlisted the public relations office at FERD headquarters in her efforts to safeguard the female ferry pilots. The captain in charge responded with an energetic campaign plan, as well as a personal observation: "Cochran is determined to take the WASP program down with her if she is turned down in her efforts to militarize the WASP."

The squadron leader at Long Beach, B. J. Erickson, and another of the seasoned originals, Florene Miller, were assigned to temporary duty as pilots on a regularly scheduled Air Transport Command route between Romulus and Chicago. Before leaving his command, General Tunner had arranged for this experiment to evaluate the performance of women as transport pilots. Nancy objected to the scheme because she was convinced it would further rile the men lobbying for the WASP's jobs.

B.J. and Florene both passed the check for first pilots and maintained an on-time schedule without incident. Nonetheless, women at the controls of a C-47 apparently made a few of the passengers anxious, so the two WASP were usually in the cockpit with the cabin door closed before the military personnel boarded. Still, now and then, they couldn't resist a prank. They completed all landing procedures while taxiing so that once the transport had reached a stop, they only had to kill the engines and unsnap their seat belts before sauntering down the aisle while the dumbfounded passengers were still in their seats.

After several weeks B.J. and Florene were offered a choice. Would they prefer to continue as transport pilots or return to their ferrying group? They jumped at the chance to abandon the monotonous three-hundred-mile route across Michigan and return to Long Beach where they could fly a tempting variety of aircraft.

By the end of September the Ferry Division's women were delivering three-fifths of all pursuit aircraft, including every fighter made by Republic Aircraft. Now that the division was in danger of losing its WASP, Brigadier General Robert Nowland, who had replaced

Tunner, and his senior officers began telling everyone who would listen that the women pilots were invaluable, irreplaceable. Eighty-four percent of the women were qualified on pursuits, and during a single month, Florene Miller recorded sixty-eight hours and forty minutes in delivering pursuits, nearly twice the average.

Meanwhile the Allies seemed to have victory in Europe within their grasp. Bombing was destroying the German industrial centers. Both Belgium and France had been liberated and ground forces were driving into the Netherlands and Germany. At last the bloody island-hopping strategy in the Pacific was supplemented by the long-range Superfortress, and the Japanese were slowly retreating.

The total casualties suffered by the Army Air Force since the outbreak of the war were approximately 42,000 planes and 72,000 men. As large as these losses might seem, they were far below those forecast—and the AAF apparently had sufficient pilots for present needs.

In September the women's OTC course at Orlando was closed and the women stationed at Buckingham as pilots for the B-17 gunnery training missions were all transferred to maintenance facilities to test repaired Fortresses. Four went to Las Vegas Army Air Force Base to join the WASP squadron there. They kept to themselves at one end of the nurses' barracks and performed their duties, rarely crossing paths with the other women pilots. Ruth Craig Jones and the others never got to know them.

Two of the B-17 pilots went to March Field, California, where Marge Harper Watson had been exiled after her marriage. Marge was flying a B-26 target tug and wondering if her squeamish stomach meant she was pregnant. She thought it was interesting that one of the husky Fortress pilots had brought a young puppy with her.

Then, on October 3, all the women pilots at Las Vegas, as well as Marge and every WASP on active duty, received two letters from AAF headquarters. The first, from Jacqueline Cochran, began, "To all WASP: General Arnold has directed that the WASP program be deactivated on 20 December 1944. Attached is a letter from him to each of you." She detailed what was expected of individuals to assure a tidy departure and thanked them for their contributions to their country and for establishing women's place in aviation. Cochran added, for the benefit of the Ferry Division, "Those who wish to continue to fly for the Army Air Forces will be disappointed."

General Arnold explained that the present circumstances meant that if the women pilots continued in service, they would be replacing instead of releasing the nation's young men. "I know the WASP wouldn't want that," he wrote. "I want you to know that I appreciate your war service and that the AAF will miss you. I also know that you will join us in being thankful that our combat losses have proved to be much lower than anticipated, even though it means the inactivation of the WASP.

"My Sincere thanks and Happy Landings always."

Not too long afterward the major in charge of training called Ruth into his office. "I have just received permission to give the Air Medal to someone from my command," he said, "and I'd like you to have it."

"What for?" she asked.

"Well, because you always do a good job."

"So does everybody else in the squadron."

"Yes, but I want *you* to have the medal."

"What could I tell the others?" Ruth asked. "I don't want it."

JACKIE'S ULTIMATUM had given both General Arnold and herself an escape from a tight spot. Neither of them had expected to run into such rough weather over the Women Airforce Service Pilots. The war was winding down, and Arnold knew the time had come to start turning off the giant aerial combat machine he had nearly killed himself to build. Thousands of civilian male pilots were already out of work and in imminent danger of being drafted into the infantry—unless they could find other essential flying jobs. The WASP occupied one thousand such jobs in the Ferry Division and other AAF commands. On top of all this 1944 was an election year and members of Congress were scrounging for vote-catching issues.

There was no legitimate reason to ride out a public storm or be buffeted by scandal over the WASP. For months Air Staff had avoided taking a stand until the opportunity for a women's air corps had come and gone; so Arnold made the speeches while Cochran handled the administrative details of scrapping the women's military aviation experiment.

MARGE STEVENSON had been electrified by the news Grace brought back from her visit to Sweetwater. The Women Airforce Service Pilots program was accepting eighteen-year-olds. A chance to fly to help win the war—like Grace! Marge announced that she was not going back to Linwood. Instead she was applying to the WASP—immediately. All right, their father agreed, but in the meantime he put Marge to work as a bookkeeper in his bank in Holdenville.

She had to wait months for a class, but at last, in April 1944, Marge entered the women's flight school at Avenger Field. Spirits were high. General Hap Arnold had been on post only weeks before to deliver a commencement address. The curriculum had just been extended to seven months and now included military procedures and courtesy. Graduates needed to salute properly because legislation to commission them as second lieutenants in the Army Air Force Reserve was pending in the Congress. And the new Santiago-blue dress uniforms!

Marge became "Stevie", and she and her 44-W-4 classmates worked hard to keep their spots. They had to transmit Morse code at sixteen words a minute. The ground school crammed two years of physics into a week. Lieutenant La Rue had built an obstacle course that could turn out junior commandos. And establishment officers were always addressed as "miss."

Unruly spring storms delayed the rookie's flying, and they had to make up lost time on the weekends—but the Stearmans were a wonder, so they didn't care. Colored flags hoisted on a pole near the tower signaled weather conditions. White was favorable; yellow, dual instructions only; red, no flying. At the auxiliary fields smoke pots called off flying.

New classes arrived in May and June. Then on June 26 Hap Arnold announced that WASP recruiting was over and that the flight school would close after the students presently in training graduated. Congress had refused to commission the WASP too. Stevie and the rest weren't sure what this meant. Had they been lucky enough to get in under the wire or was the washout rate about to soar?

When the trainees got their only weekend pass, most headed for Dallas for bright lights and, once in a while, singing in the streets.

[208]

Occasionally on a Sunday, just for a change of scene, a group would take the train two or three stops down the line to Big Springs or Abilene, where they would descend and walk around before taking a return train to Sweetwater.

Mrs. Deaton kept a sharp look out for fresh trouble, anything that might reflect on the character of Jackie's girls. She was particularly wary of the two primary forms of sinfulness in Texas: whiskey and sex. She discovered that a couple of prostitutes had set up business at the Blue Bonnet Hotel and were masquerading as WASP, just to add shine to their wares. Gossip had plagued Oveta Culp Hobby's WAC from the start, so this was serious.

By that afternoon Deaton had confined all the trainees to Cochran's Convent until further notice and had posted a copy of the order in the town square for everyone in Sweetwater to read. As days went by, with no bona fide WASP anywhere in sight, Deaton's tactic forced the whores to change their advertising. Meanwhile the trainees, who hadn't a clue why they were being cooped up, were ready to stage an insurrection.

At Avenger Field the administrative staff was composed of four female establishment officers, under the direction of Leni Deaton, and a cadre of a dozen AAF officers. Almost without fail the cadre were married men, and the rare bachelor warranted a write-up and photo in the field newspaper, *The Avenger*. The instructors remained off-limits, and the social climate was grim, even though Deaton still tried to ease the man shortage by importing AAF cadets for occasional Saturday-night dances. But most of them were only eighteen or nineteen, absolute kids as far as the trainees were concerned. However, the women discovered that on summer weekends, there were always swimming parties at Lake Sweetwater with army officers who were based nearby. Chilled watermelon laced with whiskey was a picnic specialty.

On August 4 the seventy-two members of Class 44-W-6 graduated, and Jackie Cochran and her aide, WASP Helen Dettweiler, appeared for the first time in the new WASP summer uniform.

> From this field they say you are going
> After seven months you're getting out of here
> And you're going to a field where there's menfolk
> And passes and night life and beer.

Three days later in Washington Jackie publicly challenged General Arnold to have another try at militarizing the WASP.

In September, as the nights began to cool, Avenger had celebrated visitors. Some of the American women who were serving in Britain's Air Transport Auxiliary and were stateside on leave came to call. Two former ATAs were at the field: Kay Van Doozer, one of the establishment officers, and Emily Chapin, who was part of the last class. And besides, the callers wanted to see what was up. Each of these renowned women dropped by Stevie's bay to greet Grace's baby sister. Her classmates were dazzled.

Twelve days before Stevie's October 16 graduation General Arnold announced the deactivation of the Women Airforce Service Pilots—as of December 20, 1944. Over half the class had washed out, and only fifty-three received their silver wings. The commencement speaker was Lieutenant Colonel Roy P. Ward, Avenger's new commanding officer. The Big Spring Bombardier Band was absent for the first time in a year, and there were no distinguished guests.

After taking graduation leave in Holdenville, Stevie boarded the train for six weeks of active duty. All the cars were smoky and jammed with uniforms. There was a young soldier sitting next to her, and he was drunk. He must have mistaken her Santiago blue for a nurse's uniform and he talked for hours. He was going home after months of combat and death—and he was terribly afraid. Stevie couldn't think what to say. Awhile before his stop the soldier staggered to his feet. " 'Scuse me," he muttered, weaving away from her. She always wondered whether he got off or not.

THE MISSION of Avenger Field's school was to produce pilots to ferry primary trainers, so graduates only held airmen's certificates with appropriate horsepower ratings for lower-powered planes. This restricted effective use of WASP personnel within the Flying Training Command, as well as the Air Transport Command.

As a matter of practice, however, the women were transitioning into larger types of aircraft at many airbases and by June 1944 regulations were amended to authorize them to pilot any army ship their station commanders felt they were qualified to fly.

Early in September 1944 Jackie tried to get more WASP into engineering tests on the B-17, but the general in charge of bomber transition told her that he had to check off every man he could on the B-17 and that every minute spent checking off girls on four-engine equipment was simply wasted.

WASP ANN BAUMGARTNER had been temporarily transferred to Wright Field, Dayton, Ohio, the air force's research facility, to test equipment and flight gear being designed for women. When the job was over, Ann talked Wright Field's commander into letting her stay on in flight operations. She wasn't sure if she would ever get to fly again, but every day at Dayton was like looking into the future of aviation. The planes, weapons, and technical systems of tomorrow were being created and tested all around her.

Eventually Ann finagled her way back into a cockpit, checking out equipment prototypes and aviation innovations right alongside the male test pilots. The Germans, the British, and the Americans were all experimenting with jet engines, and in September Ann got a chance to take the controls of the screaming YP-59 twin-turbine jet fighter—and became the only woman to solo in a jet for almost ten years.

ON SEPTEMBER 20, 1944, the 10,000th Thunderbolt rolled off the assembly line at the Republic factory on Long Island into a cheering crowd of workers and dignitaries. Women Airforce Service Pilots from the 2nd Ferrying Group flew all of the P-47s to the docks in New Jersey, and they drew straws to see who would get this one. Teresa James won.

While a band played, Jackie Cochran broke a bottle of champagne over the pursuit's thick nose for the motion picture cameras and exclaimed, "I christen thee 10 Grand!" And Teresa James left a note with the aircaft's paperwork before it was shipped to the European theater: "To the pilot of the 10 GRAND, you hit the Jackpot. May every mission be a GRAND one and every chance a winner. Good Hunting."

Within a month Teresa's husband's B-17 was shot down over France. Other bombers in the formation sighted parachutes, but none of the crew was ever found.

THE WOMEN of the Ferry Division were crushed by Hap Arnold's October 3 announcement. Since they had been hired originally as civilian pilots, there was a suggestion from FERD headquarters simply to rehire them. When General Arnold got wind of this, he immediately sent the following memo to air force commands: "You will notify all concerned that there will be no—repeat—no women pilots in any capacity in the Air Force after December 20 except Jacqueline Cochran. I do not want any misunderstanding about this, so notify all concerned at once."

Ferry Division leaders maintained that 117 of its women were pursuit pilots and that it would take months of training in Browns-ville, at approximately $9,336 per pilot, to replace them—or $1,085,312 for all 117! The loss of the women pilots would be a hardship on the operations of their ferrying groups and would ham-per the mission of the division. The Ferry Division requested that the women be discharged gradually while their replacements were being trained. Air Staff replied that the continued employment of WASP pilots after December 20 could not be approved.

Liberty magazine editorialized, "It's not the women who are hys-terical." The *New York Herald Tribune* objected to deactivating the pursuit WASP. The newspaper contended that the United States could not afford to throw away their experience: "If we still do not need them, a lot of top-side people in the service whose judgment I respect are 100 percent off the beam. Great Britain still needs her top-flight women pilots. So does Russia. And—unless I'm just a chronic pessimist about this war—so does the United States."

LELA LOUDDER had been stationed in Lubbock, Texas, for nearly two months, running errands in a twin-engine cargo plane. Late one night, during the first week in November, the phone rang for her. Jo Naphen was calling from Dallas and she was crying. "Tommy is missing," she sobbed. Jo had had a date to meet their former baymate, but when she arrived from New York, nobody knew where Gertrude "Tommy" Thompkins was.

The women from their bay had stayed close even after Jo washed out of training, and they were all proud when Tommy was selected for pursuit school at Brownsville. She had finished the thirty days' transition the month before, along with two other WASP from the 5th Ferrying Group, Dallas Love Field.

She and Jo had been planning a reunion. Not only had Tommy just qualified to fly the hottest ships in the air force, she had written Jo that she was a new bride with a diamond as big as a rock! Only when Jo reached Dallas, she discovered Tommy and her P-51 Mustang had disappeared after takeoff from the Los Angeles Municipal Airport over a week before, on October 26, 1944.

Jo was beside herself, so Lela figured she had to wangle a way to get to Dallas. By morning she had both a pass and a plane—as well as haze, scattered rain, and poor visibility across most of north Texas. She would have to get to Dallas on instruments. Even though Lela had been a Link instructor and had spent ample time practicing under the hood, this was the first time she had ever actually piloted a plane with instruments. As she headed east through the soup, Lela thought, the real thing is different, and Love Field is busy—all the time. Her eyes were glued to the gauges in the cockpit. Once she was on the ground, however, Jo was so glad to see her, Lela forgot how scared she had been.

A missing aircraft report on Tommy's P-51 had been filed with the ATC in Washington and FERD in Cincinnati. The flight of Mustangs she was assigned to left Los Angeles on the morning of October 26 headed for the European embarcation point at Newark, but her plane had a faulty cockpit latch, and she was delayed until four in the afternoon while it was repaired. Meanwhile the weather turned sour, and Tommy took off in instrument conditions, with strong winds and a layer of haze extending to 2,500 feet. The tower lost contact with her almost immediately. She was not reported missing for several days because no individual flight plan had been recorded, and a foul-up in the paperwork sent to the tower had omitted her ship's number from the forty-five aircraft that cleared the airfield that afternoon.

The account of Tommy's disappearance in the Los Angeles newspapers said her husband, an American flying for the Brits who had been listed as missing in action for two years, had just been declared dead by the U.S. State Department. But Jo, Lela, and the others from their bay knew that Tommy had recently gotten married again, to Henry Silver, a Hollywood producer.

After a search, no trace of Tommy was found, and the air force assumed she had gotten off course. Maybe the Mustang's compass was bad. Maybe she had headed west, out to sea, rather than east toward the mountains.

Over forty years later, in 1985, two hunters in a remote spot in the California mountains came across the wreckage of a World War

II P-51 Mustang. Oddly enough, the skeletal remains of the pilot wore a large diamond ring and a wedding band on the left hand. The dog tags positively identified Tommy.

WINTER WEATHER had already caused a backlog of pursuit deliveries. Nearly a hundred P-51s were stuck in Los Angeles, and twenty pilots had been borrowed from the Third Air Force to get them moving. The WASP at Long Beach sent a radiogram offering their services on a volunteer dollar-a-year basis until the situation was alleviated and sufficient replacements had been trained. Similar offers followed from other WASP squadrons, but instead of accepting the women's help the air force loaned the Ferry Division 161 combat pilots for a thirty-day tour of duty. Scuttlebutt indicated that this was an entire pursuit squadron that had been about to depart for overseas.

Army Air Force headquarters ordered each station employing WASP to write a comprehensive account of their activities and send—ASAP—a roster of WASP personnel, listing their home addresses, pilot's license number, and highest horsepower rating. Each woman was allowed to keep one complete uniform and set of insignia and would be issued a certificate of service along with her pilot qualifications.

The women pilots were flying every available mission, adding hours to their log books and catching memories. Whenever and wherever they could, the women tried to transition into bigger and better airplanes. As the time grew short, a B-25 bomber pilot wired home: CAN YOU USE A GOOD UPSTAIRS MAID WITH 800 FLYING HOURS?

The commander at Las Vegas Air Force Base gave his four B-17 WASP a four-day pass and a plane to go to Los Angeles to see if they could find pilots' jobs at one of the aircraft plants in the area. They returned empty-handed and discouraged.

The War Department undertook an official inquiry to determine the future plans of the women pilots. Almost all wanted to continue flying, but with the glut of pilots, few had any job commitments. When she was interviewed about plans after deactivation, Hazel Ah Ying Lee said she would be joining her husband, a pilot in the Chinese air force, and flying for China.

The WASP staff executives attached to the Eastern Flying Training Command at Maxwell Field established the Order of Fifinella, an association for the Women Airforce Service Pilots after deactivation, and tried to acquire a complete roster, with addresses, of all the women on duty with the various commands. One of this staff, Kay Dussaq, had been a reporter on *The Avenger*, and she started a newsletter filled with information and support for the WASP.

Always an organizer, Kay also began a study of job possibilities for the women pilots after December 20. She had use of an AT-6 for a cross-country survey and, on the night of November 26, 1944, was on her way from Washington to Cincinnati on an instrument clearance when she was killed in a crash.

THE STATION REPORTS began to come in by early December, and ninety percent of them gave the women pilots a thumbs-up. The objections reflected the gripes of belligerent commanding officers. For example, the opinion from Shaw Field, South Carolina, was that the women hogged center stage and were carried away with "the thrill of being a WASP." The only common complaint was summed up perfectly in the report from Minter Field, Bakersfield, California, which said the WASP did a superior job "if they were left alone to fly" and not placed on detached service by Air Staff for additional training.

The eight WASP working at the Republic factory in Farmingdale, Long Island, delivered 1,987 Thunderbolts to Newark between June 8 and the end of November 1944. The control officer found the women to be exceptionally well suited for flying pursuits and, due to their smaller stature, they were more comfortable in the limited confines of the cockpit. On several occasions individual WASP delivered as many as five aircraft to Newark in a single day.

There were no cases of social disease either reported or treated among WASP personnel at any of the stations. Even though the ban on mixed ferry crews was informally dropped in the spring of 1943, there was never a hint of scandal in the press and only a few proven instances of the practice being abused—just enough, unfortunately, for the major in charge of operational planning at FERD headquarters to joke: "It became a standard answer for any delayed aircraft."

The flight surgeon of the Ferry Division, Lieutenant Colonel Andres G. Oliver, summed up the replies from various medical officers in a report that agreed with Dr. Monserud's findings from Avenger: "The stamina and physical endurance of the WASP pilots engaged in ferrying activities have been remarkable. . . . Cases of emotional disturbances as a result of flying stress have been surprisingly rare . . . because of their sex and a certain consciousness of the dignity of their position as female ferry pilots, the WASPs cannot 'do the town' in quite the same manner as the male pilots after they have made a series of pursuit deliveries under considerable strain." In short, the WASP didn't go on benders.

HAZEL AH YING LEE had completed the Ferry Division's pursuit school in September and returned to the 3rd Ferrying Group, Romulus. She had been away for most of the past six months. In the spring she went to instrument training in St. Joseph, Missouri, then to OTC in Orlando for a month, and soon afterward to Brownsville. At Romulus, pursuit pilots delivered the P-39 Aircobra from Bell Aviation factory in Niagara Falls to the Russians in Great Falls, Montana, and later in the war they ferried the enlarged version, the P-63 Kingcobra.

In late November 1944 Hazel Ah Ying Lee flew a Kingcobra west over the grimy, churning waters of Lake Erie into a sullen, steel sky. A fierce Arctic wind thrust an early winter storm across the Canadian border and closed down all the airports in Montana, North Dakota, Minnesota, and Wisconsin. Ah Ying got caught in Bismarck, North Dakota, where the Missouri River abandons the high plains and heads straight south, fast. After the storm moved on, Ah Ying could see a horde of grounded aircraft with pilots sweeping the ice and snow off the wings. She stood with a broom in her hand, discussing the options with another WASP who had gotten caught in the mess. Should she take a direct route or make a dogleg through Billings and then north along the leading edge of the Rocky Mountains? Ah Ying picked the longer route, hoping the backlog of planes would clear by the time she reached Great Falls.

When Ah Ying reached East Base, Great Falls, about two in the afternoon, the air was still chock-full, and there were at least a dozen P-63s in the traffic pattern. On the downwind leg she called the tower for landing instructions and began her final approach. When she was two or three miles from the boundary of the field, the controller spotted another Kingcobra on the same approach, slightly above and swiftly overtaking Ah Ying. The distance between the fighters was closing fast, and the tower ordered, "Two planes on final, pull up and go around."

Ah Ying acknowledged, but the other plane remained silent and lowered its landing gear. Alarmed, the tower tried again to contact the second aircraft as Ah Ying began to pull up. The controller shouted frantically into his microphone and flashed a red light to both ships. Just short of the runway the silent, deadly Kingcobra straddled Ah Ying, and as the planes collided, the wing tank of the upper ship exploded, merging the two in a shower of flames. Both aircraft plunged to the ground and skidded down the runway, trailing fire. An officer who had been watching raced behind the planes, and as they ground to a halt in a lethal splash of gasoline, he leaped into the blazing wreckage and dragged Ah Ying's burning body from the cockpit. He pulled her clear and smothered the searing flames with his arms and hands.

Almost instantly, an emergency crew roared up to the crash sight and extinguished the fire while the pilot of the other plane was rescued. He was a young AAF lieutenant from the 5th Ferrying Group in Dallas, and he sustained major injuries. Later he was able to tell the accident investigators that the radio in his Kingcobra did not work—and that he was very sorry about Ah Ying.

In spite of her burns, Ah Ying hung on for a time in the base hospital. When she died, the air force had difficulty deciding whom to notify. Her files showed the next of kin to be Major Yin Cheung Louie, her husband, who was with Chiang Kai-shek's air force in Chengtu Szechaw, China. The only other listed contact was a woman on Long Island, who could not be located.

The confusion in the WASP ferrying squadrons during the final days kept her friends who knew about her family in Portland from discovering the air force's problem. Ah Ying's body was stored in the military morgue.

On November 24, 1944, Hap Arnold's B-29 Superfortress attacked Tokyo and only two planes were lost. About this same time Nancy Love was invited to the final graduation ceremonies at Avenger Field, which was billed as a tribute to the work of the WASP. On one corner of the invitation she penciled, *No answer as far as I'm concerned, NHL.*

On December 1, after only three hours of instruction, Nancy Love became the first woman to check out on the C-54 Skymaster, a four-engine transport. The air force had commandeered thirty-four of these planes from the airlines at the beginning of the war to haul cargo and was able at last to return some of them to the commercial fleet. During her final weeks with the Ferry Division, Nancy delivered three of the big ships.

On one coast-to-coast trip, with a WASP copilot and a black puppy, she turned a Skymaster over to American Export Airlines at La Guardia Airport. This was the first of the large planes the company had received, and the executive staff turned out for its arrival in full force. They were speechless when they came on board and discovered the cozy crew in the cockpit.

During her two years with the Ferry Division Nancy Harkness Love realized many of her personal goals. She checked out in almost every one of the prominent military aircraft used during World War II. Nevertheless she felt for the rest of her life that the air force had let the other women ferry pilots down and that they had been grounded because Arnold insisted on hooking them to Jackie Cochran's scheme.

MRS. DEATON had the task of closing down Avenger Field just as the facility was finally completed. There were two new hangars and new barracks. The runways, which had been under construction since the first class reported in April 1943, were finished, and electric runway lights had even been installed.

The last class, 44-W-10, would graduate December 7, 1944, three years to the day after Pearl Harbor. Word went out to all the Sweetwater alumnae to return to their "home hive" for the formalities, and more than a hundred answered the summons, including several WASP staff executives. There were four generals, with a full complement of military aides, and Lieutenant Colonel Ward, the base commander, acted as master of ceremonies.

During his talk General Barton Yount, who had helped Jackie set up the women's flight school and who had been the boss of the majority of the WASP, praised their contributions. "The service pilot faces the risk of death without the emotional inspiration of combat. And the WASP have died. . . . They have demonstrated a courage which is sustained not by the fevers of combat but by the steady heartbeat of faith—a faith in the rightness of our cause and a faith in the importance of their work to the men who do go into combat."

General Arnold told them that the WASP were more than a pioneering venture. They were a noteworthy accomplishment in aviation. "Frankly I didn't know in 1941 whether a slip of a young girl could fight the controls of a B-17 in the heavy weather they would naturally encounter in operational flying. . . . Well, now in 1944, more than two years since the WASP first started flying with the air forces, we can come to only one conclusion: The entire operation has been a success. It is on the record that women can fly as well as men." He went on to say that the AAF hadn't built a plane the women couldn't handle. The WASP had proved that women pilots could fly wingtip-to-wingtip with their brothers, and more important, they had buckled down to the monotonous, the routine flying assignments that the hotshot young men hated, and had done these jobs extremely well. In conclusion Hap Arnold added, "This is valuable knowledge of the air age into which we are now entering."

When her turn came, Jackie told the graduates how proud the Women Airforce Service Pilots had made her. "My greatest accomplishment in aviation has been the small part I have played in helping make possible the results you have shown." The generals and the graduates stood in an ovation.

> We wanted wings, then we got those goldarned things
> They just darned near killed us
> That's for sure.
> They taught us how to fly
> Now they send us home to cry
> 'Cause they don't want us anymore.
>
> We earned our wings, now they'll clip the goldarned things.
> How will they ever win this war?

That night Avenger Field was deserted except for the sixty-eight newly winged and forgotten WASP who had neither been given duty assignments nor been discharged. The next afternoon Colonel Ward ordered the women to the flight line with full gear. "These trainers have to go down to San Angelo to be stored," he told them. "You're trained ferry pilots and you are going to deliver them."

Surrounded by a group of ecstatic pilots and fighting back a grin, Colonel Ward warned the group that he had no written orders and that his career was on the line. "There had better not be a scratch on one of these airplanes."

Trainees had flown most of these planes into Avenger from Houston in the spring of 1943, and the last class of women pilots was flying them out again. Colonel Ward followed in Avenger's transport, *Fifinella*, to sign off on the paperwork and return the women pilots to Sweetwater.

During the final weeks morale at the WASP stations slumped. In some cases there was no work to do. Base operations cut back on their tasks, knowing they would be leaving—or the women pilots were fresh from training and it was too much trouble to find duty slots for a short period of time. Even at locations where they still had more than enough to do, it was difficult to keep the blues away.

The WASP had to account for all their government-issued gear and equipment. Often after they turned their Santiago blue in to supply, the uniforms were thrown in the trash bin. At least the Army Air Force was providing transportation home.

At Long Beach forty-five women ferry pilots scheduled missions up to the very last, and Las Vegas AAFB was planning a going-away bash. At Williams Field, Lela Loudder's first station, the WASP were given twenty-four hours to clear the base.

By December, 1,074 Women Airforce Service Pilots had graduated from training, and 916 remained on duty—141 with the Air Transport Command, 620 with the Training Command, and the rest with the domestic air forces, the weather wing, and miscellaneous AAF commands. They had flown over sixty million miles, averaging thirty-three hours' flying time each month. Thirty-eight of them had given their lives for their country.

During twenty-seven months of service the women in the Ferry Division flew seventy-seven types of aircraft on 12,650 missions, covering 9,234,000 miles. Nancy Harkness Love said of their role, "Ours was the only women's service which was subjected, in the line of duty, to the same hazards as men."

Because the initial trial of women in military aviation was conducted during wartime, when opportunities for testing were so limited, the verdict was tarnished by the clash between the military mission and the experiment. The majority of the Women Airforce

Service Pilots expected to become part of the armed services, just like the WAC and the WAVE, and lead the way for other women who dreamed of flying. Instead they were deprived of the benefits under the G.I. Bill of life insurance, medical coverage, educational assistance, and home mortgages—and they were grounded. It would be thirty-four years before women would pilot military planes again.

The Women Airforce Service Pilots were only the first American women who had answered their nation's call to military service in a time of national peril that would be shuttled back to home and hearth. The duration was ended for the WASP. Bewildered and hurt, they went home on December 20, 1944, to spend Christmas with their families and to sort out what had happened.

EPILOGUE

The First Women Military Pilots

ON DECEMBER 7, 1944, as the final WASP class, 44-W-10, was graduating with ruffles and flourishes, a twin-engine AAF transport plane with seventeen passengers left Omaha, Nebraska. The transport's destination was Tinker Field, just south of Oklahoma City. Two WASP who had recently resigned, Margaret Marian Isbill and Virginia M. Hope, and a former Sweetwater classmate, Verna Mary Turner, were on board. Shortly after takeoff the plane crashed in flames, killing all the passengers. Since the women were only hitch-hiking civilians, air force investigators took scant notice of their deaths despite inquiries from Cochran, and years passed before most of their comrades knew they had been killed.

Isbill, Hope, and Turner were swept through the bureaucratic cracks, clean away, in the prevailing rush and confusion as the WASP deactivated. They were lost and forgotten. All of the women pilots faced a similar fate. World War II would grind on for nine additional months, and the Army Air Force and the country had more important things to worry about. Besides, Jackie's girls had come to such an awkward, uncomfortable end that most of the major players, and certainly a somewhat embarrassed air force, wanted to tidy up quickly, put the women pilots on file, and get on with more heroic endeavors.

The Air Transport Command, the Training Command, and the Army Air Force finished their separate reports on the Women Airforce Service Pilots within ninety days after deactivation. Given the degree of animosity while the women were on duty, the command reports were amazingly objective and fair. In each case the authors pictured the women pilots as casualties of conflicts beyond their knowledge and control, innocent bystanders caught in the cross fire between strong personalities and super-egos. The author of the ATC report suggested that both Nancy Love and Jackie Cochran were victims, not only of male bias and competition between the various AAF commands, but of the clumsy, inept way in which high-ranking officers dealt with women. The Army Air Force document frankly admitted that these antagonisms had a regrettable effect on the WASP. "It may be that these unfortunate occurrences will be longer remembered than the contribution to the war effort or the testing of women pilots' abilities."

Early in the spring of 1945, the WASP histories and reports were filed—in the government archives—as classified information, something to be kept secret. The Army Air Force then heaved a collective sigh and completely forgot that women had ever been in the cockpit of military planes, had ever flown hot pursuits and heavy bombers.

KAY D'AREZZO returned to her parents' home in Austin. In the Pacific American troops leaped from one island to the next following a bloody, deadly path, closing in on Japan. In January they landed on Luzon in the Philippines and six weeks later Corregidor—the Rock—was back in American hands.

Kay enrolled at the University of Texas. As often as allowed, she

[223]

sent Al the twenty-five words the Red Cross could deliver to American prisoners of war. Once in a while she still received a brief note from him, although there was now difficulty in getting messages to and from Japan. Just as before, she never mentioned what she had been doing, the flying. Besides, it was over, ended.

When Kay left her young husband in the Philippines in February 1941, her father had predicted she wouldn't see Al again for at least five years. Well, it had been four.

After President Franklin Delano Roosevelt died suddenly on April 12, 1945, the nation was in shock. Then, eighteen days later in Berlin, Adolf Hitler killed himself, and on May 7 the remnants of the Third Reich surrendered unconditionally to the Allied Forces. America turned her full attention to the Japanese home islands. A naval blockade cut off supplies and food to the four main islands, to weaken the population, starve the Japanese before the American invasion. Hap Arnold's B-29s rained fire, incendiary bombs, on the major cities, one by one, leveling homes and business and killing thousands.

Four and a half years, Kay thought. How much longer?

On August 6, 1944, without warning, the atom bomb was dropped on Hiroshima from a United States Army Air Force B-29, the *Enola Gay*, piloted by Colonel Paul Tibbets. The bomber met with no fighter resistance and no flak. The astonishing, terrifying new weapon was a surprise to the entire world.

Kay was aghast. What was it—the atomic bomb? What did it do? *Where* was Al's prison camp?

Still the Japanese held out. On August 9 a second atomic bomb was dropped, this time on Nagasaki. *Where* was Al?

On August 15, 1945, the Japanese surrendered at last, and World War II came to an end. Kay was in class when the word came. She jumped to her feet, shouting, "My husband is coming home!" Captain Al D'Arezzo was coming home. She *knew* he was.

Many weeks passed before all the American prisoners in Japan were liberated and Al got to the States.

Four years and eight months. It had been four years and eight months, and Al said he had known all along that Kay was in the WASP. The word, or the rumor, penetrated the prison camps that American women were flying for the Army Air Force. Al told his pals, everyone in fact, that his wife was an army pilot. He *knew* she was.

Captain D'Arezzo picked up his military career, playing catch-up for the years he had spent as a prisoner while his West Point classmates made major or better. As they moved from army post to army post, Kay and Al raised a son and a daughter, who grew tall, very tall, like their parents.

AFTER THE WASP SQUADRON at Las Vegas AAFB shut down, Ruth Craig Jones had no reason to go back to Oklahoma City. The principal at her high school had kept his word: she had no job. She and Skip struck out for California. Maybe they could find jobs in a defense plant, she reasoned, and Ruth's husband, Lee, might come to the West Coast first, on his way home—once the war was over.

The morning of December 20 they headed west in their car, toward Los Angeles, but Skip did the driving. Ruth had a pitiful hangover. One of the few things she remembered about their farewell party was drinking old-fashioneds mixed in a tall ice cream malt glass.

Ruth and Skip found employment right away building the planes they had been flying. Their supervisor was surprised by the pair's mechanical ability, how much they knew about aircraft. Both were given a raise the first week. They volunteered for the swing shift and learned to install the guns, the weapons, because this work paid best.

A little over a year later Lee and Ruth Jones were in Oklahoma City. She was teaching at a different school, and he ran one of his family's drugstores. Ruth bought a small airplane, a Cessna, with six other WASP who had settled in the city.

WHEN THEIR WASP WINGS were clipped, Lela Loudder and Nell set off, away from west Texas, to find work. They got jobs at an air force base canteen in New Mexico. Unfortunately neither of them realized they'd have to *stand* all day. Lela's feet lasted three days; Nell's made it for four.

Next Lela ferried scrap, tired military aircraft stripped of almost everything that worked, to aviation junk heaps. It was risky business. After a delivery or two, when the receiving crew was amazed she'd arrived in one piece, Lela moved on again.

[225]

After the war was over, Lela went to work as an American Airlines stewardess. This job was tolerable while it lasted, because sometimes she flew with a crew who were friends from the naval air station at Corpus Christi. Just for fun the captain would let Lela take the controls of the DC-3 while he sat in the back and kidded with the passengers.

A year later she got married. Stewardesses weren't allowed to have husbands, so Lela had to leave American.

ON DECEMBER 20 twenty-year-old Marjorie Stevenson went home to Holdenville, Oklahoma, and thought about what to do next. Her father wanted her to finish college. "School?" she demanded. "What do I have in common with schoolgirls?"

She moped around the big house on Hinkley Street while her father listened and waited. One afternoon, at Sunday dinner, she announced that she was enrolling in the University of Oklahoma. "I thought so," her dad said, and Marge wondered if he'd known all along she would do what he wanted.

Her sister, Grace, came home from England in January 1945. After almost three years of living on starchy war rations, she weighed 175 pounds. The steamer trunks her mother had sent with her to Bristol stayed in England. The only clothes she had were her wool ATA uniforms, because they were all that fit. Mrs. Stevenson was horrified!

Grace spent a couple of months in Holdenville on a strict diet ramrodded by her mother. Slimmer and trimmer, Grace returned to Spartan Aviation in Wyoming as an instructor. She didn't stay for very long, however. After all those glorious British Spitfires, Grace couldn't abide being stuck in a Piper Cub. She quit her job— and she never flew again.

Marjorie graduated from college and married a former AAF flyer. In partnership with another couple they bought a fast, flashy Staggerwing, just like the one Jackie Cochran used to fly.

SKIP CARTER went back to teaching girls' physical education in Oklahoma City. Millie Davidson married yet another Army Air Force flyer. Marie Genaro moved from New Jersey to Dallas, Texas, with her husband. Pat Pateman worked around airports and then joined the new United States Air Force in 1948. Helen Richey, the

ATA-girl who came back to join the WASP, committed suicide soon
after the end of the war. Ah Ying's body was in storage at the
military morgue in Great Falls, Montana, for almost a year while
the air force endeavored to locate her husband in China. And in
Nashville a small airport in the hills northeast of the city was named
for a local belle, Cornelia Fort.

AFTER the Women Airforce Service Pilots were dismissed, Jackie
Cochran stayed on in Washington to write a final report as director
of women pilots. She began by thanking her generals, particularly
Hap Arnold, whose vision she said made the women's program possible, and then she set about justifying her actions. For starters she
felt that instead of operating the WASP through regular AAF command channels, the results would have been better if the program
had been classified as a special project—under the complete control
of the director of women pilots. Cochran also declared she was
simply following Arnold's orders when she deactivated the WASP,
and she felt the only way to keep from playing favorites was to
deactivate *all* the women pilots on December 20. They all had to
stay or they all had to go, no matter how badly the Ferry Division
needed the women who were ferrying pursuits.

While experimental in nature, Cochran wrote, the Women Airforce Service Pilots proved themselves. "It is no longer a matter of
speculation that graduate WASPs were adapted physically, men-
tally, and psychologically to the type of flying assigned." Fifty percent of all WASP on duty six months or more qualified as Class III
pilots. Even the Ferry Division, she reported, expressed pride in the
work of *all the women ferry pilots*, most of whom came to them
from the Women's Flying Training Detachment. Of 1,074 graduates, 900 WASP were on active duty until the final day. Cochran
insisted that the women had deserved militarization and veterans'
benefits.

In the summer of 1945, with the WASP episode behind her, Jackie
Cochran became the Pacific correspondent for *Liberty* magazine.
She was in hot pursuit of the end of the war, lusting to be in on
the kill. Jackie witnessed the Japanese surrender in the Philippines
and was the first American woman inside Japan following V-J Day.
She went to China, met Madame Chiang Kai-shek and Mao Tse-
tung, and then crossed India and Egypt to Rome, where she real-

[227]

ized the dream of every devout Catholic when she had an audience with His Holiness the Pope. By November she was attending the Nuremberg war-crimes trials in Germany. When Jackie Cochran returned to the United States at the close of 1945, she was awarded the Distinguished Service Medal for her contributions during the war. The medal was presented to her by General Hap Arnold.

Afterward Jackie went home, like millions of other civilians in those days, back to her cosmetics business, to flying, ranching, golf. And to her husband, Floyd Odlum, whose health was failing. Before long he was an invalid.

Jackie started air racing, setting records again. The Odlums' California ranch house teemed with famous personalities, politicians and military bigwigs, including the next president, Dwight David Eisenhower. In 1953, with illustrious test pilot and World War II ace Colonel Chuck Yeager as her private coach, Jacqueline Cochran became the first woman to break the sound barrier. The same year her autobiography, *The Stars at Noon*, was published. The book was a personal fable written with a peppy style and laced with Very Important People. It included a short, gossipy version of the WASP story, again with many thank-yous all around to her generals and her girls.

Regardless of a long list of celebrated aviation accomplishments, Jacqueline Cochran never achieved the public adoration she sought and deserved. More than anything else, the ragamuffin little orphan wanted America to love her, as it loved Amelia Earhart. Unfortunately in Cochran's day women with sass and grit weren't in vogue. She was ahead of her time in every way.

Even so, most of the veterans of the Women Airforce Service Pilots remained devoted fans, including those who surmised, as they grew older and wiser, that their fairy godmother had shut down the WASP because the program had to be her way or no way. Still, in her reach for the stars, Jackie lifted the first women who trained as military pilots to heights of adventure that otherwise would have been beyond their grasp. The WASP were able to test their limits, find out things about themselves they would never have known, while playing high, wide, and handsome among the clouds. And without realizing what they were doing at the time, Jackie's girls also made a revolutionary statement about the physical and mental capabilities of women—even if the government would keep the information buried in classified files for thirty years.

Jacqueline Cochran's life is well documented in public places, always with a spotlight on the central figure and her achievements. After her death in 1980 Jackie's private papers went to the Eisenhower Library in Abilene, Kansas. Her memorabilia is on permanent display in Arnold Hall at the United States Air Force Academy, where she served as a director. Additional copies of her papers, photographs, and awards were carefully disseminated among other museums across the country, from the Ninety-Nines organization in Oklahoma City to the Smithsonian in Washington.

ONCE the Ferry Division's women were grounded, Nancy Love stayed on duty for a time to assist with writing the Air Transport Command's report. Nancy finished her wartime service with another women's aviation first. She went on a flight around the world, during which she was at the controls at least half the way, including the leg going over the Hump—the 20,000-foot-high supply route over the Himalayas that had claimed the lives of 850 airmen during the course of World War II.

In July 1946 Bob and Nancy Love became the first couple in history to be decorated at the same time for their military service. Nancy was presented with the Air Medal for her pioneering work with the Ferry Division, and Bob added a Distinguished Service Medal to his other decorations.

After eleven years of marriage the Loves had the first of their three daughters in 1947, and Nancy withdrew to private life and became a mom. Bob founded Allegheny Airlines. Later the Love family moved to Martha's Vineyard, where Bob owned a shipyard on the harbor. Nancy crewed for Bob on their sailboat, rode horseback with her daughters, and enjoyed an occasional visit from one of her WAFS. The first couple of aviation limited their flying to taking the children off-island for doctor and dentist appointments.

Nancy Harkness Love died of cancer in October 1976 at the age of sixty-two. She was one of the most accomplished women flyers the world has ever known, but compared with the deluge of information about Jacqueline Cochran, there is almost nothing about her or her achievements in museums. Her daughters remember

playing dress-up in their mother's World War II leather flying
jacket, but nobody seemed to know what became of it. Nearly every
relic from Nancy's days of fame seems to have disappeared in the
bustle of family life.

By 1989 only a single box of personal papers survived. The box
contained a few photographs, news clippings, a wedding invitation, the scrapbook her father kept about Nancy, and some handwritten lists: the names of women with commercial pilot's licenses
in 1940; airplanes, perhaps the ones Nancy had flown; more names,
the eleven girls who died under Nancy Love's command—and some
small reference to each one, a news story or a photo.

THE DAY AFTER the Women Airforce Service Pilots were deactivated, on December 21, 1944, Hap Arnold was promoted to general
of the army. He had another severe heart attack in January 1945,
but he hung on and didn't retire from active duty until six months
after the war, when the loose ends were tied up. By that time the
Army Air Force had demobilized two million people and tens of
thousands of airplanes. The stress of war and four heart attacks in
two years had ruined his health. Hap Arnold was a casualty of
World War II, as surely as if he had died in combat.

In September 1947 General Arnold saw his life's work realized
when Congress made the air force a separate military service. He
suffered a final, fatal heart attack in January 1950, at the age of
sixty-four. In spite of the public embarrassment, Arnold always felt
the WASP were a sound idea and that their record supported his
judgment "that in any future total effort the nation can count on
thousands of its young women to fly any of its aircraft."

EVEN IF NOBODY CARED or remembered, WASP had proved that
bright, healthy American girls could learn to fly the army way just
like their brothers, and now that the war was over, just like their
brothers, they went enthusiastically back into civilian life. Victo-
rious American youth rushed headlong into life and love, out into
the suburbs with their new families. The G.I. Bill, which had been
denied to the WASP, allowed thousands of veterans to attend college and to build lives they'd never dreamed of before.

In 1948, just after the United States Air Force was established,
the former Women Airforce Service Pilots were quietly offered non-

flying, reserve commissions as second lieutenants. At the same time Jacqueline Cochran became a lieutenant colonel in the USAF Reserve, and before her retirement in 1970 she finally realized her ambition when she was promoted to full colonel. Nancy Love was also designated a lieutenant colonel in 1948, and several of the WAFS originals, including Betty Gillies, were commissioned as majors.

Nevertheless by the time the air force made the offer of commissions, most of the first women to fly military aircraft were deep into another phase of their lives, either up to their necks in baby diapers or buried under a stack of college textbooks. The days when they flew army planes had slipped dreamily into the past, just as they had for most Army Air Force veterans. A USAF Reserve commission, particularly as a nonflying officer, didn't interest the majority of them anymore.

Still, a few former WASP, about three hundred, did accept the United States Air Force's offer, and more than two dozen of these continued trailblazing for women in the military and made careers in the air force, retiring as majors or lieutenant colonels.

From 1945 until 1951 some of the WASP tried, in fits and starts, to get together, to hold regular meetings, but they finally gave up. Life offered more pressing demands. For more than twelve years the WASP were dormant. Then from 1964 to 1969 one determined woman, Martin "Marty" Wyall, from the last WASP class, 44-W-10, devoted five years to pulling an organization together. Her family was nearly grown, and at this stage in her life Marty's sense of history turned the women pilots' pioneering accomplishments into a mission. She started updating addresses and successfully arranged meetings in both 1964 and 1969.

By 1972 enough WASP had been roused to hold a thirtieth-anniversary reunion at Avenger Field in Sweetwater, Texas. Former flight instructors, the establishment officers, Army Staff, anyone who had been part of those thrilling, difficult days, was invited. Dedie Deaton took charge of the local arrangements. Bruce Arnold, the general's son and a retired air force colonel, came from Washington in his famous father's stead, and Jackie Cochran rolled into Sweetwater in a plush mobile home. More than three hundred Women Airforce Service Pilots, most into their fifties and many of them grandmothers, paraded down Sweetwater's main street, and

[231]

the press took pictures, just like the old days. A marble monument was placed in the square on the courthouse lawn.

Like other veterans' groups, the WASP discovered at Sweetwater that it was fun to be together again, to talk hangar talk, to sing the old songs, to remember the friends and the adventure and what it meant to fly—to be army pilots. They promised to meet every two years.

Over drinks at the Blue Bonnet Hotel or walking on the flight line at Avenger, they also wondered at the voices of feminism rising in the land. What about the women of World War II, all the challenges, all the victories? Wasn't it time the nation remembered the WASP?

Teresa James, a USAF major, confessed she had been trying on her own to get veterans' rights for the WASP, conducting a lonely, expensive, one-woman lobby. Only a few months before, the congresswoman from Hawaii had introduced a WASP bill to the House Veterans' Affairs Committee, but the chairman wouldn't even allow it on the floor of the House for a vote.

Teresa was discouraged. She asked for help. The response was spontaneous and unanimous. It was high time to take action, to right a wrong—but in this remarkable collection of women there was of course more than one opinion about what to do next. Some went to Jackie for assistance. If I couldn't do it, she told them, neither can you. Others who knew that Bruce Arnold had been a legislative liaison for the air force plied him with drinks and sentiment. They struck pay dirt. Bruce Arnold promised to champion the WASP cause in his father's name—and a long battle was joined in Congress.

Because of the women's movement, by the mid-1970s increasing numbers of young women were signing up for the all-volunteer armed forces. The first girls were admitted to the nation's elite service academies. In September 1976 ten women began training to Hardfly for the United States Air Force at Williams AAFB, Lela Loudder's original posting. These were the "first women military pilots," said the Pentagon press release. No, not the first! The WASP were insulted, and the group working with Bruce Arnold pushed furiously, rapidly forward.

Before the month was over, an amendment was added to a veterans' bill on the floor of the United States Senate that would grant the WASP full military status and make them eligible for veterans' benefits—thirty-two years after they had been deactivated and sentenced to obscurity. It was sponsored by Senator Barry Goldwater, a former World War II Ferry Division pilot who had been based at New Castle AAFB and had flown with the women ferry pilots. Most of his colleagues were surprised to hear women had served as pilots during the war. Goldwater urged them to correct a past wrong, and the WASP amendment passed the Senate.

However, before it could come to a vote in the House, the veterans' organizations came out against the amendment, just as they had in 1944. This was a raid on their benefits, they contended— think how many other groups of civilians, the Civil Air Patrol, the Merchant Marine, also served during the war. The WASP amendment would bring all of them to Washington looking for money. The House Veterans' Affairs Committee killed the proposal.

Feeling sure the veterans' clamor would fade, the House and Senate both promised Senator Goldwater a hearing on the WASP during the next session of Congress.

In October when the WASP held a reunion in Hot Springs, Arkansas, their membership roster included over eight hundred names—judges, volunteer chairwomen, military officers, professors, community leaders, writers, and lawyers. These women had come to a season in their lives when they had the time, the influence, and the money to attempt to set the record straight. The Women Airforce Service Pilots had been *the first women military pilots* in the nation's history. The group of bright, determined women who had gathered in Hot Springs planned their campaign.

The Women Airforce Service Pilots, World War II, had a pair of dedicated champions in Bruce Arnold and Senator Barry Goldwater. Arnold knew his way around Capitol Hill and he pledged to keep his father's promise to the women pilots. Hap had intended for the WASP to be part of the air force. Senator Goldwater vowed to keep up the fight, to attach a WASP amendment to every piece of legislation under consideration by Congress during the upcoming session if necessary.

The WASP set up a Washington command center in the Army-Navy Club, and in March 1977, when the WASP amendment was introduced again, it was cosponsored by every woman member of Congress. Nancy Batson Crews and Teresa James, both originals, narrated a documentary film, *Silver Wings and Santiago Blue*, that told the WASP story. The women pilots' cause caught on with television and newspapers, and the armed services weekly, *Stars and Stripes*, kept track of the amendment's progress. All across the country WASP circulated petitions and mounted a letter-writing campaign. Those gathered in the nation's capital worked hard to show members of Congress who and what they were, with scrapbooks, correspondence, photos, and official documents saved and treasured for more than thirty years.

In May Dora Dougherty Strother, a Ph.D. and chief of human factors engineering at Bell Helicopter, who was one of the two women Paul Tibbets taught to fly the B-29 Superfortress, testified before the Senate Veterans' Affairs Committee. Dozens of WASPs, some in their Santiago-blue uniforms, were in the chamber to lend support. Dr. Strother was also a lieutenant colonel in the USAF Reserve and she calmly and deliberately presented a chronicle of WASP aviation accomplishments. They had flown every type of aircraft the Army Air Force used during World War II, and chalked up over sixty million operational miles, equal to two thousand times around the globe. In less than one year, the thirty-five women stationed at New Castle AAFB had delivered 3,000 planes. In addition, she said, WASPs ferried every P-47 produced by Republic during the last six months of 1944.

Dr. Strother told the committee the women pilots had trained, lived, and worked under military discipline. They had worn uniforms and carried side arms to protect classified equipment. From the first the Army Air Force records and correspondence discussed plans for the women pilots to be brought into military service, and the women reporting to Avenger Field were told to expect to be commissioned. She closed by asking the committee to grant the WASP recognition as military pilots, de facto Army Air Force officers during World War II.

In September an important witness appeared before the committee: William Tunner, the former head of the Ferry Division, Nancy Love's boss and Jackie Cochran's nemesis. "Certainly someone today can partially correct the unfairness we showed by making veterans of these women who served so faithfully and well, and with little complaint," he said. Margaret Ann Hamilton Tunner, the retired USAF general's wife since 1950 and a member of the WASP, sat by his side. His testimony was followed by Senator Goldwater's, who declared, "The only thing wrong with those girls was that they were girls."

Both the American Legion and the Veterans' Administration continued to oppose the WASP legislation vehemently, both in their testimony and in their actions. A large majority of the members of Congress were veterans themselves, so this constituted a powerful lobby against the women pilots.

Jackie Cochran was notably absent from the hearings. She had a bad heart and perhaps an attack of old resentments. In 1975 she had testified before a military inquiry board about training women as pilots, particularly at the United States Air Force Academy. She had said that, based on her experiences, women would be unlikely to make careers in aviation. They would leave the service after their initial commitment was over for personal reasons, and the expensive education would be wasted. Contradicting what she had written in her final report and her book, Cochran told the officers how disappointed she was because the women she taught to fly during the war, for the most part, simply went home, married, and settled down.

Meanwhile the Pentagon, in the person of Assistant Secretary of the Air Force, Antonia Handler Chayes, decided to support the Women Airforce Service Pilots. The armed services had to continue enlisting women in sizable numbers or abandon the idea of an all-volunteer force. The Defense Department was spending hundreds of thousands of dollars in advertising trying to convince women of the opportunities available and that they could expect to get a fair shake in the military. "Be all you can be," promised the army. What would a public defeat for the WASP do to recruiting?

Once the Senate and House hearings were over, serious behind-the-scene maneuvering and deal making got under way. Several congressmen who were hired hands of the American Legion and the Veterans' Administration attempted to drop the WASP legislation out of committee before it came to a vote. However, two influential members of the House of Representatives, Margaret Heckler and Lindy Boggs, swung into action and, with the support of the Defense Department, managed to schedule the amendment for a vote in the House on November 3, 1977.

[235]

Just before the vote Bruce Arnold was putting together an information pamphlet for the members of Congress when he discovered in one of the WASP's personal papers a discharge notice that read "honorably served in active Federal Service in the Army of the United States." *In the Army of the United States!*

With this official military discharge in hand, Arnold worked out a compromise with the conservative members of both veterans' committees. If the air force would certify the WASP as de facto military personnel, the chairman of the House Veterans' Affairs Committee would agree to support the legislation on the floor.

On November 3 the House passed the WASP amendment to the G.I. Bill Improvement Act of 1977, and the Senate approved the legislation the following evening. Relief washed over the Women Airforce Service Pilots watching from the Senate visitors' gallery. Tears rolled down the cheeks of one who sat proudly in Santiago blue and silver wings. With a smile, Bruce Arnold reached over and shook her sleeve, "Stop that!" he commanded. "You're in uniform."

PRESIDENT JIMMY CARTER signed the WASP legislation into law on Thanksgiving Day, November 23, 1977.

On May 21, 1979, thirty-four years after the end of the war, the United States Air Force offered official recognition by issuing the first honorable discharge to a WASP.

In 1984 each woman pilot was awarded the Victory medal, and those who had been on duty for more than a year also received the American Theater medal.

In May of 1990 a delgation of three dozen Women Airforce Service Pilots met in Moscow with members of the Night Witches, the Russian women who flew as combat pilots. Commemorating the fiftieth anniversary of Russian involvement in World War II, the women marched with other veterans in the traditional May Day parade in Red Square. Afterward they recounted their experiences and memories through translators—and with their eyes and hands shared hopes for world peace.

As with many others of their generation who forged their characters during World War II, the true legacy of the WASP is found in their lives, the opportunities they expected and accepted for

themselves and others through the years, and their exuberant vision
of unlimited human possibility.

> To serve; to add my strength to theirs
> Who give their all;
> To Fly; to do my part
> Is all I ask.

$\mathcal{I}$N $\mathcal{M}$EMORIAM
1942–1944

Members of the WASP who died in the service of their nation.

Jane Champlin, 43–4

Susan P. Clarke, 44–2

Margie L. Davis, 44–9

Katherine Dussaq, 44–1

Marjorie D. Edwards, 44–6

Elizabeth Erickson, 44–6

Cornelia Fort, WAFS

Frances F. Grimes, 43–3

Mary Hartson, 43–5

Mary Howson, 44–4

Edith Keene, 44–1

Hazel Ah Ying Lee, 43–4

Paula Loop, 43–2

Alice Lovejoy, 43–5

Lea Ola McDonald, 44–3

Peggy Martin, 44–4

Virginia Moffatt, 43–2

Beverly Moses, 44–5

Dorothy Nichols, 43–2

Jeanne L. Norbeck, 44–3

Margaret C. Oldenburg, 43–4

Mabel Rawlinson, 43–3

Gleanna Roberts, 44–9

Marie Michell Robinson, 44–2

Betty Scott, 44–3

Dorothy Scott, WAFS

Margaret J. Seip, 43–5

Helen Jo Severson, 43–5

Ethel Marie Sharon, 43–4

Evelyn Sharp, WAFS

Gertrude Thompkins Silver, 43–7

Betty P. Stine, 44–2

Marion Toevs, 43–8

Mary E. Trebing, 43–4

Mary L. Webster, 44–8

Bonnie Jean Welz, 43–6

Betty Taylor Wood, 43–4

These names appear on a memorial plaque that was created by
sculptor Jewel P. Estes, 44–10 Trainee, and is located at
the Frontiers of Flight Museum, Dallas Love Field.

And the cofounders of women's military aviation:

Jacqueline Cochran, 1906–1980

Nancy Harkness Love, 1914–1976

$\mathcal{A}$UTHOR'S $\mathcal{N}$OTES

Chapter One: In June 1941, the Army Air Corps was renamed the Army Air Force (AAF). A year later, the Air Transport Command (ATC) was formed out of two other military air transportation components and put under the control of the Army Air Force. The Ferry Division (sometimes called the Ferrying Division) became part of the Air Transport Command at this time. For clarity, these organizations are referred to by the final World War II designation.

Also in 1941, the Civilian Pilot Training Program (CPT) was changed to the War Training Service (WTS) and technically girls were no longer admitted.

Chapter Two: Prior to March 1942, the Women's Army Corps (WAC) was called the Women's Auxilary Army Corps (WAAC).

Chapter Four: The unit number for the Women's Flying Training Detachment was 319th while it was located in Houston, and it was changed to 318th after the move to Avenger.

After leaving command of the women's training detachment, Major Walter Farmer was assigned to the 416th Bomber Group and promoted to lieutenant colonel. He was killed on a mission over France on August 6, 1944 at the age of twenty-eight.

Chapter Six: Mrs. Deaton's staff at Avenger was composed of four female establishment officers. There were normally thirty to forty civilian flight instructors and during the course of the WASP training program three or four of these were women.

The trainees earned $150 a month, less $1.65 per day for maintenance, the army term for room and board.

The study of the women pilots by Captain Nels Monserud, M.D., is entitled *Medical Considerations of WASPS*; the work combines studies at Avenger Field with reports from the airfields where the WASP were stationed as operating personnel.

Chapter Seven: In the late 1970s, B. J. Erickson London's daughter became the first woman pilot for Western Airlines.

Sources

Research Facilities and Museums

Air University, Albert Simpson Historical Research Center
Maxwell Air Force Base, Alabama

Frontiers of Flight Museum, the Delphine Bohn Collection and the Historical Archives at the University of Texas at Dallas
Dallas, Texas

International Women's Air and Space Museum
Centerville, Ohio

National Archives, Motion Picture and Sound and Video Branch
Alexandria, Virginia

The Ninety-Nines, International Women Pilots, Historical Archives
Oklahoma City, Oklahoma

Nolan County Historical Society Museum
Sweetwater, Texas

Sources

Oklahoma Air and Space Museum
Oklahoma City, Oklahoma

Smithsonian Institution, National Air and Space Museum
Washington, D.C.

United States Air Force Academy Library, Special Collections,
Lieutenant Colonel Y. C. Pateman Collection
Colorado Springs, Colorado

USAF Museum, Research Center
Wright Patterson Air Force Base, Ohio

Books

Arnold, H. H. *Global Mission*. New York: Harper & Bros, 1949.

Cochran, Jacqueline. *The Stars at Noon*. Boston: Little Brown and Company, 1953.

Coffey, Thomas. *Hap, Military Aviator*. New York: Viking Press, 1982.

Dailey, Janet. *Silver Wings and Santiago Blue*. New York: Pocket Books, 1985.

Earhart, Amelia, arranged by G. Putman. *The Last Flight*. New York: Orion Books, 1988.

Hynes, Samuel. *Flights of Passage*. Annapolis: Naval Institute Press, 1988.

Jablonski, Edward, and the editors of Time-Life Books. *The Epic of Flight: "Women Aloft."* Alexandria, Va.: Time-Life Books, 1982.

———. *The Epic of Flight: "America in the Air War."* Alexandria, Va.: Time-Life Books, 1982.

La Farge, Oliver. *The Eagle in the Egg*. Boston: Houghton Mifflin, 1949.

Lomax, Judy. *Women in the Air*. New York: Dodd, Mead, 1987.

Monde, Bennet B. *A History of Avenger Field, Texas*. Master of Arts thesis, Hardin Simons University, Abilene, Tex. 1983.

Mondey, David, general editor. *The International Encyclopedia of Aviation*. New York: Crown Publishing, 1977.

Rogan, Helen. *A Mixed Company*. New York: Putman, 1981.

Myles, Bruce. *The Night Witches*. San Francisco: Presidio, 1981.

Piercy, Marge. *Gone to Soldiers*. New York: Ballantine Books, 1987.

Scharr, Adele. *Sisters in the Sky*, 2 vols. Gerald, Mo.: The Patrice Press, 1986, 1988.

Shepard, Jim. *Paper Doll*. New York: Alfred A. Knopf, 1986.

Stewart-Smith, Natalie Jeanne. *Women Airforce Service Pilots*. Master's thesis, Washington State University, 1981.

Sulzberger, C. L., and the editors of American Heritage. *American Heritage Picture History of World War II*. New York: Crown Publishing, 1966.

Tanner, Doris Brinker. *Cornelia Fort*. Tennessee Historical Society, 1981.

Tunner, William. *Over the Hump*. New York: Duell, Sloan & Pearce, 1964.

Van Wagenen Keil, Sally. *Those Wonderful Women in Their Flying Machines*. New York: Rawson, Wade Publishers, Inc., 1979.

Waters, Andrew W. *All the U.S. Air Force Airplanes, 1907–1983*. New York: Hippocrene Books, 1983.

Wolfe, Tom. *The Right Stuff*. New York: Farrar, Straus & Giroux, 1979.

Wood, Winifred M., and Swain, Dorothy. *We Were WASP*. Glade House, Coral Gables, 1945.

Yeager, Chuck, with Leo Janos. *Yeager*. New York: Bantam, 1985.

Register of Graduates, United States Military Academy. West Point: Association of Graduates, USMA, 1988.

Texas: A Guide to the Lone Star State. Compiled by Workers of the Writers' Program of the Work Project Administration; American Guide Series. New York: Hastings House, 1940.

Government Documents

Women Pilots with the AAF, 1941–1944, AAF Historical Office, Headquarters, Army Air Forces, March 1946.

History of the Air Transport Command, "Women Pilots in the Air Transport Command," Historical Branch, Headquarters, Air Transport Command.

History of the WASP Program, Army Air Forces Central Flying Training Command, Historical Section, AAF CFTC.

Final Report on Women Pilot Program to Commanding General AAF by Jacqueline Cochran, Director of Women Pilots.

318th AAF Flying Training Detachment, Avenger Field, Sweetwater, Texas by L. Leoti Deaton, Staff Executive Historian.

Various AAF Base histories of the WASP and AAF Form 5s on wartime casualties.

AAFB newspapers, including *The Avenger*.

Sources

Congressional Record and transcripts of House and Senate Veterans' Affairs Committees.

Newspapers and Periodicals

Aerospace Historian
Air Force magazine
American History Illustrated
American Way
The Boston Globe
Chicago Daily Times
Confederate Air Force magazine
Dallas Morning News
Flying
Ladies' Home Journal
Liberty magazine
Life
Martha's Vineyard Gazette
Nashville *Tennessean*
Nashville *Banner*
Newsweek
New York Herald Tribune
The New York Times
The New York Times Magazine
Ninety-Nine News
Skyways
Stars and Stripes
Texas Highways
Time
U.S. Air Services magazine
Viva
Vogue
Washington Daily News
Washington Times-Herald
Woman's Home Companion
World War II Times

Women Air Force Service Pilots

WASP "Songbook," WASP roster, and WASP newsletters.

WASP Region I Meeting, USAF Museum, Dayton, Ohio, September 21–23, 1989.

WASP Region II Meeting, Bartlesville, Oklahoma, June 2–3, 1989.

Opening of the Frontiers of Flight Museum, Dallas, Texas, June 21, 1990.

Miscellaneous

Oral Histories, USAF Historical Research, Maxwell Air Force Base, Alabama.

Silver Wings, Public Broadcasting System documentary, 1980.

INDEX

ABOUT THE AUTHOR

MARIANNE VERGES is a nonfiction writer who specializes in personalities and popular culture. Her articles have appeared in magazines and newspapers in New England and the Southwest. Because she is married to an aeronautical engineer turned airline executive, Ms. Verges is a veteran observer of aviation history and its effect on American traditions and lifestyles. *On Silver Wings* is her first book.